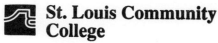

Confronting Columbus

Confronting Columbus

An Anthology

EDITED BY

John Yewell, Chris Dodge, Jan DeSirey

McFarland & Company, Inc., Publishers
Jefferson, North Carolina, and London

British Library Cataloguing-in-Publication data are available

Library of Congress Cataloguing-in-Publication Data

Confronting Columbus : an anthology / edited by John Yewell, Chris
    Dodge, Jan DeSirey.
        p.   cm.
    Includes bibliographical references and index.
    ISBN 0-89950-696-8 (lib. bdg. : 50# alk. paper) ∞
    1. Columbus, Christopher.   2. Columbus, Christopher — Influence.
3. America — Discovery and exploration — Spanish.   4. Indians — First
contact with Occidental civilization.   I. Yewell, John, 1954–
II. Dodge, Chris.   III. DeSirey, Jan.
E111.C777   1992
970.01'5 — dc20   91-50937
                                                                                    CIP

Alternative Cataloguing-in-Publication Data

Yewell, John, editor.
    Confronting Columbus: an anthology. Edited by John Yewell,
Chris Dodge, and Jan DeSirey. Jefferson, NC: McFarland & Co.,
copyright 1992.

    PARTIAL CONTENTS: 1492–1992: a historian's perspective, by
Howard Zinn. — Discovering Columbus, by John Mohawk. — A note on
the Tainos, by Jose Barreiro. — The second voyage, by Hans Koning.
— Conquered women, by Verena Stolcke. — Rereading the past, by
William Bigelow. — King sugar, by Eduardo Galeano. — Columbus in
high schools, by James Loewen. — Libraries and the Quincentennial, by
Chris Dodge. — Blacks, indigenous people and the churches, 1992, by
Jean Sindab. — Victims of an American Holocaust, by Steve Charleston.
— Bibliography. — Resource directory.

    1. Columbus, Christopher, 1451–1506.   2. Columbus, Christopher,
1451–1506 — Influence.   3. Columbus, Christopher, 1451–1506 — Study
and teaching.   4. Columbus Quincentenary, 1992–1993.   5. Native
American Holocaust (1492–1900).   6. Taino Indians — History.
7. Explorers, Spanish — Western Hemisphere.   8. Imperialism,
European — Western Hemisphere.   9. Western Hemisphere —
Exploration — Spanish.   10. Western Hemisphere — Exploration —
European — Study and teaching.   11. Racism — Western Hemisphere —
History.   12. Slavery — Western Hemisphere — History.   13. Sexism —
Western Hemisphere — History.   I. Title.   II. Title: Columbus
confronted.   III. DeSirey, Jan, editor.   IV. Dodge, Chris, 1957–
editor.   V. Zinn, Howard, 1922–   1492–1992: a historian's perspective.
VI. Mohawk, John. Discovering Columbus.   VII. Barreiro, Jose. A
note on the Tainos. VIII. Bigelow, Bill.
    970.015

Manufactured in the United States of America

McFarland & Company, Inc., Publishers
  Box 611, Jefferson, North Carolina 28640

Acknowledgments

To Sandy Berman, for every possible reason....

And to Bill Bigelow, Don Irish, Ricardo Levins Morales, Jeff Nygaard, Peter McDonald and Jack Weatherford, for their contributions of source material, fact checking and editorial guidance.

Table of Contents

About the Contributors

José Barreiro, Guajiro from Cuba, is editor in chief of *Northeast Indian Quarterly* at Cornell University.

Bill Bigelow teaches at Jefferson High School in Portland, Oregon. During the 1991–92 school year he coordinated Rethinking Columbus, a teacher-training project of the Network of Educators on Central America.

Steve Charleston (Choctaw) is the Episcopal bishop of Alaska.

Ward Churchill (Creek/Cherokee Métis) is associate professor of American Indian Studies and Communications at the University of Colorado/Boulder, co-director of Colorado AIM, and co-author (with Jim Vander Wall) of *Agents of Repression* (South End Press, 1988) and *COINTELPRO Papers* (1990, South End Press).

Jan DeSirey is a Minnesota librarian who co-edits *MSRRT Newsletter*, an alternative news and review source intended for activist library and information workers.

Chris Dodge co-edits and publishes *MSRRT Newsletter*.

Jan Elliott (Cherokee) is director of the Committee for American Indian History and editor of *Indigenous Thought*.

Uruguayan author **Eduardo Galeano**'s latest title is *The Book of Embraces* (Norton, 1991).

Hans Koning is a Dutch-American novelist, and writer of historical and political nonfiction. Among his novels are *A Walk with Love and Death* (filmed by John Huston), *The Petersburg-Cannes Express*, *The Kleber Flight*, and — most recently — *Acts of Faith*.

James Loewen has a Ph.D. from Harvard in sociology and has taught race relations at Tougaloo College and the University of Vermont. He spent

1990–91 as a senior postdoctoral fellow at the Smithsonian Institution researching *Lies My Teacher Told Me*, a critique of American history.

Peruvian archaeologist **Luis Guillermo Lumbreras** is president of the National Museum of Peru and author of *The Peoples and Cultures of Ancient Peru* (Smithsonian Institution Press, 1974).

John Mohawk, Seneca historian, is a lecturer in American studies at SUNY–Buffalo.

Jean Sindab is the director of Economic, Environmental Justice and Hunger Concerns Programs at the National Council of Churches. She previously served as executive secretary with the World Council of Churches for five years, working on global racism, land rights, and indigenous peoples' issues.

Verena Stolcke is a social anthropologist and teaches at the Universitat Autónoma in Barcelona. She is the author of *Marriage, Class and Color in Nineteenth Century Cuba*.

Robert Allen Warrior (Osage) is currently completing his Ph.D. at Union Theological Seminary in New York City. He is a freelance journalist whose works have appeared in the *Village Voice,* the *Progressive, Sojourners, Christianity and Crisis, News from Indian Country, Lakota Times, Native Peoples,* and *Native Nations.*

John Yewell is a freelance writer and editor.

Howard Zinn is a historian and playwright. His latest book is *Declarations of Independence* (HarperCollins, 1990).

Introduction

John Yewell

This book focuses on material which challenges the popular historical accounts promoted by, for example, the organizers of the official Christopher Columbus Quincentenary Jubilee Commission. While the basic standard for inclusion used by the editors was relevance to the issue of Columbus, his legacy, and the five hundredth anniversary of his arrival in the Western Hemisphere, a special emphasis was placed on writing that tried to put truth back on speaking terms with a sense of right and wrong. In style and content the editors have tried to steer the difficult course between the murky shoals of academia and the bright but treacherous reefs of journalism. The reader will notice that the two most popular, and in our view spurious, questions revolving around Columbus—his ethnicity, and the precise location of his landfall— are ignored here.

The United States honors two people with holidays bearing their names: Martin Luther King, Jr., who gave his life combating the legacy of slavery, and Christopher Columbus, who initiated it in this hemisphere. One goal in putting together this book was to promote the truth about Columbus (without merely demonizing him) in order that readers might overcome entrenched mythology and ultimately put an end to the perpetuation of this tragic irony.

Nineteen ninety-two is a crucial time in the effort to correct the historical record about Columbus. To paraphrase Mexican novelist Carlos Fuentes, North American school children are still being raised on the notion that when Columbus arrived in the Caribbean he was greeted by joyful natives hopping up and down on the sands like long-shipwrecked sailors and crying out joyfully "We've been discovered!" The real story is one of subjugation and greed, a history still being played out in Central and South America and, yes, the United States. If the opportunity to teach the truth about Columbus during the Quincentennial is neglected, posterity will be right to ask why.

The editors have not been interested in balance, but in pursuing truth. "Balanced" history gives equal weight to murderer and victim. "Balance" grants five minutes to Hitler and five minutes to the Jews. "Balance" stigmatizes the pursuit of truth and perpetuates sanitized historical records.

Certainly we who are alive today cannot restore to life the millions who died of new diseases or were slaughtered outright by Columbus and those who followed him. We cannot rewrite the history of slavery, initiated by Columbus and continued by his sons and cultural heirs. It is impossible to turn back the clock, to ask the first Europeans who arrived in this hemisphere to treat the indigenous peoples of that time and place with mutual respect. We can only with great difficulty try to undo the terrible ecological legacy that colonialism and exploitation have wrought. But we can at the very least stop lying to our children by coming to terms with the ignominies of the last 500 years.

Those years have favored the mythologizers of a fair-haired and heroic Christopher Columbus. The burden of proof is shifting, and Columbus's defenders are increasingly being challenged to prove their point. Does it suffice to say that Columbus was a product of his times, times which were brutal? If he is mere product, then it stands to reason that he did not rise above those times, usually a prerequisite for greatness.

To judge Columbus either by the "standards of his day," whatever those were, or by today's mores, whatever they are, presupposes one of two fallacies: that the mores of Columbus's age were generally despicable and accepted as such at the time — no one who has read the eloquent accounts of Bartolomé de las Casas can accept this rationalization — or that today's mores are inherently more advanced than those of 500 years ago. Only the methods of slaughter have changed.

Ward Churchill's arguments on the question of culpability, contained herein, are particularly compelling.

Whatever the mores of his times, surely Columbus and others knew that murder was wrong, that Christ himself would never condone slavery, a practice as abhorred in many parts of Europe and the rest of the world (places actually visited by Columbus) at the time as it was practiced in others.

The only standard the editors see as meaningful is one of a higher order, in which excuses for slavery and genocide have no place. They are tolerated in part because the present often dismisses past crimes as having occurred in historical "contexts." It should not be acceptable to citizens of the present time that we too be pardoned for our sins by future historians, that the tyrants of the 20th century, a century singularly cruel and for which brutality has no peer, be rehabilitated by those historians as products of their times. This cycle of contemporary acquiescence and historical dismissal should be broken. The pursuit of truth demands the acknowledgment of wrong, whenever and wherever it happened. The alternative is the repetition of those wrongs. Such atrocities continue today, in different forms and in different guises, around the world, and should be justly condemned by future historians.

This cultural blind-spot, this dogged refusal to put before the mind's eye the image of millions of people dead before an onslaught of superior technology and disease, this tenacious misology regarding Columbus and the very specific crimes he himself committed, is the most galling manifestation of the official acceptance of Columbus.

Columbus did not arrive in the Western Hemisphere bearing diplomatic credentials, or present himself as an emissary or representative of one government or people to another. Nor did he acknowledge the humanity of the peoples he met. He knew he would encounter occupied lands, whether by the "Great Khan" or others, and came intending to take possession of them anyway. He went from island to island claiming each in turn for the Spanish Crown, subjugating the peoples as he went while not even knowing where he was. As the antecedent of the perpetrators of the American Indian Holocaust, Columbus is as onerous a symbol of cultural arrogance and exploitation as any, and as such is an issue for Americans and non–Americans alike. The manner in which the United States recognizes the Columbus Quincentenary will be a measure of the nation's progress away from racism and colonialism.

Reconciliation with American Indians must begin with an acknowledgment of the racism of Columbus and those who followed him. But beyond that initial step are questions far more important to Native Americans, such as treaty rights, sovereignty, religious freedom, and land and resource management. Our society must stop ignoring these concerns and begin to take them seriously.

Americans have peculiar notions about geography and history, and a notoriously poor grasp of both. When people of color are massacred, be it 500 years ago or 5,000 miles away, the response of the West is in general tepid. Innocent, dead, dark-haired Iraqi babies is one thing; dying fair-haired Kurds is another. It is time Americans and all people tried to picture what happened to the indigenous peoples of the Western Hemisphere and to the enslaved Africans brought there after the arrival of Columbus as if it were happening today, in their own front yards, to themselves. This book attempts to do that.

"They are the best people in the world and above all the gentlest. . . . They are so naive and so free with their possessions that no one who has not witnessed them would believe it. When you ask for something they never say no. To the contrary, they offer to share with anyone. . . . They are well-built, with good bodies and handsome features. . . . They do not bear arms, and do not know them, for I showed them a sword, they took it by the edge and cut themselves out of ignorance. . . . They would make fine servants. . . . With fifty men we could subjugate them all and make them do whatever we want."

— *Columbus, from the log of his first voyage*

"They spared no sex nor age; neither would their Cruelty pity Women with child, whose bellies they would rip up, taking out the Infant to hew it to pieces. They would often lay wagers who should with most dexterity either cleave or cut a man in the middle, or who could at one blow soonest cut off his head. The children they would take by the feet and dash their innocent heads against the rocks."

— *Bartolomé de las Casas, from* History of the Indies

The chapter heading quotations were selected by the editors.

1492–1992:
A Historian's Perspective

Howard Zinn

If there's anything I detest more than another, it is that spirit of historical inquiry which doubts everything, that modern spirit which destroys all the illusions and all the heroes which have been the inspiration of patriotism through all the centuries. —Chauncey Depew, president of the New York Central Railroad and agent for the Vanderbilt fortunes, at Carnegie Hall on the 400th anniversary of Columbus.

I'm here to celebrate with you the Quincentennial of Columbus. You know, big plans are being made for this. Many states have established commissions. You probably know that President Reagan established a commission back in 1985 for the observance of the Quincentennial. It was a little embarrassing though, because he appointed this man Goudie, who was a Florida real estate developer—Who else? A natural choice. He resigned last year because some House subcommittee was investigating him. You thought only people like us are investigated. [laughter] Sometimes they investigate people like that, when they get really flagrant. He was letting out contracts to real estate friends of his, then it turns out he had trouble with the courts, and that he had lost his real estate license. Anyway, he's gone.

Of course Reagan knows a lot about American history and Native Americans. He used to listen to the Lone Ranger, [laughter] and from that he derived his knowledge of American Indians. In the last part of his presidency you may remember he visited Moscow. He had refused to meet with a number of Indian representatives to discuss the conditions of Indians in the U.S., so they followed him to Moscow and showed up at some meeting he was having at Moscow U. He was slightly embarrassed. Three of these representatives were

A transcript of a speech by Howard Zinn at Cowles Auditorium at the University of Minnesota, Minneapolis, April 12, 1991.

there, and they raised their hands, and I guess he was a little surprised they spoke English. [laughter] And then the moderator said:

> Mr. President, I heard that a group of American Indians have come here because they couldn't meet you in the United States of America. If you fail to meet them here will you be able to improve, to correct it, and to meet them back in the United States?

Reagan: "I didn't know that they had asked to see me," — there was a lot Reagan didn't know. [laughter] Then he says, as if to educate this Moscow audience:

"Let me tell you just a little something about the American Indian in our land. We have provided millions of acres of land for what are called 'preservations,'" and then he stopped and said "I should say 'reservations.' We have done everything we can to meet their demands as to how they want to live. Maybe we should not have humored them in that." [groans] Please, a little respect for the president. [laughter] "And you'd be surprised: some of them became very wealthy, because some of those reservations were overlaying great pools of oil. And you can get very rich pumping oil. And so, I don't know what their complaint might be."

I just thought I'd start off with Reagan, and finish with Reagan as fast as I could.

All these plans are being made. One of them, a group in New York, is planning a marriage between the statue of [incredulity] . . . — there are a lot of very intolerant people around here — between the statue of Columbus, which is in Barcelona, and the Statue of Liberty. Really. I don't make these things up, even though I'm a historian. . . . [loud laughter and applause]

There was, as some of you may remember, a Quadricentennial. There was a big celebration in New York, and Chicago had a huge one. People came, and there was a big hoopla. Grover Cleveland started off the ceremonies. But there was no opposition recorded to the Quadricentennial a hundred years ago. Now, of course, what is happening around the country is that there is opposition, there is resistance, there is counter-information. . .

Perhaps he was anticipating a hundred years beyond his time what was happening, but at the Quadricentennial there was a speech made at Carnegie Hall by Chauncey Depew. You can tell from the name he's a member of the left. Chauncey Depew, president of the New York Central Railroad, agent for the Vanderbilt fortunes, said:

> If there's anything I detest more than another, it is that spirit of historical inquiry which doubts everything, that modern spirit which destroys all the illusions and all the heroes which have been the inspiration of patriotism through all the centuries.

I'm just glad he's not around to see this meeting. [laughter]

People are surprised when you begin to talk about Columbus and what happened back then in 1492, 4, 5, 8, 9, those years that Columbus and his brothers and the rest of their crew were doing their work, their wonderful work of discovery, in the New World.

It was new to them. It wasn't new to the people who were here...

The big problem with history is not that people tell you lies, although of course sometimes they do, but most of the time the big problem with history is what is left out. And what is left out can be so important as to cast the entire story into a great lie, even though you've been told some true things. And so, I confess to you that I did not know anything about Columbus beyond what school kids know until after I had my Ph.D. in history. Really. I'm a trained historian, whatever it means to "train" a historian, [laughter] and I'd gone all through my historical education right up through the doctorate at Columbia University and no one ever corrected the story of Columbus that I had got at elementary school. What I got later on was a more sophisticated, slightly more detailed, slightly more polysyllabic version of what I had learned in elementary school. And ... this is a real confession: it wasn't until I started doing work on this *People's History of the United States* that I learned about Columbus...

It's not that I was astonished, because by this time I was not astonished by things that I learned about people who were supposed to be important and famous and great... I wasn't astonished in the general sense, but I was astonished very specifically. It was new material for me.

So I'm not surprised now that the overwhelming number of reactions to this *People's History* are about Columbus. The mail that I get from around the country starts off with Columbus. This may mean that's all they read of the book. [laughter] I don't like to think that. What's more likely is that it's the most startling thing. It's just that people do not learn this, people do not know this. It's only very recently, in the last few years, that people have begun talking about this, that a literature has begun to appear...

Hans Koning wrote a book called *Columbus: His Enterprise.* It's a small book, very neat, and a very vivid account of Columbus. And there's a new book by Kirkpatrick Sale, called *The Conquest of Paradise,* which is a very detailed account of Columbus's voyages and also of all the hoopla that has followed Columbus through the centuries down to the present day.

So what did I learn? I learned that when Columbus arrived he was greeted by the Indians on this island in the Bahamas. You know there's a lot of controversy over exactly where Columbus landed. This is a big thing. This is the kind of thing that makes the front pages of the newspapers. (I saw on) the front page of the *Boston Globe:* "New Discovery About Columbus." I thought, wow, finally they're gonna come out with it. [laughter] The new discovery was: that Columbus landed 60 miles to the south of where people thought he had landed. The *New York Times* had an editorial on Columbus. I thought: an editorial on Columbus, maybe now . . . The editorial was about how nobody knows what Columbus looked like.

This is the kind of history that makes the front pages or the editorial pages. We're accustomed to that by now.

I remember reading a front page story in the *New York Times*. You know, historians are always looking to see if they'll put something on the front page that's in [their] field. A front page story in the *New York Times* revealed the disease that Martin Van Buren had before he died.

Who was Martin Van Buren? A little research discloses that he was president of the United States.

What has not made the front pages of the newspapers, and what I have not seen yet on television . . . is the fact that when Columbus arrived he was greeted by the Taino Indians — I called them Arawak Indians in my book. It's really embarrassing after you've written something and you discover that you didn't get the name right.

They came out and greeted Columbus, these strange creatures alighting from these boats wearing these funny things and these odd looking implements. They went up and greeted them with gifts. Columbus talked about this a number of times in his journal, about what the Indians were like that he encountered. He wrote a letter to one of his patrons back in Aragon just after he returned from his first voyage:

> As soon as they see that they are safe and have laid aside all fear they are very simple and honest and exceedingly liberal with all that they have, rather than refusing anything that he may possess when he is asked for it, but on the contrary inviting us to ask them. They exhibit great love toward all others in preference to themselves, they also give objects of great value for trifles and content themselves with little or nothing in return. I did not find, as some of us had expected, any cannibals among them, but on the contrary men of great deference and kindness.

And at another point in his journal:

> They are the best people in the world, and above all the gentlest. They are without knowledge of what is evil, nor do they murder or steal. They love their neighbors as themselves and they have the sweetest talk in the world and are always laughing.

In the very entry in his journal where he talks about how nice they are he says, "With fifty men we could subdue them and make servants of them."

And of course that's what they did. And more.

Las Casas described it — he saw with his own eyes what the Spaniards did while he was there: dashing of babies against rocks by Spanish soldiers, the atrocities they committed, the rapes, the disembowelments. Columbus said they were gentle and nice people, but they weren't treated as people; they were treated as inanimate objects...

Hans Koning in his book writes:

> We are now in February 1495. Time was short for sending back a good "dividend" on the supply ships getting ready for the return to Spain. Columbus therefore turned to a massive slave raid as a means for filling up these ships. The brothers rounded up 1500 Arawaks—men, women, and children—and imprisoned them in pens in Isabela, guarded by men and dogs. The ships had room for no more than 500, and thus only the best specimens were loaded aboard.

Of the 500 slaves, 300 arrived alive in Spain, where they were put up for sale in Seville.

Of course Columbus was looking for gold. He saw little bits of gold in their noses and their ears, and he was very anxious to please. I love it when I hear people talk—mostly important people in the government or in business—about the sanctity of the profit motive... The profit motive operated very strongly with Columbus. And for it he sent the Indians out in quest of gold so he could have gold to bring back to his sponsors in Spain. They had a quota of gold that they had to get in three months, this is for everybody over 14. If they didn't bring back this quota their arms were hacked off with axes so they could bleed to death as an example to everybody else...

So, butchery took place in Hispaniola. The Spaniards were armed with things that these Indians had never seen, had no notion about. They marauded through the island to put down any signs of ... non-compliance with their demands or resistance to their enslavement. Horses, dogs, crossbows. The Tainos did not know what a sword was when the Spaniards first came. Columbus notes that they didn't know that these were weapons and so they reached out to touch the swords and they cut themselves because they didn't know it was sharp.

Las Casas describes having seen the Spaniards just sharpen their swords, they went out looking for a group of Indians to [test their sharpness] on, and there follows a massacre that horrifies them. And las Casas became a strong protester against this and demanded that something be done.

Of course reform laws were passed which were meaningless, as many reform laws are.

But when you tell people this they are surprised.

Every semester for about the last eight years I get about 25 letters from a high school in Tigard, Oregon, from a class taught by this teacher who apparently forces these kids to read my book. [laughter]

He probably also forces them to write letters to me after they've read my book, in which they ask me questions. Half of them say, "Wow, I never knew

this stuff," and others say, "Who are you?" "What's wrong with you?" [laughter]
One writer said, "Do you believe in God? I noticed that in your whole book,
your whole 600 pages of American history, you don't mention God once." I'm
gonna correct that, of course. [laughter]

One wrote:

> You say that Columbus physically abused the Indians that
> didn't help him find gold. You've said that you gained a lot of this
> information from Columbus's own journal. I'm wondering if there
> is such a journal, and if so, why isn't it part of our history? Why
> isn't any of what you say in my history book or in history books
> people have access to each day. [applause]

Now, it could mean two things, right? He could be writing in indignation: "Why don't they tell us these things in our history books?" Or he could
be saying: "Come on now. Nobody else has told me this. Where did you make
this up?"

But you can't blame him. You can't blame people being surprised and
shocked... [Is] the media, with all of its power, capable, in this country of
free expression, of hiding one of the most fundamental facts about the genesis
of western society in this hemisphere? It's not surprising. This is what people
get, from kindergarten up through college.

The main biography of Columbus is written by Samuel Eliot Morison,
the "distinguished"—every time I use the word "distinguished" I want to put
quotation marks around it—Harvard professor who was enamored with
Columbus—so much so that he sailed across the Atlantic trying to follow Columbus's traces. And he wrote this great long history of Columbus in which
he mentions genocide—it's there, it's just there, somewhere, you know. It's
as if you wrote a book about Hitler and you wrote about his great accomplishments. He solved the unemployment problem in Germany, he built
tremendous architectural works, and a fantastic highway system, and he was
a magnificent orator, and then somewhere in this book about Hitler you have
a few lines about how he was responsible for the deaths of many millions of
people.

Morison was a flamboyant writer. This endeared him to a lot of people
because a lot of historians are sort of dry as writers. Some of you may have
noticed... [laughter]

He [wrote]:

> Never again may mortal men hope to recapture the amazement,
> the wonder, the delight of those October days in 1492 when the
> New World gracefully yielded her virginity to the conquering Cas-
> tilians.

It's interesting from the standpoint of the argument that goes on among historians about presentism; some of you may be familiar with that. The argument involves someone saying to someone else: "Now look . . . if you're writing about the past, you shouldn't write it from your present point of view, you should try not to impose the present and present values on this period." You're writing about a period in which people butchered one another, you really have to put yourself back in that time. The mores were different.

The mores were different? Then people butchered one another. It's amazing how that argument goes on. You mustn't look at Columbus from the standpoint of today, you see. But what defeats that argument is that if you go back to that day there are people who criticize and speak. Obviously, Columbus's values were not the only values present in the world in 1492. Las Casas had his values — and of course the Indians had their values.

Here's las Casas taking a different point of view:

> I believe that because of these impious, criminal, and ig-
> nominious acts God will visit His wrath and His ire upon Spain,
> for her share in the blood-stained riches obtained by threat and
> usurpation accompanied by such slaughter and annihilation of
> those peoples.

There was a German historian in the 1960s who wrote a cultural history of the modern age, taking a long view of the history of human culture, and judging the 500 years since Columbus. He says: "The 500 years of this modern age is one of the most rudimentary, childish, and primitive periods in the history of the human experience."

The only word I object to is childish.

But he caught something there, something about the culture of these 500 years which troubles him.

By the way, if you look in the *Columbia Encyclopedia* and you look at the entry on Columbus — which is a long entry, naturally — you will not find a word about atrocities, about killings, about enslavement — nothing. . . Of course it's the *"Columbia" Encyclopedia.*

The importance of all this, I guess, is not simply to set the record straight on Columbus and what happened in the 1490s on Hispaniola. . . Some people think that this is what history should be doing. History should be constantly setting and resetting the record straight on some past period of history just to get the facts right about what happened. But there's no real point, in my opinion, in getting the facts right, unless there's some important purpose behind it. . . There must be some meaning to this. There must be a reason why it's important to bring these things out about Columbus.

It's not to denounce Columbus. It's too late for that. It's not to have an imbroglio about Columbus Day and have a big battle about what really happened then, and was Columbus a good guy or a bad guy. Who cares? It's too late to make a character judgment about Columbus — he's not asking us for a letter of recommendation. [laughter] There must be something beyond that.

I think the importance is that this is the beginning of a 500-year period of what is called, usually with gratitude and admiration, "Western civilization." This is the beginning of 500 years of progress — this is the modern age, speeding ahead in geometric waves — progress far beyond what had been made in the millennia before. Five hundred years of enormous, swift progress of the development of technology, industry, and the advancement of science. It's true, just as it's true that Columbus was a great navigator and explorer.

What also marks these 500 years — and that's why adding the facts about Columbus is important — is that they are 500 years of conquest by the western powers, represented first in that one instance by Spain, but very soon by many others. Five hundred years of conquest, of exploitation, of enslavement, of violence, of war, of colonialism. It seems to me that to hide the truth about Columbus is to hide the very sort of genetic truth about Western civilization and what it means and what it has meant for so many people.

All of . . . the terrible things that have happened in these 500 years — of which Columbus gives us a preview — all of this is justified by the idea of progress and material advancement. And it's also always given sort of a moral justification; in Columbus's time it was a religious justification. God was somehow involved in all of this.

In our times we still invoke God — that is, governmental leaders invoke God — again and again to back them up . . . This moral justification — "We did this for liberty"; "We did this for democracy"; "We invaded this country to stop the invasion of another country"; "We killed these 100,000 people to prevent the killing of more people." Always doing terrible things to prevent more terrible things — except that the terrible things that we do are immediate and certain, the more terrible that we claim we are preventing are in the distance and hazy and uncertain.

This process that went on for 500 years of conquest and violence is reinforced and intensified, made easier to happen, by racism, which is right there at the start by simply finding that these other people to whom you are doing these things are not really like you, not really human beings, and therefore you can do whatever you want to them.

And also [by] nationalism: [We say] "These people are on the other side of the river, they're on the other side of the boundary line, they're someone else, they're not under our flag, they're under their flag, they don't pledge allegiance the way we do, they pledge some other kind of allegiance." So we've been beset by this . . . complex ideological justification which has been going on now for a long time.

It started in Spain and Portugal. At that time the Pope divided the world between Spain and Portugal. Spain and Portugal were the colonial powers, and then the others followed . . . The Dutch, the French, the English, the

Germans, the Russians, the Japanese and the last of course to come on board — and not the least — is the United States of America...

Let me just talk a little about the Columbian legacy in the United States of America, since there isn't time to talk about it in all the other parts of the world, and all the things that all the other imperial powers did in their history.

With the United States of course it started very soon after Columbus with the very first settlement, maybe Jamestown in 1607, and in 1619 the first black slaves. If you want to have another esoteric argument among historians you can argue about whether or not they were slaves or servants. Historians love to argue about things like this.

But they were in effect slaves and they were the first slaves in the beginning of a long slave trade, and the beginning of a long period of slavery. It's very easy of course to forget that in the history of this country we've had more years of slavery than of non-slavery. We've had slavery for more than 200 years, and the 13th amendment was just a little over 100 years ago... What's interesting is that we can have slavery and still be a democracy ... still be considered one of the most advanced countries in the world, where we have representative government, separation of powers. We have this marvelous on-paper democracy, which has, people will admit, its little flaws, like slavery... [laughter]

Indians are not so easily enslaved; it's their territory. It's easier to enslave blacks, brought from Africa in chains, torn from their language. The Indians: this is their turf. Not so easy — although it's tried — to enslave them. And besides, by this time you don't need them: you have black slaves.

So with the Indians, the main problem is to get rid of them — which this country ... the country of the Declaration of Independence, of Jefferson and the founding fathers ... proceeds to do. So our continental expansion takes place across a great land which is inhabited by Indians, although it doesn't look that way on the map.

I remember the maps in my classroom somewhere back then, which were labeled "Westward Expansion." It showed the different colors for the Louisiana Purchase, the Florida Purchase, the Mexican Cession, and all of that. It was as if westward expansion was a biological thing. We just expanded, from being a thin line of colonies along the Atlantic coast to the Pacific Ocean, we just expanded. And how did we expand? By purchases and cessions.

The Florida Purchase. It was quite a while before I learned that it wasn't like a commercial deal. Andrew Jackson went into Florida with his troops and killed a number of people, and then Spain was persuaded to, quote, "sell" Florida to us, although no money ever passed hands.

The Mexican Cession. Well, that also looked benign. Mexico ceded that great southwest territory up to California, Colorado, New Mexico, that great southwest... But then I did learn: Why did they cede it to us?

Friendship? [loud laughter] Latin hospitality? [laughter] An early good neighbor policy? [laughter]

I learned about the Mexican War. We instigated a war with Mexico, that's what you have to say. It was a disputed territory; we sent soldiers into the territory; there were clashes. Polk, our president — another one of those Martin Van Buren types [laughter] — wanted California. He planned something just like Lyndon Johnson planned the Gulf of Tonkin episode. Some people think this thing in Iraq was planned. . .

So we take 40 percent of Mexican territory after a brutal and bloody war — a war which is not particularly palatable to the soldiers. When I did my *People's History* and I came to the Mexican War I said, I want to look at the Mexican War from the standpoint of the victims, from the standpoint of the Mexicans and of the GIs who fought in the war. I discovered how many GIs deserted, how many didn't want to fight in the Mexican War, how the Massachusetts volunteers came back to Boston with their ranks decimated — half of them were dead. They came back to a victory dinner and they booed their commander off the place. [applause] We need more victory dinners like that.

Then there was the Louisiana Territory. I remember how proud I was . . . as a kid. If any of you saw the map: we doubled the size of the country just like that with a terrific deal we made. We bought this huge territory, going from the Mississippi to the Rockies, and: it's uninhabited. [laughter] Well, we could tell that by looking at the map.

It's interesting: the Indians are invisible people. They don't exist. And once you have started with that, then you don't have to be told — I certainly wasn't told, and young people learning history are not told — that we fought hundreds of wars to annihilate the Indians, to get rid of them. We removed them from places where they lived, removed the Cherokees and the Choctaws, and the other five "civilized tribes," removed them from the southeast, pushed them west on that infamous Trail of Tears, 4,000 of them dying along the way. Sixteen thousand people forced by the Army to go west.

Annihilate the buffalo herds to remove the sources of the food in the middle of the country on the Great Plains. Push the Indians farther and farther away, those who aren't killed, push them into something we called "Indian Territory" in Oklahoma. At last: now this is your territory, this is Indian Territory.

Then oil is discovered in Indian Territory.

And then it's no longer Indian Territory. Just as when gold was discovered in north Georgia the Cherokees had to get out of north Georgia, and had to be pushed out of there.

We still sometimes do things for oil. [laughter] It's worth it. How could we live without oil?

So we became a great continental power. Then we moved outside the continental limits and became a world power. In 1898. There's that one period of American history where the textbooks tell you straight out, unabashedly... They almost always have a chapter in American history textbooks: "The Age of Imperialism"—lasting from 1898 to 1903. [laughter] And then we go into Columbus's territory: We go into Cuba to help the Cubans, because we always go places to help people... We went to Cuba to help free the Cubans from Spanish rule just as went into Iraq to free the Kuwaitis from Iraqi rule. We're always going into places to free people from other people's rule.

There was that splendid little war with Spain, a quick war, three months. Very few casualties. Even most of our casualties were not caused by battles; most of them were caused by poison beef sold to the Army by contractors: Swift and Armour. Tins of beef left over from the Civil War. I'm serious. Thousands of soldiers died of disease. A few hundred died of battle wounds. The profit motive—I'm sorry to mention the profit motive again.

Of course, there was an opportunity to take Puerto Rico. It's not far from Cuba. A little cannonading and Puerto Rico is ours.

From then on there's nothing to stop us. Sure, there are people who live in these places, but we were a kind of superior civilization by then. We were going to bring democracy and Christianity and civilization everywhere to these miserable people.

And so we pick up Hawaii halfway across the Pacific—and now we're really getting far from home. And then the Philippines, which is on the other side of the Pacific, which is off the coast of Asia, off the coast of China, although McKinley doesn't seem to know this. He doesn't know where it is. [laughter] And by the way, some of you may remember this famous episode: McKinley invokes God to explain why the United States took the Philippines instead of leaving it to the Filipinos.

Spain was in control of the Philippines, the Filipinos wanted freedom from Spain, but McKinley says, "I didn't know what to do with the Philippines, but I walked the floor night after night, and I got down on my knees and prayed to God, and God told me to take the Philippines." [derision] You sound skeptical. [laughter]

But of course God didn't give the same message to the Filipinos. They fought. It wasn't a splendid little war, like in Cuba. The Filipinos fought a bitter, bloody, a kind of pre–Vietnam War full of atrocities in which ten-year-old Filipino children were slaughtered... And finally, after years and years, the Filipinos were subdued and United States control was established.

It was around this time that they began talking in the United States of the U.S. as a world power. The first books that used that phrase, "United States as a world power" came out about 1906. By that time we ... had created Panama. We wanted Panama ... and Theodore Roosevelt took Panama. The early part of the 20th century was a period of the United States moving into the Caribbean, moving into all the countries in Central America, the American corporations moving in, railroaders, banks, United

Fruit, the Marines moving in when things weren't going well enough for United Fruit or the corporations or the banks, and governments established, over-thrown, or protected, according to whether [they] would play ball with us, not according to whether [they] were democratic or liberty loving, or anything like that.

I just have to read this to you. This [was] in the *New York Times* last week. The Kurds are fleeing Iraq, and you know what's happening with all of that. This is a quote:

> Administration officials explained [in explaining why the United States was letting the Kurds be attacked by the Iraqi army] that they found themselves torn between two principles of American foreign policy. One principle is that international borders and the territorial integrity of nations have to be respected for the sake of world stability, no matter what kind of governments happen to rule within those borders. The other principle is America's long-standing commitment to human rights and self-determination.

Now only a public that has been deprived of history could believe that. [loud, sustained applause]

I believe the only reason that the Bush administration has been able to get away with what it has been doing, is that the administration and their spokesmen who dominate the airwaves [applause] — and the media who allow them to dominate the airwaves — all of them have . . . collaborated in keeping history out of the newspapers and off of the airwaves, because it would only take a smattering of history for the American people to reject what has been told to them as excuses and rationale for making war in the world today. [applause]

I emphasize that because it seems to me that what is going on here in this meeting, and what will go on in subsequent meetings, what's taking place around the country, and what people who are socially concerned have as their responsibility, is to fill in that historical vacuum that exists, and to spread the word. I don't believe that the American people are innately brutal, or bad, or want to do terrible things. But I do believe that they are victims of tremendous misinformation, lies, deception, and most important, omission of important data. And I believe that once the people in the United States . . . learn about these things, they have the courage to become critical, even of their own government.

This was shown during the years of the Vietnam War, where there wasn't a quick and immediate victory, but the . . . people in the United States became more and more aware of what was going on. They began to see the pictures of what the United States Army was doing. They saw on television the burning of huts, Marines setting fire to villages. They saw Vietnamese women holding children in their arms, cowering in fear before Americans armed with automatic rifles pouring this rifle fire into the bodies of old people, women and children. They saw this, and they revolted against [it].

I'm simplifying it — it's more complicated than that. But I believe that was an important factor in the turning around of American public opinion. It took several years, but . . . that common sense of the American people, based on this recognition of something they had not known before, lead them to dispute the government and no longer to believe in the government. All the polls and surveys by 1975 showed that the American people . . . distrusted the government, had no faith in what the government was telling them. It will take that kind of presenting of information to a public which has been denied that information to make an important change in what is going on in this country . . .

Let me recommend to you a book . . . by Eduardo Galeano, called *Open Veins of Latin America*. It is a book which surveys five centuries of what the United States, what the American government, has been doing in Latin America. It's not an ordinary book; it's an eloquent, passionate, powerful and very well-documented history of Latin American relations these 500 years.

It's important to listen to the voices of people from Latin America, like Galeano and many many others. It's important to listen to the voices of Indians who are speaking out, although it was thought some years ago that we had really annihilated the Indians . . .

But in the sixties and seventies the Indians began to speak up, they began to be heard from again. Remember, they occupied the site of Wounded Knee, and defied the American government to remove them. [applause] And a consciousness of American Indians as an exploited and oppressed group in this country is still at a level that needs very much to be enhanced.

I recently got a letter from a man I met who teaches in California. He's an Indian who in fact is working on something to take place in California in 1992 in connection with Columbus. . . I know he wouldn't mind me repeating this:

> I'm a father of five children that have all experienced the institutional racism of American society. All my children are bright, having grown up in an academic environment, and yet they have fundamental problems realizing their full potential, since they are first and foremost American Indians. Teachers have initial low expectations for my children. I remember going to a parent's night in a Los Angeles elementary school where my children are in attendance. The teacher said that my daughter was shy, but she was doing remarkably well in all of her subjects since her first language was Spanish. Shocked by this assessment, my wife and I informed the teacher that our daughter's first language was English, and her second language was Navaho. We realized that the teacher had stereotyped our daughter as Hispanic from the start, and had not

even paid enough attention to her during the first two months of
class to even set her superficial stereotypes straight.

I tell you this to indicate how still alive is this problem of racism in the
United States in regards to Indians. And I don't even have to talk about its
continued existence with relation to Blacks and Hispanic Americans and so
on.

[Another] teacher who wants to set the record straight about Columbus
starts his class off by going over to some kid and taking her purse. She objects
and says, "You took my purse." And he says, "No I didn't; I discovered it."
[laughter] And then he goes on and talks and has them read material about
Columbus. And these students wrote letters, letters of their own discovery,
the letter of a young person who has learned something startling and interesting, letters of indignation in which they say, "Why have I been lied to
all this time?" "Why are they lying to us?" "What are they trying to hide?"
"What are they trying to do to us?" "I think they're trying to make us super-
patriotic. I think they want us to accept whatever the government says. No,
I'm gonna think about this more from now on."

It's possible for education to go on, for people to learn things. . . . I think
we have a great opportunity with this Quincentennial to raise issues, to have
discussions and meetings, [to] recapture history and connect our history with
what is going on in the United States today, to talk about the meaning of progress, and to challenge this much-vaunted American industrial technological
progress. All the material things that we have, all this great industrial progress, was made . . . at tremendous human expense: at the expense of Black
slaves, at the expense of Chinese and Irish laborers on the railroads, at the expense of people who work, [of] girls who worked 16 to 18 hours a day in textile
mills. All this talk about progress, about technological advance, doesn't talk
about the human cost of that advance, or the cost in terms of what happened
to the land and the life on the land—the ecological cost. It's an opportunity
to bring all that up and talk about that.

We only have nine years or so till the next century. Maybe we can do
enough things in these next nine years to open up the new century with a new
kind of society, a new kind of world, a new kind of feeling among people, for
a world community. I think it's possible at least to start in that direction.

Discovering Columbus:
The Way Here

John Mohawk

At their first entrance they commanded them to swear fealty and obedience to the King of Spain, and those that would not come in and submit themselves to the will of such unjust and cruel men, they proclaimed rebels.... The blindness of the chief Governors of the Indies not permitting them to discern, that no man can be called a Rebel who is not before a Subject. — Bartolomé de las Casas, from *History of the Indies.*

The legend of Christopher Columbus's "discovery" of the Americas in 1492 is one of the most widely shared stories in the world. Columbus's story has been reinvented, certain specific events have been selected and whole trends of the time have been ignored. The resulting pattern is intended to explain and celebrate the events of the time as part of a glorious history of Western civilization.

The obvious fiction of a "discovery" of lands occupied by millions of people for tens of thousands of years underscores the ethnocentrism evident in most historical accounts. Columbus is portrayed as an enormously talented individual who, with a bit of luck, embarked on a journey to find a commercial water route to Asia and who instead arrived at the islands of the Caribbean. What followed, according to popular accounts, was the migration of Western civilization to these previously "unknown" lands and the subsequent development of modern civilization. The idea of "discovery" tends to render invisible all that existed in the Americas prior to 1492, including the peoples who occupied those places. Their fate at the hands of the Europeans becomes more and more irrelevant until what remains is the story of waves of successful "pioneers" who found virgin shores and who, through adventure and hard work, brought about the world we live in today.

Reprinted from View from the Shore *published by* Northeast Indian Quarterly, Fall 1990.

World history, as told by Western historians, has until recently been the story of the evolution to modernity of European-originating societies. This is why the history of the Americas begins in so many accounts with Columbus's voyages. Previous voyages had been made, but such voyages did not result in European colonization and therefore are only curious footnotes to the real story. The existence and previous histories of the American Indians similarly are not part of the story of the triumph of the West and are therefore relegated to a status of exotic and more or less irrelevant digressions. The celebration of Columbus's voyages, as experienced in contemporary times, has been largely an embrace of an historical myth which reinterprets actual events and the context of those events in ways which explain how things got to be the way they are to the exclusive benefit of the conquerors. The Indians are almost as invisible as the trees or the parrots of the islands in a story which has only one significant player — the Europeans — and a single genesis — European civilization — at the foundation of modernity.

Columbus was born in Genoa around 1451, about the time the Gutenberg press was invented. Little is known about his childhood and adolescence except he was the son of a middle-class wool weaver and he undoubtedly learned the craft himself. In 1451 Genoa was a city-state on the west coast of what would later become the nation of Italy. Columbus's native language was Genoan, a local dialect distinct from Italian. Christopher Columbus was destined to become one of the most famous and celebrated men in history, but the fact of his fame and celebration emerged long after his death in obscurity at Valladolid, Spain, in 1506.

At the time of Columbus's birth, Genoa was a small but significant power in the Mediterranean. His life of adventure at sea began during the summer of 1476. He joined one of five ships owned by the Di Negro and Spinola families of Genoa bound for England to trade wine and other goods from the Mediterranean for English goods — primarily wool, the commodity which brought England into the expanding European market.

The little caravan was met off the coast of Portugal by 17 ships flying French colors. France was allied to Portugal in a contest against Spain (actually the kingdoms of Castile and Aragón) and, under the complex system of such alliances and hostilities the French naval commander designated the Genoan ships as enemy craft. In an afternoon of heavy fighting Columbus's officers, rather than allow their cargo to fall into enemy hands, set the ship ablaze. Columbus, wounded, swam to shore (he later said it was six miles) and soon found himself a member of a colony of Genoese immigrants in Lisbon.

Columbus adapted quickly to his new circumstances and was soon sailing the Atlantic under Portuguese colors. In 1476 or 1477, Columbus was aboard a ship which visited Bristol and Iceland. He would later state his ship journeyed 100 leagues (over 300 miles) beyond Iceland into the deep North

Atlantic. During this journey he observed the prevailing winds of those climes, an observation which would later enable him to find his way home from the Caribbean. A legend has it that during this journey he met Bishop Magnus Eyjolsson. His journals, written some years later, indicate he visited the Guinea (African) coast during these years. He also visited the Canary Islands and Galway on Ireland's western coast. It is probable he visited the Cape Verde Islands prior to 1492.

Not long after his arrival in Portugal, Columbus married a Portuguese woman, Felipa Perestrello Moniz, of modest estate but noble family. She was the daughter of Bartolomeo Perestrello, a former captain in the Portuguese navy and governor of the little island of Porto Santo located about 30 miles from Madeira Island in the Atlantic. This father-in-law, who had died in 1457, had been among the company of adventurers who first sought to colonize Madeira Island around 1417.

Columbus's life story is one of the great personal adventures of all time. He was a bold-hearted explorer, a keen observer of the forces of nature, especially wind and water, a reader of the skies and clouds, and a gazer, for practical purposes, upon the stars. He was a seller of books, a cartographer, and possibly the best dead-reckoning sailor who ever lived. And he lived in a time when to be all these things was possible, when the ships and the technology of navigation — however modest they seem to us today — enabled Europeans to go where no European had been before, or at least had returned ready to repeat the journey.

The mid-15th century was a momentous time in European history and a period which deserves some reflection. Europe is as much an idea as a physical continent. It has become a continent, not because it is geographically separated from the great land mass of Asia, but because it was the home of Latin Christendom.[1] For untold centuries, stretching back to the time of the classic civilizations of Mesopotamia, civilizations of the Africa-Asia-Europe land masses centered around well established and often flourishing trade routes in the Indian Ocean and the South China Seas. A 15th century traveler would have found more of the refined arts, creature comforts, and general trappings of an advanced civilization in India or Japan or, as the Europeans well knew, China.

European imaginations played an important role in the developments which were to follow.[2] Christian cosmology portrayed the West as inheritors of a mandate from Christ, and through Him from the surviving (and carefully edited) texts of the Old Testament. This idea provided an identity in the West and a tailored explanation of the origin and purpose of Western society which modern anthropology recognizes in other peoples as mythology.

In the 11th century Pope Gregory VII moved to unify Christendom under the papacy when he declared papal supremacy over the emperors. The unifying effort was, in political terms, a failure but it did produce at least two momentous results: the Crusades, which were essentially foreign wars fought to regain real estate in Jerusalem to prepare for the second coming of Christ, and a revitalization of the ideology which invented a connection between the cultures of Western Europe and a continuation of the ancient civilizations of the Mediterranean, Greece and Rome.[3]

The culture of the West was forged through a long history of conflict and violence, the roots of which stretch into the ancient civilization of Mesopotamia. The Assyrians, for example, were a conquering civilization that had developed extremely successful military technologies and techniques, including the phalanx, a military formation which produced stunning victories against less well-organized fighting styles. This history of organized violence resulted in experimentation with and perfection of these techniques and technologies of the ancient civilizations.[4] European warfare produced a history of succeeding military technologies that inflicted stunning casualty rates and murderous military victories celebrated as conquests.

This tradition of militarism had been accelerating during the two centuries preceding Columbus's birth. During the 13th century the Mongol mounted archer was the most formidable warrior, the primary implement of Mongol military successes. Mongol armies were called home before they were able to complete the conquest of Western Europe. Their invasion was the last serious external threat Europe experienced.

Europe, more than any place in the world, turned its attention to the development of increasingly effective and destructive military arms. Crossbows were invented which were capable of dismounting a man at 100 yards. The longbow, which Henry III brought to France in 1346 during a bloody campaign to extend his rule to the continent, crushed the flower of French knighthood. At Agincourt in 1415 more than 6,000 French knights fell in futile charges against a small band of English archers. It was a moment when the yew tree of England was the atomic bomb of its age. The longbow could launch 10 missiles a minute and was deadly at 100 yards, but its place at the center of the stage of military developments was relatively short lived. Edward III is credited with the introduction of another weapon to European warfare, the fire tube. Within two centuries, firearms were the central fact of life in European warfare and ". . . the age of man-powered warfare had drawn to a close."[5]

The world's first naval arsenal was founded in Venice shortly before 1300 at about the time Marco Polo's account of his adventures in the Orient was published. The naval arsenal was the result of a joint venture in which commercial insitutions joined with government to produce sea craft which served both military and mercantile purposes. Commercial investment in such enterprises was made possible by the existence of considerable fortunes amassed through trade in the Adriatic and Mediterranean seas. Italy was the center of this marine trade and would also become, not coincidentally, a major producer and supplier of arms to the continent. Thus did three tendencies emerge in Italy at the same time: the coordination of efforts between the military objectives of the state and the commercial interests of the bankers and traders, the growth of an arms industry, and the design and production of more efficient and well-armed sea craft. The result of these developments was "[a] remarkably flexible and efficient system of warfare, relating means to ends according to financial as well as diplomatic calculations by the end of the 15th century."[6]

The impact of gunpowder on warfare would cause parallel developments in other areas of human endeavor. Although sails had been invented centuries earlier, the need for wider-beamed ships able to mount and reload cannon soon led to total concentration on sailing technology and the abandonment of the oared galley in the same process which made the other machines of war — the mounted archer, the phalangite — obsolete.

The new technologies of warfare developed farther and faster in Western Europe than anywhere else in the world because of the confluence of existing technologies, the cultural diversity which made some experimentation not only acceptable but inevitable, and intense local competition which by tradition was settled through violence. By the 15th century, Europeans were the world's master firearms manufacturers. Indeed, European military dominance was so complete that in the succeeding centuries a European army would suffer a major defeat in battle only once by a force not similarly armed, a remarkable record in light of the number of conflicts which span five centuries.

Taxation began as the method of financing a standing and professional army to combat wandering bands of armed men who occasionally appeared and supported themselves through plunder of the countryside and populace. By Columbus's day, professional armies were fairly standard and would be necessary to any renewed military assaults on the Holy Land, an objective Columbus mentions in his log as a motivation for his voyages. The evolution of centralization of taxation powers and professional standing armies were major developments toward construction of the modern nation-state. As McNeill has stated, "[T]hese (economic) linkages combined esprit de corps with bureaucratic subordination, loyalty to a commander and . . . also to the state."[7]

The introduction of new weapons set into motion an arms race which has continued to the present. As new military technologies were introduced the players were forced to buy the new weapons and adopt the new techniques or face annihilation on the battlefield. Each new offensive weapon was countered with a defensive weapon or formation. Huge cannonballs capable of smashing projectiles through thick masonry walls were countered with earthworks which proved impervious to cannonballs. As states grew in size and wealth, the ambitious among them acquired the weapons and armies which helped to spur their growth during periods when offensive weapons overwhelmed defensive ones.

Commercial activity was a major source of taxable wealth, altering the economies of sovereign states. Growing overseas commerce required the development of technologies which would make oceangoing cargo ships safe from piracy. The new source and level of wealth dramatically and irreversibly changed the character of medieval Europe, which had been essentially a decentralized, agrarian society.

The new conditions combined the need for an effective standing military with an increasingly focused effort toward developing commercial ventures which would either be taxed or themselves monopolized by the crown and would thus provide the necessary cash to pay the military and to purchase or develop the latest military technology. Modern nation-states became possible when commerce generated enough wealth to provide for a paid standing army which would do the will of the sovereign without question and without need of reciprocity.

It is not an accident that Isabella of Spain became queen by seizing the royal treasury. She knew an army traveled not only on its stomach but also on the purse of the person giving the orders. The ethic, in this environment, urged princes to take whatever action was effective, within the rules, to secure revenues which would enable the expansion of the state. In Latin Christendom, the Papacy played a role in generating the rules. The rules, as with modern international law, were obeyed or not obeyed according to the inclinations and circumstances of the people making the decisions.

Christopher Columbus's Apprenticeship

Of his many discoveries, Christopher Columbus's discovery of Felipa Perestrello and the Perestrello family traditions clearly marks a turning point in his career. Her family introduced him to life on the Atlantic islands and the peculiarly reckless culture of the Portuguese adventurer-sailors. During this period, he noticed that more Portuguese seamen were dying in Guinea (the African coast) than in Portugal. The spirit of high seas exploration, encouraged and sponsored by the Portuguese Crown at times as enlightened speculation, made the Portuguese Europe's pioneers of the oceans. The Crown guarded information about the details of seamen's voyages as state secrets.

The Atlantic island of Porto Santo was discovered by João Gonçalves Zarco and Tristao Vas Tiexeria when they were blown off course from the Guinea coast into the deep Atlantic. They claimed it for Portugal. In 1419 or 1420, the Portuguese Crown granted Bartolomeo Perestrello the title First

Captain of Porto Santo and directed that he colonize it. He carried ashore a pregnant pet rabbit which soon escaped. The Porto Santo he discovered was an island of grass and trees, but the rabbits, which he thought might enrich the fauna, devoured all the grass and were impossible to contain. There were so many rabbits, the plan to colonize the island was abandoned and Porto Santo was left to the rabbits.

Madeira, meanwhile, grew and prospered, and some years later Perestrello was encouraged to return to Porto Santo to resume settlement. This time he was more successful. The island was temporarily somewhat prosperous but following Perestrello's death in 1457, Porto Santo went into decline. The reasons for the decline are sometimes listed as plague, droughts, epidemics and famine, but human ecological mismanagement should properly be added to the list. Although vegetation was sparse at discovery, several varieties of trees provided materials for various enterprises. By the end of the 15th century, however, Porto Santo is described as an arid land almost devoid of plants.

Following the marriage, Columbus and his bride emigrated to Porto Santo and lived on land that had been owned by her father. The little Atlantic island was part of the frontier of Portuguese exploration and a port of call for the storytellers and adventurers on the high seas. Perestrello's widow provided her son-in-law with her husband's collection of charts, the family provided the lore of explorers into new lands, and the seamen provided fantastic stories of great adventures.

There is evidence that during this period Columbus traveled to and lived on other of the Atlantic islands, including the Azores. He learned of pine logs washing ashore on these beaches, logs unlike any known in the islands. There was a report of the corpses of two people who had washed ashore whose appearance was different from that of Europeans. Rumors persisted (and persist)[8] that a dying Portuguese sailor had struggled ashore with tales of a landfall to the west and described islands he thought were located off the coast of Asia.

Conquest of the Canary Islands

When the Portuguese "discovered" the Canary Islands they encountered what was to them an unprecedented set of circumstances. The Canaries were inhabited by an indigenous population of about 80,000 known as the Guanches. According to the Spanish, they were a giant race of people, some attaining six feet six inches in height. Their ancestors had arrived many centuries earlier, almost certainly from North Africa. Sometime after their arrival they abandoned the custom of sea travel, and although their islands were close enough that they could see from one to the next, they did not travel among them and they had no way of communicating from one island to the next.

The European military invasion of the Canary Islands commenced in 1402. There was no recorded reason for the attack other than to claim the islands, and the Guanches failed to submit. The Christian objective (the Europeans of this period referred to themselves more often as Christians than as Europeans) provided an ideological framework for the developing environment of militarism which made possible the forging of modern nation-states. A key element of this process, the on-going international arms race, meant essentially that only those peoples possessed of an organized state capable of entering the race were recognized as a legitimate state at all. The Guanches possessed no such organized state and had no access to the arms of the continent.

The colonization of the Canary Islands was carried out not by settler colonials but by professional armies acting to secure resources for the purpose of generating profits to support the state. Once European powers expanded past the borders of Europe to new lands, commercialized militarism took on new meaning and founded an age of colonization directed by European nation-states for the purpose of expanding their power.

Although Europe was experiencing a period of unprecedented development of military technology, Latin Christendom was a place under siege by the 15th century. A good argument can be made that much of Europe was in a state of cultural depression. Over two centuries the Black Death had reduced whole areas of the countryside. Populations were just reaching pre-plague levels in 1450. Islamic forces held areas of Iberia and significant portions of Eastern Europe. Christendom had waged an 800-year war against Islam with generally mixed results.

There had been some positive developments. The most exciting was the publication of Marco Polo's account of his travels and adventures in Asia, dictated while Polo was a prisoner in Genoa. Polo's account of his adventures in Asia left an impression that Christendom had lost a great opportunity to spread the Gospel in China. He described Asia as a place where gold was plentiful, and which held an inexhaustible potential for trade.

The China of the imagination may actually have been less impressive than the China of reality. But for a twist of fate which may never be fully or satisfactorily explained, Chinese mariners could have "discovered" America's Pacific coasts before 1492. It is very possible, even probable, that Asian sailors and fishermen reached the Americas for centuries prior to Columbus's day. Asian sailors and their craft certainly had the potential to do so and there is a legend that at least one Chinese captain reached Mexico. There is evidence of pre–Columbian artifacts of Asian origin in Central America. Some of the Indian cultures of the Pacific northwest coast possess art and dress which looks strikingly similar to styles found in Asia, a peculiar coincidence in view of existence of a seafaring tradition and winds which could have easily brought people to distant shores from Asia and, possibly, from America to Asia. But no tradition of an idealized Europe with streets of gold enchanted Chinese emperors and sailors and none were apparently making heroic efforts to discover sea routes to go there.

Trade and commerce were ancient habits in the South China Sea and the Indian Ocean. On land, principalities headed by men the West has forever insisted on calling "warlords" arose and vied for power over great populations. One of these succeeded in reuniting greater China under what would become the Ming Dynasty (1368–1644). Unification created opportunities for growth and coordination of effort. By 1420, three decades before Columbus's birth, the Ming navy boasted some 2,800 ships of the sea. Some 1,350 of these ships were combat vessels and 400 were described as "large floating fortresses." There were another 250 "treasure" ships which could travel long distances.

The largest Chinese vessels were about five times greater in tonnage than were later Portuguese vessels to reach the Indian Ocean at about the time of Columbus's third voyage across the Atlantic. The Chinese navy boasted more guns, manpower and cargo capacity and carried men with more seamanship in vessels more seaworthy than anything of Columbus's or Magellan's command.[9]

Despite these apparent advantages, the Chinese did not set out across the Pacific to the Americas to conquer and colonize even though they did seem to have most of the necessary tools at hand. One theory is that China may have been too successful in centralizing power at home to undertake such an enterprise. The Chinese empire was, at the beginning of the 15th century, extensive to the point of being unwieldy. Although they exhibited a tendency to establish colonies, China withdrew from aggressive expansion because of resistance abroad and problems maintaining order closer to home.

There may have been another contributing reason. Despite assertions that all people act similarly under similar circumstances, evidence suggests that people in different cultures act out of different motivations. The Chinese did not possess the same motivations for overseas colonizations as the Portuguese or Spanish.

In Spain, an impoverished nobility yearned for wealth and significance with a fever later witnessed in the Americas. They left their homelands eagerly and readily set out on incredible adventures of hardship and danger. One might say the European pot was bubbling and ready to boil over. The Chinese pot, quite possibly, was not.

During the early years following contact with China, Europeans nurtured high hopes for the future of Christianity there. The Great Khan had exchanged letters with the Pope, had received Franciscan and Dominican missionaries and even built monasteries for them, three in his capital.[10] Europeans were dramatically heartened by these events. They envisioned a Christian Asia of unimagined power and opulence as an ally with a potential to place Islam between two powerful Christian forces.

Christian optimism about potential success in proselytizing China was premature. European attitudes during this period are instructive, however. This was an era which preceded the rise of racism in the West, and early European visitors were genuinely flattered at the reception they met in the courts of the emperors. When they returned home, they retold their story with a vigor which was not without a stirring of the imagination of not only the listener but also the storyteller.

Tartar attitudes toward Christianity seem somewhat pluralistic from a modern point of view. They were not for Christianity or against it. The Great Khan, conqueror of China and pretty much all the world he cared about, was friendly to Europeans and to others as well.

Christian ambitions in China were thwarted by the expansion of Islam and contact was cut off with the fall of Constantinople in 1454. The sudden extinction of the road to China was a shock. Isolation from China heightened the sense of siege which had arisen through centuries of conflict. It was an inevitable conflict, born of the universality of the Christian culture. Unlike many cultures of the world which accept the reality that different peoples harbor and nurture a variety of beliefs about the truths of human existence, a core of Christian belief was characterized by its jealous universality. Christianity asserted not only belief in the divinity of Jesus Christ but also that this doctrine was intended for all human beings.

The idea of a compulsive universality — that Christian truths were absolute and permitted no deviations among believers, non-believers, or peoples who had not yet encountered the faith — was one of the foundations of Western thought. Christianity was not only the faith of their forefathers, it was the absolute truth of God revealed. In the 11th century Christian popes had moved to unify all of Christendom under papal authority, threatening a significant and effective excommunication to those of its followers who disagreed. The Papal Revolution which brought this about happened under Pope Gregory VII beginning in 1057, nine years before the Norman Invasion of England.

This recruitment to papal authority succeeded in unifying Europe under a more or less single ideology which served as the foundation for the foreign wars known as the Holy Crusades, beginning at the end of the 11th century, to regain the Holy Lands for Christendom in anticipation of the second coming of Christ.[11] These wars were successful in reinforcing a European identity, although it can be said they were a culmination of a centuries-long process of development of ideology and identity which found its origin in the courts of Charlemagne during what is known as the Carolingian Renaissance. An

important element of this ideology of "renaissance" was the claim of an inheritance to the glories of the ancient empires. The ancient empires were a
time of dramatic centralization of power and thus the renaissance provided
an ideological framework which created centralization of power as a mission
of the emperors. The Papal effort to forge all Europe into a single state by
coercing emperors with the threat of spiritual extinction ultimately failed.
However, the ideology of the glories of empire eventually helped to inform
the emerging development of the ideologies of the nation-state.

The ideological claim to universality during the 12th century impelled
Christendom into renewed and revitalized conflict with Islam, a culture with
a tradition of universality of its own. When Constantinople fell, Christendom
suffered an ideological as well as commercial setback. In Italy the Levant
trade had developed private fortunes which were now motivated to invest in
maritime explorations of new routes to their traditional markets. Spain was
engaged in a vigorous war against the Moslem kingdoms of Iberia during the
1480s. On December 4, 1489, Baza, an important Muslim post, surrendered.
An anecdote is told of King Boabdil's vision of the future of his Moslem kingdom:

> He put a gold platter in the middle of a large carpet, and asked
> his courtiers to seize the platter without stepping on the carpet. No
> one could see how to do it. He then rolled the carpet and lifted the
> platter, explaining that their last stronghold, Granada, would be
> compelled to surrender after the Catholic Kings had seized all the
> seaports like Baza, through which Granada could obtain essential
> supplies. Queen Isabel and Ferdinand were rolling up the carpet.[12]

Portugal under Prince Henry the Navigator's father, the Infante, had initiated a modern overseas empire. Portugal had laid claim to the Cape Verde
islands, the Madeira and the Canary Islands. They had discovered (or
rediscovered) the Azores islands and laid claim to all the African coast south
of Cape Bojador, known then as Guinea. On Madeira they planted Spanish
grapes which ultimately provided the world with Madeira wine and Portugal
with profits therefrom. By the middle of the 15th century, Madeira was
Europe's most successful colony and the world's major producer and exporter
of sugar.

Columbus was obsessed with the idea of a journey across the sea westward to China. This ambition consumed him. He had married into an in-
fluential and wealthy Portuguese family and was making a living trading
Madeira sugar and products of the Cape Verde islands. He was, from every
account, reasonably prosperous in 1480. Thereafter, all his energy, including
his wealth and the time he could have devoted to his businesses, was consumed
in the quest for financing for a voyage west across the Atlantic. By 1484, or
1485, when he left Portugal, he was deeply in debt.

Columbus calculated and promoted a theory of the width of the ocean to coincide with his theory that it was crossable in an age when oceangoing vessels carried water in wooden casks which rendered it undrinkable after about 40 days. His calculation of the distance to Cathay (China) was dead wrong. Erasthenes had calculated the circumference of the earth at about 25,000 miles and he had it about right. The informed wisdom of the day held that to venture west from Spain would be to encounter a sea so wide that all aboard would perish before reaching land. Had there been no land, these calculations would have proven true and Columbus would have perished at sea, a forgotten footnote to history. From the viewpoint of his own scholarship, Columbus's successes were based primarily on his enormous good fortune.

Others had long before crossed the Atlantic to what would later be called America. The ancients could well have made the journey. Certainly the idea of Atlantis may have come from ancient mariners who had made the crossing, had entered and passed through the Sargasso Sea, and at least one or two had possibly returned to tell the story. If such events had happened, however, they were irrelevant to Columbus and his contemporaries in the late 15th century. The details of how to accomplish this task, if such details had ever been known, had long been forgotten. The journeys of the Vikings in the North Atlantic, even if known to Columbus, would have been of little help. Even if there had been a Portuguese captain who had made such a journey, and if Columbus had personally interviewed him, the story would have been added to many such tales of islands and landfalls in the deep Atlantic which had proven elusive and ultimately simply incorrect time and again.

We celebrate Columbus (those who do celebrate his achievements) because he found land, but finding land was incidental. More important were his discoveries of truths about the ocean seas and winds. Such discoveries were significant in themselves, and indeed did much to create the modern world. Those who celebrate Columbus, therefore, celebrate the creation of the modern world and many who read this will find it difficult to accept that there are those who do not wholeheartedly embrace the details of modernity's development. Of the people who lived in the 15th century, few will deny, Columbus is probably the most famous, at least in the West. What Columbus did that set him apart from the others was to provide the information necessary to make crossing and recrossing the Atlantic possible at a moment when the confluence of military and navigational technologies combined with political evolutions to create conditions that would dramatically alter the history of the world.

Three things contributed to Columbus's claim to greatness. The first was his astute observation, gained from his voyages to the North Atlantic and the Guinea coast, that the prevailing winds in the north blew east across the Atlantic to Europe and to the south blew west, always west. The second was the fact that European sailing and military technology had advanced far beyond that of any other people in the world and Columbus carried aboard his ships technologies (including a tradition of literacy which could record his every move) mostly unavailable to his predecessors. The third was the development in Europe at that moment of the commercialization of militarism which made such voyages and the subsequent discoveries not only possible but also compelling in terms of practical conquest. The development of the commercialization of militarism is extremely important and lives with us still.

From previous sailing experience, Columbus had seen that at certain latitudes the prevailing winds blew west and and at other more northern latitudes on the Atlantic the winds blew east. Thus he had reason to believe if he sailed west there would be a wind to carry him forth and another, along with a more northerly route, to bring him home. It is very likely he wasn't the only observer of these facts, but would prove to be the most important one. For centuries, as long as sailing vessels were the principal vehicles of the seas, ocean travel from Europe would depend on these facts. The second fact about Columbus was equally important: in a day of vague maps and ideas about longitude and latitude, Columbus was the finest mariner at the skill of "dead reckoning." He was able to retrace his course with what can only be described as astounding accuracy.

The common wisdom holds that Columbus set forth on a journey westward to find China. That much is generally true and accurate. That people thought the world was flat is simply a misconception which makes the telling of the tale more exciting. Educated people had long thought the world was round.

Western historians would weave a cocoon of mythology around the story of Columbus as had been done with countless other heroic figures, and would in time anoint the story as historical fact. Columbus's story is generally told as an adventure to find new routes to Asia, but the context of a quest which culminated generations of the development of a world market economy and the commercialism of militarism is largely ignored, its implications unexplored. Columbus's major task in assembling the voyage was to convince the Crown and the banks of the viability of his proposal.

Can it be that the celebration of Columbus's "discovery," in full view of the historical context, is one of the great propaganda victories of history? The colonization is a story of military conquest carried out by a people possessing vastly superior arms against sometimes practically unarmed populations, of subduing and sometimes exterminating those populations, of appropriating their land and their labor to the ends of the conquerors.

The Doctrine of Discovery, an agreement among the competing military states of Europe, ensured that whichever of them first encountered a place, that power had first rights to explore and colonize that place. It soon became

the practice that this "right of discovery" applied whether the place was occupied by people or not. In fact, under such principles the existence of distinct
peoples became legally irrelevant.

In the early centuries of the modern era this doctrine was one of the foundation blocks of the modern interstate system under which the nation-states
of the world agree to recognize each other's rights over and against the
numerous peoples of the world. Today there are about 168 nation-states and
some 3,000 to 5,000 indigenous cultures in the world.[13] The nation-states
claim to own and have rights of domination over every acre of the globe,
claiming as their citizens people they have not yet contacted,[14] and claiming
a right over their land and persons which arises out of this very ideology. The
Doctrine of Discovery was simply a theory of the right of exploitation. Even
today indigenous peoples have no rights to exist as distinct peoples under international law. This absence of rights to dignity and culture, land, and ultimately existence, was and remains one of the central features of the process
of "discovery." We who celebrate an informed version of how the modern
world came to be the way it is may wish to carefully reevaluate the significance of such ideologies in our own time.

Chapter Notes

1. The area designated Eastern Europe was homeland to the Eastern or Greek
Orthodox Church. These designations are more correctly cultural/historical than geo-
graphic.

2. Imagination has played a powerful role in European history. The origin of
the identity of Europeans as Europeans — a people with a history and purpose which
transcended geography — clearly arises from that culture's metaphysical tradition.
Although it can be argued that many cultures have such traditions, none has so influenced the evolution of the modern world as this one.

3. We will return to a discussion of the Crusades and the idea of renaissance
shortly. I mention these trends here as part of an opening list of significant parts of
the story of the events leading to the Columbus enterprise. An interesting discussion
of the early manifestation of the ideology of renaissance is found in Philippe Wolff,
*The Awakening of Europe: The Growth of European Culture from the Ninth Century to the
Twelfth* (London: Cox and Wyman, 1968). The following work discusses the role of
the imagination in creating national identities; although it focuses on a much later
period, it makes observations which inform the above discussion: Benedict Anderson,
Imagined Communities: Reflection on the Origin and Spread of Nationalism (Thetford [US]:
Thetford Press, 1983).

4. A discussion of how the history of Western Europe was in fact distinct from
that of the classical civilizations of Greece and Rome (and others) is found in Harold
J. Berman, *Law and Revolution: The Formation of the Western Legal Tradition.* (Cambridge,
Mass.: Harvard University Press, 1983), esp. 1–45. The continuity between the ancient civilizations and Christian Western Europe was at least in part an invention of
later ideologies. For a discussion of an apparent continuity of at least some military

technologies and traditions, see Robert L. O'Connell, *Of Arms and Men: A History of War, Weapons and Aggression* (New York: Oxford University Press, 1989).

5. O'Connell, p. 105.

6. William H. McNeill, *The Pursuit of Power: Technology, Armed Force and Society Since A.D. 1000* (Chicago: University of Chicago Press, 1982), p. 77.

7. Sometimes these marauding bands were the erstwhile standing armies which had not been promptly paid. "Professional" armies date back to the Assyrians whose armies were paid from the spoils of victory, a policy which required that armies always be in the field against an enemy. The emergence of professional armies in Europe in the 14th and 15th centuries resulted from an arms race which altered the rules of war. Ancient peoples generally fought wars, so they said, over women and revenge. Civilizations fought sometimes over disputes involving territory. The Crusades were launched ostensibly for ideological reasons, but the Crusaders also seized territory.

8. McNeill, p. 44.

9. "But even if the idea of guns as well as of gunpowder reached Europe from China, the fact remains that Europeans very swiftly outstripped the Chinese and every other people in gun design, and continued to enjoy a clear superiority in this art until World War II." McNeill, p. 81.

10. Daniel Sargent, *Christopher Columbus* (Milwaukee: Bruce, 1941), p. 31.

11. The First Crusade was 1096 to 1099.

12. McNeill, p. 99.

13. See Bernard Nietchmann, "The Third World War," *Cultural Survival Quarterly* 2, 3 (1987), pp. 1–16. Nietchmann states that these fundamental inequities are being played out in wars around the globe as nation-states continue to attempt to subdue and dominate indigenous peoples.

14. Consider, for example, the situation of Brazil's claim to sovereignty and control over the territory of a single Indian group, the Yanomami. Brazil claims as its citizens these and other Indians who have not yet heard of Brazil nor heard a single word of the Portuguese language. Brazil makes decisions about Yanomami territory under an international system which simply does not recognize indigenous peoples as having rights as a group against the powers of a nation-state, no matter how obviously excessive and unfair those powers might be. Under the principles of international law which descend from the Doctrine of Discovery, indigenous peoples have practically no group rights as distinct peoples.

A Note on the Tainos

José Barreiro

They do worship some covetous and unfaithful Deity, and ... taking up a little Chest filled with Gold, he [said]: "Behold here the God of the Spaniards."— The Taino lord Hatuey, in hiding on the island of Cuba, as quoted by las Casas, 1511.

Christopher Columbus, whose name literally means "Christ-bearing colonizer," wrote in his diary shortly after the landfall that he and his sailors saw "naked men" (there were also women), whom they found "very healthy-looking." Landing at Guanahani, in the Bahamas, and sailing on to Cuba and Bohio (Haiti/Santo Domingo), renamed Española, Columbus soon noted a widespread language and system of beliefs and lifeways. Conferring with various caciques (chiefs), he heard them call themselves "Taino" (Tyler, 1988).

Taino (the term actually describes the sachem families from among the island Arawaks) culture was dominant throughout the Caribbean, a sea and island world that was in turn cradle of Taino civilization. In agriculture, seafaring and cosmology, Ciboney and Guanahatabey (western Cuba), Macorix and or Ciguayo (Bohio) and even Carib (Lesser Antilles) all followed the material and much of the psycho-spiritual framework of the Taino. The original Caribbeans spoke Arawak. The people of the Arawak language family still comprise one of the more widespread American indigenous cultures, with relatively large kinship nations in the Amazon and Orinoco river basins of South America. Throughout the Caribbean, usually in remote mountain ranges and coastal promontories, remnant groups and communities of Taino-Arawak and Carib descendants survive to the present. Aspects of the animistic and material culture of the Taino-Arawak have been adopted by the mestizo populations of the Caribbean and are interwoven into the Euro-African fabric of the island's folk universe.

Reprinted from View from the Shore *published by* Northeast Indian Quarterly, *Fall 1990.*

The word Taino meant "men of the good," and from most indications the Tainos were good. Coupled to the lush and hospitable islands over a millennium and a half, the indigenous people of "La Taina" developed a culture where the human personality was gentle. Among the Taino at the time of contact, by all accounts, generosity and kindness were dominant values. Among the Taino peoples, as with most indigenous lifeways, the physical culture was geared toward a sustainable interaction with the natural surroundings. The Taino's culture has been designated as "primitive" by Western scholarship, yet it prescribed a lifeway that strove to feed all the people, and a spirituality that respected, in ceremony, most of their main animal and food sources, as well as the natural forces like climate, season and weather. The Taino lived respectfully in a bountiful place and so their nature was bountiful (Jane, 1930).

The naked people Columbus first sighted lived in an island world of rainforests and tropical weather, and adventure and fishing legends at sea. Theirs was a land of generous abundance by global terms. They could build a dwelling from a single tree (the Royal Palm) and from several others (gommier, ceiba), a canoe that could carry more than 100 people.

The houses (bohios) were (and are today among Dominican and Cuban Guajiros) made of palm tree, trunk and thatch lashed together in a rectangle or sometimes a circle pattern. The islands still have millions of royal and other useful palm trees, from which bohios by the hundreds of thousands could be built. The wood of the Royal Palm is still today considered the most resistant to tropical rot, lasting untreated as long as 90 years.[1]

The Tainos lived in the shadows of a diverse forest so biologically remarkable as to be almost unimaginable to us. Indeed, the biological transformation of their world was so complete in the intervening centuries that we may never again know how the land or the life of the land appeared in detail. What we do know is that their world would appear to us, as it did to the Spanish of the 15th century, as a tropical paradise. It was not heaven on earth, but it was one of those places that was reasonably close.

The Taino world, for the most part, had some of the appearance that modern imaginations ascribe to the South Pacific islands. The people lived in small, clean villages of neatly appointed thatch dwellings along rivers inland and on the coasts. They were a handsome people who had no need of clothing for warmth. They liked to bathe often, which prompted a Spanish royal law forbidding the practice; "for we are informed it does them much harm," wrote Queen Isabella. Their general physical appearance was consistent with the appearance of other Indians of the Americas. They were rarely taller than five feet six inches which would make them rather small to modern North American eyes. They painted their bodies with earth dyes and adorned themselves with shells and metals. Men and women chiefs often wore gold in the ears and nose, or as pendants around the neck. Some had tattoos.

From all early descriptions the Tainos were a healthy people who showed no signs of distress from hunger or want. The Tainos, whose color was olive-brown to copper, reminded Columbus of the people of the Canary Islands, who were neither white nor black. He noted their thick, black hair, short in front and long in back, and that it fell over muscular shoulders. On some islands, the women wore short cotton skirts after taking a permanent man but in others all the people went naked. In parts of Cuba and Santa Domingo, some of the caciques, village or clan and nation chiefs, wore a type of tunic on ceremonial occasions, but they saw no apparent need to cover their breasts or genitals and they were totally natural about it. The Taino had plenty of cotton, which they wove into mats, hammocks and small sails and numerous "bejucos" or fiber ropes (Tyler, 1988).

The Taino islands provided a vast array of edible fruits. The Arawaks made specific use of many types of trees and plants from an estimated floral and faunal range of 5,800 species. The jagua tree they used for dyeing cotton, the jocuma and the guama for making rope, the jucaro for underwater construction, the royal palm for buildings and specific other trees for boats, spears, digging tools, chairs, bowls, baskets and other woven mats (in this art they flourished), cotton cloth (for hammocks), large fishing nets and good hooks made of large fish bones. Inspecting deserted seashore camps, Spanish sailors found what they judged to be excellent nets and small fishing canoes stored in water-tight sheds. Further upriver, in the villages, they saw large fields of corn, yucca, beans and fruit orchards covering whole valleys. They walked through the squares of villages, all recently swept clean, where they saw many kinds of drying tubers, grains and herbs, and sunlight-tight storage sheds with shelves packed with thousands of dried cassava (*casabe* or *cazabi*) torts. In one village, sailors found large cakes of fine wax, a local product (Rivero, 1966).

The Taino were a seagoing people and took pride in their courage on the high ocean as well as their skill in finding their way around their world. They visited one another constantly. Columbus was often astonished at finding lone Indian fishermen sailing in the open ocean as he made his way among the islands. Once, a canoe of Taino men followed him from island to island until one of their relatives, held captive on Columbus's flagship, jumped over the side to be spirited away.

Among Tainos, the women and some of the men harvested corn, nuts, cassava, and other roots. They appear to have practiced a rotation method in their agriculture. As in the practice of many other American indigenous eco-systemic peoples, the first shoots of important crops, such as the yucca, beans and corn were appreciated in ceremony, and there are stories about their origins. Boys hunted fowl from flocks that "darkened the sun," according to Columbus, and the men forded rivers and braved the ocean to hunt and fish for the abundant, tree-going jutia, the succulent manatee, giant sea turtles and countless species of other fish, turtles and shellfish. Around every bohio, Columbus wrote, there were flocks of tame ducks (yaguasa), which the people roasted and ate (Cassa, 1974).

Father Bartolomé de las Casas, the Spanish friar who arrived on Columbus's heels and lived to denounce the Spanish cruelty toward Indians, wrote (exaggeratedly but impressively) about "vineyards that ran for three hundred leagues," game birds taken by the tens of thousands, great circular fields of yucca and greater stores of cassava bread, dried fish, corn fields and vast gardens of sweet yams. Tainos along the coasts of Española and southern Cuba kept large circular corrals made of reeds which they filled with fish and turtles by the thousands. In part of Puerto Rico and Cuba, Jivaro and Guajiro fishermen used this method into the 1950s. The early Taino and Ciboney of Cuba were observed catching fish and turtles by way of a remora (suction fish) tied by the tail (Eugenio Fernandez Mendez, "Los Corrales de Pesca Indigenas de Puerto Rico," *Revista del Instituto de Cultura Puertorriqueña*, October 1960).

The Taino world of 1492 was a thriving place. The Taino islands supported large populations that had existed in an environment of Carib-Taino conflict for, according to archeological evidence, one and a half millennia, although the earliest human fossil in the region is dated at 15,000 years. Tainos and Caribs may have visited violence upon one another, and there is little doubt they did not like each other, but there is little evidence to support any thesis that genocidal warfare existed in this world. A Carib war party arrived and attacked, was successful or repulsed, and the Tainos, from all accounts, returned to what they were doing before the attack. These attacks were not followed up by a sustained campaign of attrition. The Taino existence was not threatened, from these accounts, any more than a modern American's existence is threatened by street crime (Tabio and Rey, 1985).

Bohio was the Taino name of Española, now Santo Domingo/Haiti. It means "home" in Taino, was in fact home to two main confederated peoples: the Taino, as predominant group, with three cacicasgos, and the Macorixes, with two cacicasgos. There was also one small cacicasgo of Ciguayo Indians on the island when Columbus arrived. The three main Taino caciques were named Bohequio of Jaragua; Guacanagarí of Marien, and Guarionex of La Vega. The two Macorix caciques were Caonabó, of Maguana, at the center of the island and his ally, Coyacoa of Higuey. Mayabanex, also a good friend of Caonabó, was cacique of the Ciguayo country. The three Taino caciques were relatives and allies and had good relations. The Taino of Jaragua had a particularly good agriculture, with efficient irrigation systems that regularly watered thousands of acres of all manner of tubers, vegetables and grains. The Macorixes and Ciguayos were strong warriors, known for a fierce dexterity at archery. They balanced the scale with the peaceful Tainos, who often fed them, and for whom in turn the Macorixes and Ciguayos fought against

the more southern Carib. Caonabó, a Macorixe cacique was married to Anacaona, a Taino and sister of Behechio.

It is true that Caribbean Indian peoples fought with each other, taking
prisoners and some ritually eating parts of enemy warriors, but even more
often they accommodated each other. As "discovery" turned to conquest, they
allied as "Indians," or, more properly, as Caribbean indigenous peoples
against Spanish troops. As a peaceful civilization, the Taino caciques apparently made diplomatic use of their agricultural bounty to appease and
tame more militaristic groups (Vega, 1980).

Indian Vision/Spanish Mission

The Tainos had many cosmological stories and fundamental cultural
principles. High among these was the organization of people to produce food
and the value of feeding everyone in each community. Whatever else can be
said of their ancient way of life, it contrasted starkly with the Spanish idea
of economics in 1500. As las Casas and others have attested, the migrations
to America occurred because no such principle was at work in Europe during
the same and later times. Even the earliest encounters of the fundamental
American indigenous thinking about this human value, which is found
throughout the continent and continues to be one of the contrapuntal
arguments between the American Indian civilization and European civilization, is fueled by Judeo-Roman-Christian precepts.

A telling event occurred when the Spanish were pressing against
Guarionex's Indians in Santo Domingo. Guarionex was one of the five main
caciques of Española. His territory in the Valley of La Vega was highly
esteemed for its agricultural productivity. In 1494–95, after Columbus imposed
a tribute of gold to be paid by every Taino man, woman or child, Guarionex
went to the first colonizer with a counter offer. Guarionex's main chiefs
gathered over 1,000 men with coas (planting sticks) in hand. If Columbus
would drop the gold tribute, they offered to plant all the food the Spanish
would ever want to eat. They said to Columbus: we will feed you here on
the island and also all of your people back in Castile. You don't even need
to work. But of course, the colonizers wanted gold or, in lieu of it, slaves
and precious woods. This documented event, where chiefs offer men with
planting sticks to appease Spanish hunger, focuses the value of land as
equalizer, with the provision of basic sustenance as a fundamental right
(Tyler, 1988).

By all descriptions, Taino life and culture at contact was uniquely
adapted to its environment. Population estimates vary greatly but put the
number of inhabitants in Española (Santo Domingo/Haiti) at between half
a million and seven million. Estimates for Cuba vary from 120,000 to

200,000, with newer estimates pushing that number up. Whether one takes the low or the high estimates, early descriptions of Taino life at contact tell of large concentrations of people, with strings of a hundred or more villages of 500 to 1,000 people each. These concentrations of people in coastal areas and river deltas were apparently well-fed by a nature-harvesting and agricultural production system whose primary value was that all of the people had the right to eat. Everyone in the society had a food or other goods–producing task — even the highly esteemed caciques and behiques (medicine people), who were often seen to plant, hunt, and fish along with their people. In the Taino culture, as with most natural world cultures of the Americas, the concept was still fresh in the human memory that the primary bounties of the earth, particularly those that humans eat, are to be produced in cooperation and shared.

Comparison of the life-style described by the early chroniclers with to-day's standard of living in Haiti and Dominican Republic for the majority of the population, as well as with the ecological degradation caused by extensive deforestation, indicates that the island and its human citizens were better fed, healthier, and better governed by the Taino's so-called primitive methods than the modern populations of that same island (Tyler, 1988).

Like all American indigenous peoples, the Taino had an involved economic life. They could trade throughout the Caribbean and had systems of governance and beliefs that maintained harmony between human and natural environments. The Tainos enjoyed a peaceful way of life that modern anthropologists now call "ecosystemic." In the wake of recent scientific revelations about the cost of high impact technologies upon the natural world, a culture such as the Taino, that could feed several million people without permanently wearing down its surroundings, might command higher respect. As can be seen throughout the Americas, American indigenous peoples and their systems of life have been denigrated and mis-perceived. Most persistent of European ethnocentrisms toward Indians is the concept of "the primitive," always buttressed with the rule of "least advanced" to "most advanced" imposed by the prism of Western Civilization — the more "primitive" a people, the lower the place they are assigned in the scale of "civilization." The anti-nature attitude inherent in this idea came over with the Iberians of the time, some of whom even died rather than perform manual labor, particularly tilling of the soil. The production and harvesting of food from sea, land and forests were esteemed human activities among Tainos. As with other indigenous cultures, the sophistication and sustainability of agricultural and natural harvesting systems was an important value and possibly the most grievous loss caused by the conquest of the Americas. It is in direct contrast with the Spanish (and generally Western) value that to work with land or nature directly, as a farmer and or harvester, is a lowly activity, thus relegated to lesser humans and lower classes. This attitude is ingrained in popular thinking in most Western countries through jokes about the "country bumpkin" and the "city slicker" which invoke superior attitudes about "dumb" farmers. In that tradition, the least desirable thing is to work with your hands.

In the Spanish annals, Española is described as the most "advanced" of the greater Antilles. Tainos in Española were known for their good communications and productive agriculture. Española was the center of Taino culture, which appears to have traveled from there to Cuba and the outer islands. Gardens, ballcourts, and huge areitos (round dances) with speaking forums and poets characterized that lush island, which was confederated into five main cacicasgos, or kinship nations.

There was little or no quarreling observed among the Tainos by the Spaniards. The old caciques and their councils of elders were said to be well-behaved and to have a deliberate way of speaking and great authority. Las Casas wrote, "the Indians have much better judgment and maintain much better public order and government than many other nations which are overwhelmingly proud of themselves and which hold Indians in contempt." The peoples were organized either to the gardens ("conucos") or to the sea and the hunt. They had ball games played in bateyes, or courtyards, in front of the cacique's house. They held both ceremonial and social dances, called areitos. Among the few Taino-Arawak customs that have survived the longest, the predominant ideas are that ancestors should be properly greeted by the living humans at prescribed times and that natural forces and the spirits behind each group of food and medicinal plants and useful animals should be appreciated in ceremony (las Casas, 1971).

Contrary to popular imagination, the Tainos were a disciplined people. Particularly during their spiritual and healing ceremonies, natural impulses were limited. In those important instances, strong abstinence over sexual activity and eating were demanded, even under penalty of death. The local cacique and his medicine man, the Taino behique, had the task of calling the ceremonial times. Among these were the famous areitos reported by Pané. These were round dances and recitation ceremonies, where thanks was given for various natural and plant spirits, and the ancient stories were told. They included the most ancient of creation time stories, of Deminán and his three skydweller brothers, the four Taino cosmological beings (four sacred directions) who walked on clouds and blue sky over the spirit world of the Caribbean. Orphaned by their virgin mother at birth, the sacred beings, called Caracaracolesin Taino, wandered the sky islands, here and there receiving creative powers from ornery old shamans who carried it from even farther back. This way, out of gourds (jicaras), they created the oceans and fish; out of a turtle, the islands; from spirit babies, toads; from toads, the rains and waters; from clay and stars, men; from jobo trees, their prayer statutes; and from the river manatee, exquisite source of sustenance, women[2] (Arrom, 1989).

At the areito, carved wooden statuettes, called cemis, representing the various forces, were polished and addressed, fed and smoked for. A tribal meditation and vision took place, often with the use of the sacred herb, cohoba, a hallucinogenic snuff compounded from the seeds of anadenanthera peregrina. In the areito, elements of the plant and animal life were remembered. There were areitos and cemis for the season of huracán, singings for the four beings, for the origin of the sun and moon, the ocean and fishes, the snake and jutia, for the guayaba, the ceiba, the corn, the ñame and the yucca. Yucca, a tuber and their main food, was the special gift, and singularly represented by the Yucahu, the Taino's identification for the Supreme or Original Being.

Columbus and His Trajectory

To Christopher Columbus, and the Spanish Catholic kingdom behind him, the voyage to the American lands sought a "discovery." The Grand Mariner was among a handful in Europe to suspect that strong wind currents blew across the great ocean, going west farther south and back east on the northern latitudes. Why he knew this, how he came to be the first to ascertain it for a major European power, what he sought and how he was thinking about potential "discoveries," define the true story, not only of Columbus, but of the thinking and tenets that guided (and justified) the colonization of the American Indian continent. Columbus knew that conquest and Spanish political hegemony would follow a promising discovery. He hoped to and did get very rich by his "discovery."

On August 3, 1492, Columbus sailed south to the Canaries (a route he knew well and where he would turn west) out of the port of Palos, in southern Spain. Thousands of Jews had sailed out of Spain, mostly from the same port, on the previous day. The inquisition was at its zenith in Spain in 1492; all remaining Jews were to convert or die. Executions by fire were still common. It was a pious, "Christ-bearing" Columbus who went forth with the Catholic King's mandate, carrying the mission of conversion to fuel his drive to "discover."

Landing in Guanahaní (renamed San Salvador), Columbus planted a Spanish flag, ordered a Catholic Mass and proclaimed himself Viceroy over the new lands. For days, large dug-out canoes full of curious Lucayo-Arawak men paddled out to the strange, giant ships. The large canoes glided quickly over the water. Caciques (chiefs) went out with warriors carrying bows and arrows and lances, but also food and other gifts. Columbus sought information about larger landfalls and about the source of golden amulets he received as presents. From his log, we know what Columbus thought about these new people and how he analyzed their worth. One can only wonder what thoughts crossed the Tainos' minds at this first encounter, what interpretation their unique cosmology could give these events.

The Tainos thought Columbus and his men strange enough to be gods, possibly representatives of the four skydwelling brothers in their creation story. The bearded men with hairy, sand-color faces, with ships of many sails and booming sticks that could cut across a swath of trees, were thought to come from the sky. Mystically overwhelmed and naturally friendly, the Arawaks' first idea was to make peace. What they had a lot of, food and simple ornaments, they gave freely. Columbus soon re-provisioned his ships' holds with fresh water, dried fish, nuts, calabashes, and cazabi (yucca) bread. During all of Columbus's first trip, in numerous encounters with Tainos, both in Cuba and Santo Domingo, the clothed visitors were welcome and the Tainos attempted to appease all their hungers. Wrote Columbus in his ship's log,

> They are so ingenious and free with all they have that no one would believe it who had not seen it; of anything they possess, if it be asked of them, they never say no; on the contrary, they invite you to share it and show as much love as if their hearts went with it ... [Jane, 1930].

There is never any sense in Columbus's writing that the Tainos are incapable, only that they were innocent and well-intentioned. He would come to know that they were completely honest, as if the ability to deceive had not developed among them. Columbus wrote that the young men wondered at the shiny things, grabbing sabers by the edge and cutting themselves for lack of experience, but that otherwise they were quick-witted, knew their geography and expressed themselves well. The Indians referred to more than "one hundred islands by name," Columbus said. Later writings of Columbus, las Casas, Pedro Mártir de Anglería and other Caribbean chroniclers gave many instances of Taino quick-wittedness and eloquence of expression. "They are a very loving people and without covetousness," Columbus wrote. "They are adaptable for every purpose, and I declare to your Highness that there is not a better country nor better people in the world than these." And also: "They have good memories and inquire eagerly about the nature of all they see." Columbus noted that after eating, the caciques were brought a bouquet of herbs with which to wash their hands prior to washing in water.

Everything seemed exotic to the Admiral, and in fact he was witness to a culture and a way of life arising from a totally different civilization. It was a quite logical and compelling culture, one with a significant sense of time and existence, but also one which has been consistently relegated to "primitive" status on the ladder of stages of civilization elaborated by Western scholars. Leaving aside the ascendancy view of civilization can one envision that Taino civilization was also in a developmental process — one with its own definitions, but just as genuine and important and universal as the European process.

Among the islands, Columbus asked directions to the court of the Great Khan, of whom he had read in Marco Polo's journals. Captive Lucayo-Arawaks, in the classic first of many future cross-cultural miscommunications, guided his way toward their "Khan," the island of Cuba, which they called Cubanakan. It would take a full season for the Tainos, happy people of paradise, to lose their essential good will for the Spanish, who increasingly demanded women, continued to take captives by surprise, and virulently announced their hunger for the yellow metal the Indians called guanín — the Spanish "oro" or English "gold."

At the entrance to the Bay of Bairiay, in eastern Cuba, the three Spanish ships hove to through a night of thick tropical rain before awakening to a "beauty never before seen by the eyes of man," according to the ship's log. That same day Columbus told his log about "green and gracious trees, different from ours, covered by flowers and fruits of marvelous flavors, [and] many types of fowl and small birds."

Though he waxed poetic, the Admiral's main task was sizing up the real estate and its inhabitants. He did so with a banker's eye. Columbus's venture was financed by powerful investors who wanted a return, and his ship's log betrays three major concerns: finding the court of the Great Khan (for trade), finding gold in quantity, and estimating the resource exploitation value of land, slaves, precious woods, woven and raw cotton and fruits. "Our Lord in his mercy," Columbus wrote, "direct me where I can find the gold mine" (Tyler, 1988).

Conquest of Española

The conquest of Española began in earnest with Columbus's second trip. Fifteen hundred adventurers, ex-prisoners, and ex-soldiers with experience in the final campaigns against North African Moors came back with Columbus in 17 ships. They came seeking their private fortunes and would be ruthless in this pursuit. The Spanish (Castillian, Aragonese, and Extremaduran) soldier of 1494 was a deadly foe. He had good steel armor and swords, arquebuses, cross-bows, trained mastiffs and excellent cavalry.

One battle had already been fought. During Columbus's first trip, his flagship, the *Santa María*, ran aground and was wrecked. As a result, a fort, called Fort Navidad, was built, and some 40 men volunteered to stay behind. They were charged with maintaining good relations with the Taino and with searching for the source of gold. They were true to the later mission, though not to the former.

Almost immediately the men broken into factions, fought each other, and proceeded to harass the Taino population, hoarding as many as five women apiece. While Guacanagarí, the local cacique, remained loyal to his promise to Columbus that he would care for the men, a band of conquistadors carried on their terror campaign deep into the territory of another cacique, Caonabó, who had made no promises. Caonabó would not tolerate the depredations and ordered attacks, first on the intruding band and later on the fort itself. All the Spanish were killed but the attack became justification for retribution upon Columbus's return.

The Spanish mounted almost immediate military campaigns against Indian villages. For several years the fights were back and forth, and by 1496, according to las Casas, only one third of Indian Española was left. Other historians assert that the pace was not quite as quick, that it took until about 1510 for that kind of extermination. Plagues played a big role in the decimation of the Indian population, first in Española, and later in Puerto Rico, Cuba, the Bahamas, and good parts of Florida. This type of biological warfare that followed human migration from Europe into the Indian populations contributed greatly to the decimation of Indian resistance.

Gold mines had been discovered. Well-armed Spanish patrols captured Indians as needed to work gruelingly in the gold mines. The wanton cruelty and disregard for human life by the 15th century Spanish in the conquest of the Indies is darkly legendary. Often, Indian miners died of starvation, though food could be had easily. As many Indians were easily enslaved through raids during the early years, the life of an Indian had little value.

Caonabó, the most respected cacique in Española, persisted a few years until captured by trickery and punished by a Columbus lieutenant, Alonso de Hojeda. Columbus had ordered Caonabó decapitated, but instead sent him to Spain as a slave (the cacique was lost at sea, in the same disaster that claimed Guarionex). Hojeda himself sliced off the cacique's brothers' ears. These types of actions precipitated general insurrection among the Tainos.

In 1496, Columbus led an assault later known as the Battle of the Vega and called by his followers the principal battle against paganism, in part to punish a cacique, Guatiguanax, who had killed 10 Spaniards and burned 40 others. Guatiguanax had taken revenge for the killing of one of his own elders, who had been torn to death by a Spanish mastiff commanded by two Spanish soldiers. Columbus captured many Indians during this campaign that he sold into slavery (Fernandez-Armesto, 1974).

One immediate factor of the invasion of the Caribbean is that Spain immediately shipped out increasing numbers of transmigrants to the newly "discovered" islands. A transmigration took hold that was similar to the Amazonian one of present-day Brazil. It is contended here that this initial migration to the Indian country of the Americas was caused by mostly the same factors that cause the transmigrations today — the landlessness and general poverty of the European peasant after displacement from land as land production became increasingly measured for its commodity value rather than its people-feeding value.

After 1502, when the gold foretold by Columbus was found in Española, migrants came by the thousands. Las Casas complained later: "Nobody came to the Indies except for gold — in order to leave the state of poverty which plagues all classes in Spain." The roads to the mines were like ant hills with arriving Spanish, wrote de Anglería. Many in the first wave were poor Spanish nobleman with parasitic ways and their even poorer servants. The Indians complained that the Spanish ate too much and worked little.

In time, the Spanish comendadors realized that they had brought too many people to the island. But it can be safely asserted that the immediate process of transmigration precipitated itself because of the misery of the inhabitants of Spain in their homeland. It will remain a consistent theme in the process of peopling the Americas with Europeans. Wrote las Casas: "Allowing too many people to emigrate from Spain has always been one of the principal reasons behind the devastation of the Indies."

The Last Spanish Crusade

Once military superiority was established, the persecution of the Indian people by the Spanish was characterized by unimaginable cruelty. The Indian had no personhood, the Spanish conquest allowed no regard whatsoever for the human life of an Indian.

"It was a general rule among our Spaniards to be extraordinarily cruel to the Indians," las Casas wrote. The Spanish men relished working their steel swords on the Taino flesh, often cutting hands off at the slightest offense. "They would test their swords and manly strength on captured Indians and place bets on the slicing off of heads or the cutting of bodies in half with one blow," las Casas told.

In a single act of revenge after an Indian attack, the Spanish soldiers captured 700 villagers and stabbed them all to death. The war cacique they hanged, as this was an abhorred form of death to the Tainos. De Anglería records that during this incident some soldiers attempted to protect the children. One soldier took a young boy in his arms, but the boy was stabbed by another soldier who came from behind with a lance. Another good soldier had a boy by the hand, and a passing soldier cut the boy's legs with his sword. When Isabella's successor, Queen Juana (the protectress) heard about this massacre, she was moved to order an investigation. Fray Nicolás de Ovando, then governnor, held a posthumous trial for the slaughtered caciques and cacicas. As witnesses, he brought in the men who did the killings.

There were many pitched battles where Indians routed the Spanish soldiers, and organized resistance persisted for 50 years, but Spanish cannon, steel swords, horses and dogs overwhelmed the Indians. One by one, Spanish captains approached the ruling nucleus of the tribal leadership. The techniques used to lure and trap the sincere Taino were strictly Machiavellian. The Spanish would sue for peace and start negotiations at which the caciques would put on large feasts. Then the Spanish would attack.

Governor Ovando did this to destroy the powerful woman cacique, Anacaona, whose people he sought to "encommend" to new Spanish arrivals. He chose Christmas day, after three days of generous feasting, dancing, storytelling and games. Anacaona had arranged a large areito, where her councilors were singing of the ancestors. At a signal from Ovando, Spanish soldiers seized Anacaona and all her nobles. The nobles were burned in a pile. Anacaona, the Taino queen, was hanged (Tyler, 1988).

One by one, the caciques of Española fell and their peoples were given over to Spanish masters, or "encomendados," who literally worked the majority of them to death. Cuba, Puerto Rico and Jamaica followed. In Puerto Rico, Caribs and Tainos joined battle against the Spanish and later migrated together to the islands in the Lower Antilles. In Cuba, the Tainos allied with the Ciboneys to mount several major rebellions. They were aided by the warnings of Hatuey, a cacique from Española, who had seen the Spanish system in his own land. Hatuey was joined by a Cubano cacique, Guamax, to initiate a general warrior resistance that would carry on to the 1530s. Hatuey, who warned other Indians that gold was the only god of the Spanish, was captured and ordered burned alive. The story of Hatuey's execution, recorded by las Casas, is still told to children in eastern Cuba.

A Spanish friar attempted to convert this first Cuban national hero, tied and ready as soldiers with lit torches approached. The friar explained about conversion, baptism and the Catholic conception of Heaven and Hell. He offered to baptize Hatuey, thus cleansing all of his sins he had perpetrated against the Christian God. Hatuey is said to have requested time to think on the offer. In the Taino culture, the dead are carried by the living and ongoing generations. They live in a parallel world and must be recognized and fed. A great deal of ceremonial attention is given this fundamental human responsibility by the Caribbean and Meso-American Indian cultures. No doubt a traditionalist such as Hatuey carried his own peoples' medicines and song into his final moment.

Hatuey finally responded: "And the baptized, where do they go after death?"

"To Heaven," said the friar.

Hatuey: "And the Spanish, where do they go?"

Friar: "If baptized, of course, they go to Heaven."

"So the Spaniards go to Heaven," Hatuey responded. "Then I don't want to go there. Don't baptize me. I prefer to go to Hell."

The story of Hatuey's execution is a persistent oral telling in Camaguey and Oriente provinces in Cuba. There is a tradition of pilgrimage to the site of the deed, a place called Yara, near the city of Bayamo. The tradition refers to the "light of Yara" that appears to visitors. The power of physical vigor is associated with this belief. Indeed, a major Cuban rebellion against the Spanish, called the Cry of Yara, started in the same area near the City of Bayamo in 1868 (Cruz, 1988).

The Greater Antilles region was settled slowly over the next 200 years. Smallpox decimated large numbers of Tainos, and malaria, brought in by African slaves, also played a role. Many Indians fled west and south. During the conquest, many of the Taino ceremonial materials were transferred to western Cuba, hidden and found decades later (Rivero, 1966).

Small veins of gold were finally found in Cuba, but the discoveries coincided with Cortés's expedition to Yucatan and his "discovery" of the Aztec and Mayan mainland. The great quantities of the precious yellow metal in meso–America obviated the urgency to settle Cuba, as Española turned to sugar cane (Cuba would follow), and Havana became a port of call for African slavery and the shipment of gold and other treasure from the Spanish Main.

Many Puerto Rican Tainos or Boriquas, among a total number of perhaps 50,000–100,000 (with a dozen caciques) and of indistinct religion and customs from the Cubeños or from Española Tainos, appear to have migrated to the islands of Lesser Antilles and possibly back to the South American mainland. Several Carib settlements to the east of them had been traditional enemies, but helped organize the withdrawal of many Tainos to the Lesser Antilles. The Spanish never penetrated the wall of Carib resistance beyond the Taino territories. As many as a third of Borinquén Tainos fled into the mountains and disappeared, and much the same can be said for Indians in Cuba and Santo Domingo.

Among the first conquistadors and other new Spanish arrivals, particularly the men from the Canary Islands and Galicia, many were known to take one or more wives among the Indian villages. There were noted alliances and nuclei of mestizajes stemming from these early intermarriages. In Santo Domingo, they settled along the Yaque River and into the Marien region. This "nascent, native feudalism . . . claimed hegemony over whole tribes . . . and was a subtle breakaway from Columbus's factoria system" (Floyd, 1973).

The concubinage system set up by the old chiefs and some new Spanish men, both in Cuba and Puerto Rico, and the "guatiao" (exchange of names ceremony) in Santo Domingo created a few somewhat ordained mestizajes, one that would sustain a core of indigenous traditions to modern times.

There were incidents of sympathetic individual Spanish men marrying Indian women and thus removing the cacicas and their particular tribes from the encomienda system. The Spanish did this mostly to gain labor and advantage and at times as a way to remove themselves from the central authority all together. For the remaining Indian caciques, it was a way to marry their remaining people and take status as one of the new people, neither white nor pure Indian Taino, but with at least the ability to establish families and hold land. The comendadors took after this practice when they could. One Cristóbal Rodríguez (nicknamed "La Lengua"), a well-known Spanish-Indian interpreter, was exiled for arranging the marriage of a cacica to a Juan Garces, "probably with the intent to remove her tribe from the encomienda system" (Floyd, 1973).

A very few Indian communities, deep in the highest mountain valleys, did manage to survive in isolation in Cuba for nearly 500 years. These are the communities of Caridad de los Indios and others in the Río Toa region.

In Cuba's Camagüey province, Vasco Porcallo de Figueroa, a particularly vigorous lieutenant from Narváez's army, took dozens of Indian wives and spawned a generation of more than 100 mestizos. Rather than continue to fight, Camagüeybax, the old cacique of the savanna, organized marriages from among his people and Porcallo's children. Later, Porcallo invited some 50 Spanish families to send young men and women to settle in Camagüey where he coupled his mixed offspring to the new arrivals. They named the new mixed generation "Guajiro," a Taino word possibly coined by the cacique Camagüeybax and meaning "one of us" or "one of our countrymen."

Porcallo and his fellow conquistadores provided no gentle model of "pater familias." Porcallo's rule was so brutal that many Taino families in the region committed suicide rather than submit to his encomienda. Near Baracoa, Cuba, at a coastal village named Yumurí, a promontory stands in mute tribute to the many Taino families who, according to local oral history, jumped to their deaths off its cliffs while taunting their Spanish pursuers (Wright, 1916).

Whither Progress?

Did the Spanish (read the West) represent progress to the Indian people? Did Indian people advance as a result of the great encounter? Or was there possibly something the West might have learned from the American indigenous peoples? The Indian populations had little opportunity to teach their culture to the newcomers. The encomienda system, which distributed whole tribes outright to conquistadores for working gold mines and tilling soil, destroyed the Tainos and surrounding peoples with genocidal tempo. Swept aside, the Indian populations retreated to remote areas as their civilization was truncated and their ancient communal patterns were destroyed. Five hundred years later, it might be appropriate to appreciate what more we might have now known had their humanity been respected and their social-cultural knowledge intelligently understood.

That the Tainos could keep their quite numerous people strong and well fed yet prescribe both agriculture and fisheries of a reduced scale, and using the softest of technologies reap sufficient yet sustainable yields of food, housing, and other resources, is a significant achievement. Labeled as "primitive" and "backward" even today, it was a system that has arguably not been improved upon.

The label "primitive" is almost always a denigrating assignation. In academic historical thinking, the so-called "primitive peoples," whether in the "savage" or "barbaric" stage, were of a lesser time (the past) from which we (the humans) are thought to have progressed. However, in contemporary development theory, the most "advanced" thinking uniformly incorporates "scale" and the concept of "appropriate technologies." Such new fields as "sustainable agriculture" and "ecosystems management," and the theoretics of "no growth" are establishing themselves in colleges and universities. Their applicability and practicability in a world of fragile ecologies are increasingly accepted. Taino life, in fact, most of what heretofore has been branded as "primitive" and thus not worth emulating about indigenous cultures, is viewed in a totally different light as humankind enters the 21st century. "Primitiveness" which should only define a people's "primary" relationship with nature, might be seen as a positive human value and activity in these ecologically precarious times.

The history of the European contact with America and its subsequent conquest has been written and rewritten — but seldom from an indigenous perspective and never from the continuity of an Indian survival over that history. Western historians have had a tendency to disregard the Indian oral sources, and many a fundamental lie about Indian culture has been carried from early written texts into the modern day. Not a few Indian elders have told their children, upon sending them to Western schools: "Remember your culture. Don't forget who wrote the history."

To the American indigenous peoples, members of a unique civilization, first sight and first contact with Columbus and his caravels could only mean that a new and yet incomprehensible manifestation had arrived. Most of the early contact stories throughout the hemisphere confirm that the indigenous response was almost uniformly friendly, curious, and extremely respectful. What came back, uniformly and abruptly, was arrogant interrogation and a superior attitude. Unrelenting brutality followed, one exploding in sexual temper and blood furies never before imagined, certainly not by the Tainos, and never equalled in all the (often questionable) annals of Sun sacrifice, cannibalism and inter-tribal warfare.

The actual brutality imposed on Indians by the European conquest is now more or less accepted history. What has not decisively changed is the notion that it was, after all, justifiable. Throughout the hemisphere, the average non–Indian American is infused early with the notion that Europe brought "civilization" to the Americas, that Amerindian peoples were mired in an early, "primitive" version of the universal historical process, that they were savages, pagans, and, most damningly, cannibals. But one still needs to wonder about the nature of savagery between two peoples, one of whom worked for and provided food as an uncommercialized staple to its members, and another which could shed copious blood for the gold of the earth.

In his ship's log, the Admiral recorded how well formed and muscular the Taino men and women were, with "no bellies, and good teeth." He noted, too, what good servants they would make, reminding King Ferdinand that slavery has been justified historically many times. To Ferdinand, as a justification for enslavement, Columbus wrote: "Many other times it has already happened men have been brought from Guinea.... They (the Tainos) will make excellent servants." Columbus speculates that a few Spanish soldiers could enslave the Tainos: "They are all naked and neither possess weapons nor know of them. They are very well fitted to be governed and set to work to till the land and do whatever is necessary. They also may be taught to build houses and wear clothes and adopt our customs.... With 50 men, all could be subdued and made to do all that is desired." Time would prove the battle more difficult than expected, though the end result would ultimately be as Columbus predicted.

This 15th century Spanish idea that non–Christian peoples could be oppressed at will is rooted in the thesis of the Cardinal bishop of Ostia, Henry of Susa, in the 13th century, who successfully postulated that, "heathen peoples had their own political jurisdiction and their possessions before Christ came into the world. But when this occurred, all the powers and the rights of dominion passed to Christ, who, according to doctrine, became lord over the earth, both in the spiritual and temporal sense" (Tyler, 1988).

Guacanagarí, a Taino cacique who befriended Columbus and was in turn sold into slavery for his trouble, twice sent Columbus face masks made of gold. I think he meant to say: "Gold is such your interest that it is what you are. Your face must be of gold; gold must be the identity your eyes look through."

Chapter Notes

1. In the middle of a housing shortage, current planning in Cuba discourages the building of bohios. They are considered symbols of the "past" and associated with "underdevelopment." In Cuba, for many years, the bohio-dwelling Guajiro was isolated and subject to harsh and arbitrary mistreatment at the hands of the Rural Guard. Eastern Guajiros in Cuba today have more access to modern conveniences but complain about government regimentation over their agricultural practices and market. They still build many bohios, some quite comfortable, out of the Royal Palm.

2. Friar Roman Pané, who wrote the earliest Native cosmology in the Americas

(Macorix field work commissioned by Columbus: Winter, 1493) uses the term "anguilas," or eels, to describe what his informants spoke of as a large, slippery, river animal "with a form similar to a woman." Given the centrality and abundance of the manatee for the peoples of the Greater Antilles, it might be assumed that the old story refers to the manatee, rather than the eel, in this fecund context.

Sources

Cassa, Roberto. *Tainos de la Española.* Santo Domingo: Editora de la Universidad Autónoma, 1974.

Cruz, Felipe Pérez. *Los Primeros Rebeldes de America.* Cuba: Editorial Cente Nueva, 1988.

de Anglería, Pedro Mártir. *Fuentes Históricas sobre Colón y América.* 1982.

Fernández-Armesto, Felipe. *Columbus and the Conquest of the Impossible.* London: Weidenfeld and Nicholson, 1974.

Floyd, Troy S. *The Columbus Dynasty in the Caribbean, 1492–1526.* Albuquerque: University of New Mexico Press, 1973.

Jane, Cecil, ed. *The Voyages of Christopher Columbus Being the Journals of His First and Last Voyages, to Which Is Added the Account of His Second Voyage by Andrés Bernaldez.* London: Argonaut Press, 1930.

las Casas, Bartolomé de. *History of the Indies.* Andrée Collard, trans. and ed. New York: Harper and Row, 1971.

Pané, Fray Roman. *Antigüedades de los Indios (1493).* José Juan Arrom, ed. Mexico City: Siglo Veintiuno, 1989.

Rivero de la Calle, Manuel, ed. *Las Culturas Aborigenes de Cuba.* Havana: Editorial Universitaria de la Habana, 1966.

Tabío, Ernesto E., and Estrella Rey. *Prehistoria de Cuba.* Havana: Editorial de Ciencias Sociales, 1985.

Tyler, S. Lyman. *Two Worlds: The Indian Encounter with the European, 1492–1509.* Salt Lake City: University of Utah Press, 1988.

Vega, Bernardo. *Los Cacicazgos de la Española.* Dominica: Museo del Hombre, 1980.

Wright, Irene A. *The Early History of Cuba, 1492–1586.* New York: Macmillan, 1916.

The Second Voyage

Hans Koning

Never again may mortal men hope to recapture the amazement, the wonder, the delight of those October days in 1492 when the New World gracefully yielded her virginity to the conquering Castilians. — Samuel Eliot Morison, historian.

There is no ship's log in existence for the second voyage of Columbus to America, but there is much material, and foremost among it the report by Diego Chanca. Chanca was one of the court physicians, and the king and queen sent him on the expedition and paid his salary. He did not stay with Columbus but went back to Spain on the first ship returning.

Geographically no other crossing, obviously, matched the first one. The mystery barrier had been broken. Henceforth, ships from many countries would sail west. Before the century had ended, Europeans would have set foot on American soil from Newfoundland (John Cabot) to Brazil. In the words of a writer of the period, "the works of Creation were doubled."

But for the native population of America, the second Columbus voyage was perhaps the crucial one. On that occasion, the pattern was set for centuries to come. The pretense was ended, the idyll over. The Indians, who had been praised for their generosity and innocence, were now called savages. The talk was of slavery and gold, rather than of brotherhood and conversion. The new relationship between the races was established.

I am not going to assert that this was all Columbus's fault. Although there was no systematic slavery within Europe at that time, enslavement of darker races had been considered a matter of course from the first contact with them. The Portuguese were buying slaves on the Guinea coast, though not catching them themselves — a moot distinction.

Dangerous as such generalizations are, a case can be made that the

Reprinted by permission from Hans Koning's biography Columbus: His Enterprise, *Monthly Review Press, New York City, 1991. Copyright 1976 and 1991.*

Spaniards from that time on became more cruel than any of the other seagoing nations of Europe — more cruel toward their own poor as well. Soon they
would be treating the Indians, in the words of Bishop de las Casas, "not as
beasts, for beasts are treated properly at times, but like the excrement in a
public square." Las Casas, who was an admirer, not an enemy, of Columbus,
said that Columbus was "at the beginning of the ill usage inflicted upon
them." (But then, when we think of children pulling coal wagons in British
mines — not in 1492 but in 1852 — even this ill usage becomes relative.)

This is not to say that the picture of Spain in America is totally black.
There were forces for the good besides Bishop de las Casas. Columbus
assuredly was not a force for the good. If an entire race stood in his way, it
had to go.

Surprisingly, Ferdinand and Isabella, the sovereigns who had instituted
the dreaded Inquisition in 1480 and expelled all Jews in 1492, seemed a force
of moderation. Their express command to the Admiral for his second voyage
was that the Indians were to be treated "well and lovingly."

It was a half-hearted command, however. These two, who always called
themselves "the Catholic Monarchs," appear not to have taken any specific
steps when the various priests who went and returned did not convert one
single Indian, and when instead the ships started returning with enslaved
men, women and children.

Only when the slave trade had stopped making profits for the Crown or
anyone else, because the Arawaks could not survive under its conditions, did
the Crown terminate the practice. By then, the Arawak nation was already
doomed.

Unfortunately, this is not the only instance in Western history where
men became humane at the very moment inhumanity lost its business advantage.

The Crossing

The report by Columbus about the first voyage — his sales prospectus,
so to speak — saw to it that this time there was no shortage of candidates for
the Enterprise. No less than 17 ships set out, with 1,200 to 1,500 men. Many
others wanted to go and were refused. The organization of the expedition,
for that time enormous, was not left to Columbus, but was carried out by
Juan de Fonseca, archdeacon of Seville, who would henceforth continue to
act as a quartermaster-general for the American sailings.

Another "*Santa María*" was the flagship for this fleet; most of the other
ships' names are not known. Some were very small, and meant for inshore
exploration. (Twelve of them were to turn around upon reaching the New
World.) The *Niña* went again, and some members of the Niño family who

owned her. The Pinzóns did not go; they were no longer on speaking terms with Columbus. Two hundred passengers, gentleman adventurers, were going at their own expense.

This fleet sailed on September 25, 1493, from Cádiz, which is some 60 miles down the coast from Palos. Again, the Canary Islands were the first port of call, and they sailed from there on October 13. Three weeks later, on November 3, they sighted land: the island Dominica in the Lesser Antilles.

The ease of this passage makes you wonder again for a moment why it had not been done long before. The answer is, indeed, illustrated by the story of Columbus making his egg stand on end: once you know how, it's simple. This is especially true with the westward voyages, which, different from the Portuguese endeavors around Africa, led through blessed climates and seas that were tempestuous only on rare occasions. The hardships of these crossings at no time took the terrifying toll of the tropical voyages.

From Dominica, the fleet went island-hopping, sailing north, past (what are now called) Guadeloupe, Montserrat, the Virgin Islands, Puerto Rico, and finally on to their principal destination, Hispaniola.

They staged brief reconnaissances on most islands. Dr. Chanca comments on their lushness, even at that time of year, the green shores, or then again mountains rising from the sea with waterfalls of dizzying height. Chanca reports that everywhere captives were taken, but he also notes that a number of Indians came freely aboard the ships. These had been captives themselves of raiding Caribs. In most places, the men were away on fishing expeditions and the women and children who could, fled. Different from the experience of the first voyage, here most villages stood empty when the Spaniards came ashore.

Their first meeting with Indians who tried to defend themselves came in mid-November, off a small island, probably Saint Martin (Sint Maarten).

The Admiral was lying offshore and a boat he had sent out was on its way back with captives. Then, as related by Chanca, a canoe appeared around the point of land with four men, two women, and a child. When they saw the Spanish fleet, they were so astounded that, in the words of Chanca, "they remained without a motion, a whole hour, at about a reach of two mortar shots from the ships."

It is a particularly clear and haunting image for me: that motionless canoe, with its seven people, just sitting and staring at the 17 ships reflected in the blue water, under a blue sky.

But to the Spaniards these people were game rather than fellow beings.

Several boats set out to get them, hugging the shore and unseen by the Indians, who were "lost in amazement." At the last moment, the Indians saw their attackers approach, and when they realized they could not get away, they took up their bows, men and women alike, to defend themselves, first from their canoe and then, when that had been upturned, standing in the shallow water.

They were overpowered and brought to the *Santa María*. One, whose stomach had been slit open by a Spaniard, was tossed overboard, but he swam toward shore, holding his guts in with his hand. The gallant Spaniards went after him, capturing him anew, and this time threw him overboard after binding his hands and feet. The Indian managed to free himself, and swam off once more. Then he was "shot through and through" from the deck of the ship and sank in the clear water.

This happened during what Columbus's American biographer Samuel Eliot Morison calls "those bright November days, the fleet gaily coasting . . . and hearty voices joining in the evening hymn to the Blessed Virgin."

Hispaniola Revisited

As Columbus was approaching Hispaniola from the east on this occasion, none of his old crew recognized it; the captive Indians told them where they were. Presently they saw the Bay of Samaná, and from then on they followed the north coast which was familiar to them, on to Fort Navidad.

Toward the end of November, late in the evening, Columbus reached the place. Remembering the wreck of his first *Santa María*, he stayed offshore and had a cannon fired. But no answer came from the fort.

In the night a canoe of Indians approached, men from the villages of Guacanagarí. They brought presents and told him all was well; but their fearfulness showed it was not.

Soon the Admiral learned through his two interpreters — survivors from the captives of the first voyage — that all inhabitants of his first colony had been killed. They had roamed the island in gangs, looking for more gold than even the ever willing Guacanagarí could find for them, and taking any woman or boy they fancied. Other caciques were less fearful than Guacanagarí, and finally the misdeeds of the Spaniards became so unbearable that those "gentle, timid souls" rose against them and killed them in a pitched battle. They then marched on Navidad where they found only ten Spanish settlers who had stayed home, each with a bevy of enslaved girls, and these were overpowered and killed too. Through it all, Guacanagarí had remained in his role of the friend of Columbus and had tried to prevent this revenge.

The evil deeds committed by the Spanish colonists must indeed have been staggering, for the first day the Admiral and his officers did not speak of retaliation — and that at a time when an Indian already had his ears cut off if he touched a Spanish article of clothing. Only Friar Buil, head of the priests who had come to convert the savages to Christian love, wanted Guacanagarí put to death "as an example." Columbus decided to wait and see. Guacanagarí was his ally, his only one.

The Admiral immediately ordered the ground of Navidad turned over with spades. Gold was still and always his first thought, and before sailing, he had given orders to those men to bury all the gold they got on the spot. It is not known if anything was found beyond the buried bodies of the Spaniards.

The Admiral then decided to set up a new settlement and had the surrounding area reconnoitered. After their experience with the Navidad men, the Indian mood was very different. No more jubilation; whenever the Spaniards reached a village, they found that all the inhabitants had fled.

Ten women, whom Columbus had captured earlier, jumped overboard and tried to escape. Four were caught with the boats as they came out of the water, but the others made it inland. Guacanagarí must have been more and more uncomfortable in what had become a role of traitor to his people, for Columbus now sent him a messenger, demanding that he find the six women and return them to the ships. (They were to be used as sex slaves for the crew.)

Against hard eastern winds and much rain, the entire fleet then proceeded along the coast, looking for a new place for a fort. They were steering in the direction of the alleged gold fields of Cibao and central Hispaniola that Pinzón had reported on the first voyage. On January 2, 1494, they anchored in a sheltered bay and started building a new fort, which they called Isabela (after the Spanish "Isabel" of the Queen's name.)

By now, according to Dr. Chanca, a third of the men had fallen sick. Although he ascribed this to the air, the water, the climate, and the general "beastliness" of the place, there was another and quite different reason, as we will see later. Apart from all the sickness, the work involved in building the fort, and the difference between reality and the picture painted by Columbus in his report, made for much resentment among the expedition. After only a few days at Isabela, Columbus decided to send a large contingent home, together with what he thought was sandalwood and pepper (it was not), 26 captured Indians, and all the gold they had scraped together from the Indians in that short time. Twelve of the 17 ships were sent right back after a rather useless voyage, and on one of them went Dr. Chanca.

Just before Chanca left, two reconnaissance parties sent out by Columbus had returned with reports of gold fields with riches beyond even Spanish greed. Chanca didn't question the finds. He ends his chronicle by assuring his readers that "the King and Queen will henceforth be the richest and most prosperous in the world, for nothing comparable has ever been seen or read of in the whole creation. . . . On the next voyage the ships will carry away such quantities of gold that anyone who hears of it will be dumbfounded."

From Isabela, Columbus promptly mounted a number of expeditions into the interior. He himself led the first one. Armored and helmeted, with swords and muskets, horses and fierce dogs, the Spaniards marched through the green valleys and up the hills of the island, banners flying and trumpets sounding. It was a most inconvenient and sweaty way of traveling that humid climate, but the idea was that a show of force would stamp out any nonsensical ideas the natives might have begun to harbor. The target of these marches was of course those gold fields in Cibao, fields "as large as Portugal" in the words of Columbus's son. He, many years later, still clung to Columbus's fantasies — fantasies fatal to the island.

In reality, there were no gold fields anywhere, just a few rivers carrying grains of gold in alluvial form.

Columbus gave orders to build a fort near those non-existent gold mines, and he named it San Tomás, presumably because of the doubting Thomases among those adventurers in his train who still didn't believe in the promised riches. He put all the weapons in Isabela aboard his flagship because he was afraid of trouble from his colleagues. He then placed the settlement under the command of his younger brother, Diego, the only man he now trusted, and set off himself for a reconnaissance of China — that is to say, Cuba.

Cuba and Jamaica

In April, Columbus, with two other ships, crossed from Hispaniola to Cuba, which he once more took "possession" of by planting a cross. Then he and his officers decided to follow the southern coastline. According to Aristotle, it is in the south rather than the north that all good things (gold and spices, that is) are found. From the south coast, they sailed to Jamaica, two days' sailing farther south. For Jamaica was called "Jamesque" by its inhabitants, and that name sounded to the Spaniards like "Babeque," another mystic place reputed to be crammed full of (even greed gets monotonous) . . . gold.

But nothing was found but Indians less friendly than the Arawaks had once been. However, they were soon taught to obey or flee, after crossbowmen from the ships had killed some of them and others had been savaged by the dogs the Spaniards had brought. This particular stratagem had first been used by Spain against the original inhabitants (long since exterminated) of the Canary Islands. Trained dogs are a terrible weapon against unarmed and naked men and women, and the Spaniards (like their French successors on Hispaniola) exulted in the results. The Alabama police dogs have a long history.

Columbus followed the Jamaican shore for a short while and then sailed back up to the southern coast of Cuba. He followed it to the gulf due south of where Havana now is. There, plagued by contrary winds and disease, he decided to return to Isabela.

In 1488, Bartolomeu Dias had rounded the Cape of Good Hope and had been well on his way to India when his crew refused to continue. Dias had returned to Lisbon, but first he had every man sign a deposition that Africa had indeed been rounded, and the way east found. With this as a supposed example, Columbus now had every man on his ships, under threat of dire punishment, sign a deposition saying (what no one knew) that there was no need to go any farther west, as the length of their voyage had proven Cuba not to be an island — no island could be that long — but the mainland of Asia!

Once more, the Admiral acted as if saying or writing something with enough emphasis made it so. In doing that, he might look like the first public relations man, a worthy, if somewhat pathetic, predecessor of Madison Avenue. But what moved Columbus was deeper, and more frightening. He seemed to be accumulating within himself that terrible ire of a man who feels that he alone is right, and that the world is forever conspiring against him, and not giving him his due.

It was a tough voyage back, which led the fleet once more to Jamaica and all around it this time, to dodge unfavorable winds.

From Jamaica they crossed to the southern shore of Hispaniola and followed the coastline. When they had made it to the southeastern tip of the island, they were lucky enough to witness a total eclipse of the moon. This, with the help of an astronomical table, gave them the time difference between their point of observation and the place for which the eclipse table was drawn, Nuremberg.

This was indeed luck, for such an event was the only way to find longitude. It was a simple method: one hour's difference in time meant 15 degrees longitude. The only error would be in measuring the time span from the observation to noon of the following day, in order to get local time. Columbus should have found that he was about five hours and twenty minutes behind Nuremberg, that is almost 80 degrees west of it. But wittingly or unwittingly his sum came out at 103 degrees west of that town. Thus, he could tell himself once more that he had indeed just been to the Asian shores.

Shortly thereafter, the three ships rounded the eastern tip of the island, and toward the end of September Columbus landed once more at Isabela. He had been away more than half a year.

Conquered Women

Verena Stolcke

While I was in the boat I captured a very beautiful Carib woman, whom the said Admiral [Columbus] gave to me, and with whom, having taken her into my cabin, she being naked according to their custom, I conceived desire to take pleasure. I wanted to put my desire into execution but she did not want it and treated me with her fingernails in such a manner that I wished I had never begun. But seeing that (to tell you the end of it all), I took a rope and thrashed her well, for which she raised such unheard of screams that you would not have believed your ears. Finally we came to an agreement in such manner that I can tell you that she seemed to have been brought up in a school of harlots. — Michele de Cuneo, an Italian nobleman and passenger on Columbus's second voyage.

Our memory is like a broken mirror. It does not reflect the world as it was, but our fragmented, partial, even personal reconstruction of it.[1] By realigning the fragments, we may become aware of aspects of our past that previously were invisible. Until very recently, our memories of the conquest and colonization of America have been angled away from the experiences of Indian and African American women. Historians have generally presented the conquest as a man's affair, an aggression and dispossession by one sector of men (Spaniards) over other men (Indians).[2] They failed to reflect the sustained assault on these women's cultural and personal integrity, or how that assault gave form to the emerging colonial society.[3]

Some historians have sought to justify the conquest by emphasizing its civilizing mission. Others have denounced the enormous human cost of imposing European spiritual and social values and political principles on the native population. Up to now little attention has been paid to the dialectical interplay between these foreign, imposed values and the realities of colonial

Reprinted with the permission of North American Congress on Latin America, 475 Riverside Drive, 454, New York, NY 10115. This article originally appeared in NACLA Report on the Americas, *Vol. 24, No. 5, February 1991. All rights reserved.*

society. Status concepts brought over from the metropolis — Spain — were reformulated in the colonies to legitimate the new hierarchical order. One of the most important of these was "purity of blood" (*limpieza de sangre*), which was transformed from a religious principle in Spain, to a racial one in America.

The very fact of the conquest, of the domination and exploitation of the local population, produced a profoundly unequal society. But that inequality need not have been codified on the basis of racial differences. In Spain, status was determined by a variety of factors: hereditary nobility, religious affiliation, sex, and even — in limited spheres — proofs of merit (skill, prowess, etc.). But in the colonies, the physical and cultural differences of the indigenous, and later African American, peoples took on a profound political and social meaning, one that marks Latin American societies to this day.[4]

Modern racism, the attribution of socio-economic inequalities to racial and therefore hereditary deficiencies, has often been interpreted as a perverse consequence of the imperial expansion of European power to other lands. It has also been common to argue that the doctrine dates only from the 19th century. Both these views are mistaken. The mistakes are due, in part, to the insufficient attention given to the racist ideological constructs of Europe, and particularly Spain, that served to justify the conquest and colonization of America.

The origin and history of the term "race" are a subject of debate. There is isolated evidence of the use of the word *raza* in Spanish, *raça* in Portuguese and *race* in French since the 13th century, although these appeared more frequently 300 years later. According to some authors the French *race* initially meant, primarily, belonging to and descending from a family or house of "noble stock," or *stirpis nobilitas,* which was translated as *noblesse de sang* ("nobility of blood") in 1533. "Race" represented both the succession of generations, "from race to race," as well as all those members of the same generation, and implied "nobility" and "quality."

In Spain, however, according to the etymologist Corominas, this sense of *raza* merged in the mid-15th century with the old Castilian (Spanish) term *raça,* meaning "thinness [*raleza* in modern Spanish] or defect in the fabric" or, simply, "defect, guilt." From the 16th century on, the term appears in Castilian commonly in a negative sense. Corominas concludes that "When the foreign term *'raza'* entered Castilian in the biological sense or the sense of a natural category, it was not surprising that it should be contaminated by the pejorative shading, especially since its application to Moors and Jews lent itself to this use," although this negative sense is not constant.[5]

The conquest of America followed closely on the Christian Reconquest of Spain from Moorish domination. In the early years of the Reconquest, Jews and Muslims could correct their defective status by conversion; baptism placed them on the same social and legal level as Christians. But this religious-cultural discrimination turned into racism toward the middle of the 15th century, as persecution of converts and the exclusion of Moriscos (converted Muslims) increased. What was emerging was "a racist doctrine of original sin of the most repulsive kind."[6]

Converted Jews and Moriscos, together with their ancestors and descendants, soon became objects of discrimination based on the doctrine of "purity of blood," which meant having no racial mixture of Moors, Jews, heretics or penitents (those condemned by the Inquisition). Non-Christian religious faith came to be considered an inherited stain of "blood" and thus ineffaceable.[7]

In the mid-15th century, the Council of Toledo adopted the first statute of purity of blood. Several religious and military orders, universities and some city councils and cathedrals also adopted them — although these were never made part of the laws of Spain. The Spanish Inquisition was founded in 1480, when the Reconquest was nearly complete. Four years later the Inquisition decreed that those who had been sentenced for crimes against Christianity would not be permitted to hold public office. Then, in 1492, the same year that Christopher Columbus set out across the Atlantic, the last Moorish stronghold, Granada, fell to the Catholic Monarchs, and Jews and Muslims who refused to convert to Christianity were expelled from Spain.[8]

The Inquisition was the sole court with immediate jurisdiction over purity of blood. Thus the Holy Office, as the ecclesiastical court of the Inquisition was known, acted as mediator between theorists of exclusion and the people, popularizing the idea that all converts were suspect.[9] Endogamy and legitimate birth became important as guarantors of purity of blood; the Inquisition reviewed genealogies for false declarations of purity. The Holy Office and blood proofs for marriage would not be eliminated until the beginning of the 19th century.

However, the statutes excluding those considered "impure" from positions of confidence and social preeminence were by no means accepted without protest in Spain. To the consternation of the nobility, who in previous centuries had happily intermingled with Moors and Jews, the only authentic pure Christians according to the new doctrine turned out to be the commoners. In the face of this paradox, doubts over the doctrine intensified in the 17th century. Opposition by jurists and theologians to the purely racial application of the doctrine grew, and the concept of purity was gradually extended to other "stains," this time of class, such as servile trades. Thus the racial doctrine was adjusted better to defend the socioeconomic hierarchy.

The notion that even before God some were more equal than others, and that the distinction was racial, was initially a Spanish product for domestic consumption. But the doctrine of "purity of blood" became most important in the colonies by the early 18th century, just as it was losing force in the metropolis. With its implications for marriage and legitimacy, it acquired new meanings with especially painful consequences for women.

From the beginning, access to the New World had been forbidden to "Moors, Jews, or their sons, or the sons of Gypsies or of a reconciled heretic or son or grandson of anyone who has been burned or condemned for heretical baseness and apostasy through the masculine or the feminine line...."[10] The purity-of-blood requirement was progressively extended. In the 16th century no distinction was made between mestizos and pure Spaniards with regard to legal and property rights. Gradually, though, mestizos were rendered ineligible for the priesthood and public office.[11] Thus in 1679 the Constitution of a seminary school in Mexico prohibited the admission of children who were not "pure and of pure blood without race of Moors, Jews or penitents by the Holy Office, nor recently converted to the faith, nor mestizos, nor mulattoes...."[12]

The remark by an English physician in the mid-19th century aptly describes the view current in the 16th century Spanish colonies: "The uterus is for the race what the heart is for the individual: It is the organ for the circulation of the species."[13]

The first consequence of the conquest was the dramatic decline of the indigenous population. There followed a prolonged debate within the Church and the colonial bureaucracy over the status of the survivors. Some theologians attempted to establish a link between them and the tribes of Israel. The Crown ended up granting the Indians the status of purity of blood except in cases where they refused to be evangelized.[14] As late as 1734, the Crown was insisting that "chiefs and their descendants retain all the preeminences and honors (both ecclesiastic and secular) that the noble hidalgos of Castile enjoy, and the less illustrious Indians or their descendants, pure in blood without mixture or any other disapproved sect, retain all the prerogatives, dignities and honors that are enjoyed in these Realms by the pure of blood, of so-called common status, with whose Royal determinations they are capacitated by your majesty for whatsoever honorific posts...."[15] Formally, then the indigenous population still enjoyed privileges (which in many cases they would lose with independence). But in practice they already suffered discrimination like the other non-white groups.

In the 16th and 17th centuries, voluntary European immigration and the forced importation of African slaves increased, along with miscegenation. Social ranking became more obviously based on racial rather than religious criteria, even as the distinctions grew more and more minute. There were slave and free Blacks, mulattos, zambos and zambaigos (descendants of Blacks and Indians), "liquid" (pure) Indians and mestizos, and several other categories for gradations of various mixes.[16] Whites, meanwhile, were divided into Peninsulars (Spanish-born) and Creoles (born in the colonies), rich and poor. Mulattoes, mestizos, and other mixed categories in particular were objects of disgrace. They inspired deep distrust because they made racial barriers uncertain, placing in doubt or actively threatening the emerging racial hierarchy.

Toward the end of the 17th century there was an increase in royal warrants seeking to resolve questions of purity of blood, granting dispensations for entry into the priesthood or occupation of posts, and confirming racial distinctions. At this time, for reasons still unclear, the indigenous population began to recover. The mestizo and mulatto population multiplied as a result of the ubiquitous concubinage between white men and Indian or Black women. Also Creole and Peninsular whites grew in number.[17]

Often the sexual excesses of the Spanish conquerors with Indian and later African women have been attributed to the scarcity of Spanish women in the colonies. However, by the mid-16th century there was no such scarcity.[18] Rapes and forced cohabitation were really demonstrations of the arrogance of the conquerors, who saw indigenous and African women as easy prey for their sexual gratification.

Cortés's behavior in this area was a model of duplicity. He took as his interpreter and lover the young Indian woman he called Doña Marina, popularly referred to as "la Malinche," or "la Chingada."[19] Cortés, already married to a Spanish woman, recognized the son he had with Malinche, but forced her to marry a soldier from his ranks. While he himself was traveling with his Indian mistress, Cortés declared, "so as to make clear the intention that the settlers of these parts have of residing and staying in them, I order all persons who have had Indians or who were married in Castile or other parts, to bring their women within a year and a half . . . under penalty of losing the Indians and everything acquired and gained with them."[20]

From the beginning of colonization the Crown issued a spate of decrees and laws requiring that all colonists who had wives in Spain bring them to America as soon as possible. Those laws remained in force until the 18th century. Their purpose was not only to settle the colonies but to safeguard their stability by whitening them.[21] Although there were difficulties in implementing this policy, proof that there was no lack of Spanish women is that by the mid-16th century the first convents were founded, where legitimate or illegitimate daughters of Spaniards who did not find Spanish men to marry were supposed to end up.[22]

Around the beginning of the 18th century, colonial society had become a complex, multicolored human mosaic of inequalities, the result of an interaction of race and class criteria. And it was perceived that way by its members, for the good of some (Creole and Peninsular whites) and the ill of others (everybody else). "Purity of blood" acquired new force as it lost any religious connotation, becoming a clearly racial notion.

Colonial society, however, was not an impermeable, closed order. On the contrary, its inherent contradictions threatened its cohesiveness in several ways. The mestizos, resulting from extramarital sexual exploitation by white men of women considered racially inferior, subverted the hierarchy.[23] Contacts between the different racial categories grew, and the fluidity of the hierarchical colonial order aggravated even further the obsession with purity of blood among the elites that were white by definition. For the elites and for those who sought to get close to them, legitimate birth from a legitimate married couple thus acquired new importance as the only proof of purity of blood. Illegitimate birth, on the other hand, was a sign of "infamy, stain, and defect" stemming from the mixture of races. [24]

The only guarantee of racial purity, hence social prestige, was marriage between racial equals. But the Church, which until the 18th century had the exclusive prerogative to perform marriages, rejected any paternal interference for possible reasons of social and or racial inequality. Freedom to marry was based on the consent of the parties. For the Church, women's sexual virtue, that is virginity before marriage and chastity afterward, was the highest good. This had to prevail over and above any paternal social whim. Blood or ritual relationship between bride and groom constituted the only important canonic impediment.

Nevertheless, as early as the 16th century there were cases when parents attempted to block a marriage for reasons of supposed social inequality. [25] In these disputes the sexual virtue defended by the Church came up against the interest of parents in protecting family purity from a marriage considered unequal.

The canonic doctrine that privileged sexual honor above social prestige was egalitarian only in appearance. The Church never managed to eradicate the sexual exploitation outside the marriage bond of women of low racial status. Interracial unions were mainly, as they were euphemistially called in the period, consensual.

By stressing sexual virtue, the Church, moreover, promoted discrimination between different categories of women in sexual terms: between those who were sexually abused by white men (generally women of inferior social status) and also penalized because they supposedly were living in mortal sin; and virtuous women (white women, or daughters of family), subject to a severe family control of their sexuality. The other side of the Church's doctrine was sexual control, especially over women. Salvation of the soul depended on submission of the body.

The ecclesiastic authorities in the colonies did not carry out these supposedly egalitarian precepts to the letter. The clergy themselves were notorious for sexual abuses. There were many cases of "solicitation," clerics forcing Indian women into bed on the pretext of saving their souls. This became one of the crimes codified by the Inquisition. One Jesuit was said to have "solicited" more than 100 women. Nevertheless, the fact that the Church's policy threatened the temporal interests of the elites is indicated by the many pre-nuptial disputes that reached ecclesiastic courts.

Toward the beginning of the 18th century the Church had increasing difficulties defending its doctrine against prenuptial interference by families, a phenomenon attributed to a growing parental obsession with racial purity.[26] Ironically, it was precisely in that period that the stress on purity of blood was declining in the metropolis. One reason for the decline may have been that the new doctrine of individual liberty and equality, which was gaining advocates elsewhere in Europe, also made some impact in Spain. In that sociopolitical climate, which was clearly in transformation, marriages considered unequal must have become more frequent.

In 1775 the Crown requested an opinion from a Council of Ministers about measures to avoid unequal marriages, given "the sad effects and most serious wrongs caused by marriages that are contracted between persons of very unequal circles and conditions," alleging that "the excessive favor given by ecclesiastic ministers to the misunderstood freedom of absolute and unlimited matrimony with no distinction made of persons and sometimes against the just resistance of parents and relatives . . . has been the principal source from which have flowed for the most part the harmful effects suffered in Spain on account of unequal marriages."[27]

In 1776 King Carlos III promulgated the Pragmatic Sanction to prevent the contracting of unequal marriages. The State thus took over jurisdiction over marriages. The free will of contracting parties to marry was suppressed, and marriage could only be performed with parental consent under penalty of disinheritance for the parties. Some authors have interpreted this sanction as a reaction of Carlos III to the marriage of his younger brother to a woman of inferior social condition.[28]

The Pragmatic Sanction was promulgated during the Bourbon reforms at a time of social and political transformations. At first view it seems paradoxical that it would be precisely in a period of liberal political opening and modernization that the Crown introduced severe controls over marriage. But laws are not necessarily the legal expression of changes in social values; there is often a dialectical relation between the two. The Pragmatic Sanction can be seen as an attempt to increase social control over matrimonial practices that seemed to threaten the established hierarchical order.

The secularization of marriage regulations resulted in the suppression of individual freedom to marry. Any matrimonial dispute had to be resolved from then on by a civil court. Several later royal decrees reinforced parental authority in matters of marriage—unlike what occurred in the colonies, where the principle of purity of blood underwent a late revival.

In 1778 the Crown extended the Pragmatic Sanction to the Indies, "Bearing in mind that the same or greater harmful effects are caused by this abuse [of unequal marriages] in my Realms and Dominions of the Indies on account of their size, the diversity of classes and castes of their inhabitants . . . and the very severe wrongs that have been experienced in the absolute and confused freedom with which passionate and incompetent youths of both sexes become betrothed."[29]

Excluded from the Sanction were "mulattoes, Negroes, natives, and individuals of similar castes and races publicly held and reputed as such" who presumably had no honors to protect. In all other cases parental consent was required. In case of parental opposition, civil authorities had the power to grant exemption.

Application of the Sanction in the colonies met with considerable opposition. People with few possessions had little to lose by marrying against the will of the family. There were those who wished to marry for love or to legitimize a premarital sexual relation regardless of social differences. But the crucial problem was posed by interracial marriages. Racial prejudices and reasons of state did not always prevail against human passions, nor did ecclesiastic moral imperatives.[30]

Several other royal decrees on the subject of unequal marriages followed that of 1778. They reveal a double controversy. The Crown favored marriages in the colonies even over parental opposition, to encourage the growth of the colonial population. Yet there was a great deal of ambivalence regarding interracial marriages on the part of colonial authorities, concerned with maintaining purity of blood. It was not initially clear who needed official permission to marry "members of the castes," i.e., nonwhites. In 1810, this doubt was finally resolved by a decree requiring nobles and other adults of recognized purity of blood who wished to contract matrimony with Blacks, mulattos, and other castes to procure a license from the colonial civil authorities. This implied a potential prohibition of interracial marriages and established that matrimony was a concern of the state. What was at stake were not only family interests but the stability of the social order. In the colonies, this meant the racial hierarchy.[31]

What consequences did this new racist turn in marriage laws have for women? When social position is attributed to inherent, natural, racial and therefore hereditary qualities, the elite's control of the procreative capacity of their women is essential for them to preserve their social preeminence. As a 19th century Spanish jurist argued, only women can bring bastards into the family. By institutionalizing the metaphysical notion of blood as the carrier of family prestige and as the ideological instrument with which to guarantee the social hierarchy, the state, in alliance with families that were pure of blood, subjected their women to renewed control of their sexuality while their sons took their pleasure with those women who lacked social status without having to assume any responsibility for it.

The Church had defended the freedom to marry in order to protect sexual virtue as a moral value in itself. The state converted marriage into an instrument to protect the social body. In a racist hierarchical society, in effect, "the uterus is for the race what the heart is for the individual."

But a reservation is in order here. It is important to remember that the legal matrimonial paraphernalia were necessary precisely because there were always men and women who defied the politico-racial order and its social and moral values.

Racism as we know it today is not wholly a result of colonial expansion. In the 19th century, "scientific" racism came to replace the metaphysics of purity of blood, helping to mask the contradiction between an individualist meritocratic doctrine and the unequal social reality of the emerging class society. Thus, racial conflict today cannot be reduced to an "anachronistic" colonial residue. But its particular form in Latin America, and its intimate connections to the control of women's sexuality, go back to the very beginnings of colonial society, when the conquest of the women was an essential part of the colonial project. The evidence is all before us. All we need do to see it is shift slightly the angle of our mirror.

Chapter Notes

1. Christoph Hein, *Horns Ende* (Berlin: Aufbau Verlag, 1985), pp. 279–80.
2. Irene Silverblatt, *Moon, Sun, and Witches: Gender Ideologies and Class in Inca and Colonial Peru* (Princeton, N. J.: Princeton University Press, 1987).
3. See Ann Laura Stoler, "Rethinking Colonial Categories: European Communities and the Boundaries of Rule." *Comparative Studies in Society and History* vol. 31, no. 1 (1989).
4. There was, granted, an ideological conflict over not only the treatment but also the conceptualization of the indigenous peoples: whether they were human, equal in essence to the conquistadores, capable of being converted to Christianity, or whether on the contrary they differed from Europeans in nature and were thus inferior. But if this were true, what criteria could justify that inferiority?
5. Joan Corominas, *Diccionario Crítico Etimológico Castellano e Hispánico* (Madrid: Editorial Gredos, 1982), pp. 800–801.
6. Henry Kamen, *La Inquisición Española* (Barcelona: Editorial Critica, 1985), p. 158. There were those in Spain who continued to believe that a baptized Jew should be considered no different from a baptized Christian.
7. As Kamen notes. "In the fifteenth century many people felt that the honor of religion and nation could be preserved only by assuring purity of lineage and avoiding the mixture of Jewish or Moorish blood." Kamen, p. 158.
8. Between 1690 and 1614, the Moriscos (converted Muslims) were also expelled from Spain.
9. Henry Kamen, *La Inquisición Española*.
10. José Luis Martínez, *Pasajeros de Indias* (Madrid: Alianza Editorial, 1983), p. 32.
11. Henry Mechoulan, *El Honor de Dios* (Barcelona: Editorial Argos Vegara, 1981).
12. Richard Konetzke, *Colección de Documentos para la Historia de la Formación Social de Hispanoamérica, 1493–1810* (Madrid: Instituto Jaime Balmes, C.S.I.C., 1958–62, 3 vols.), Vol. II, pp. 691–692.
13. Mary Poovey, "Scenes of an Indelicate Character: The Medical Treatment of Victorian Women," in Catherine Gallagher and Thomas Laqueur (eds.), *The Making*

of the Modern Body: Sexuality and Society in the Nineteenth Century (Berkeley: University of California Press, 1984), p. 145.

14. Mechoulan, p. 57.

15. Konetzke, Vol. III, 1, p. 217.

16. Konetzke, Vol. II, 1, p. 148 and 2, pp. 694–95.

17. Nicolás Sánchez Albornoz. "The Population of Colonial Spanish America," in Leslie Bethell (ed.), *The Cambridge History of Latin America* (Cambridge, England: Cambridge University Press, 1984), Vol. 2.

18. Konetzke, [vol. unknown], p. 148. See also Richard Konetzke, "La Emigración de Mujeres Españolas a América durante la Época Colonial," *Revista Internacional de Sociología.*

19. The term *chingada* (meaning in various situations screwed, failed, sloshed, and so forth), ubiquitous in Mexican slang, reflects the enormous ambivalence that surrounds the image built up of Malinche. She is represented as the victim of a rape at the same time that she is characterized as Cortés's consenting, useful instrument at the service of the Conquest. Octavio Paz described her in *The Labyrinth of Solitude* as the quintessence of Indian collaborationism. Even today in Mexico the term "malinchismo" is used to refer to a turncoat. This interpretation of Doña Marina lets the conquistador off. The victim is blamed for her own misfortune.

20. Cited by Konetzke, [vol. unknown], p. 126.

21. Konetzke, [vol. unknown], p. 128.

22. Konetzke, [vol. unknown], p. 148.

23. Asuncion Lavrin (ed.), *Sexuality and Marriage in Colonial Latin America* (Lincoln: University of Nebraska Press, 1989).

24. Konetzke, Vol. III, 2, pp. 473–74. But economic gains could up to a certain point compensate for inferior racial status. And the Crown wielded the power to excuse even that "stain." See Verena Martínez-Alier, *Marriage, Class and Colour in Nineteenth Century Cuba: A Study of Racial Attitudes and Sexual Values in a Slave Society* (Cambridge: Cambridge University Press, 1974. 2nd ed., Ann Arbor; University of Michigan Press, 1989).

25. For the case of Mexico, see Patricia Seed, *To Love, Honor and Obey in Colonial Mexico* (Stanford: Stanford University Press, 1988).

26. *Ibid.*

27. Konetzke, III, 1, pp. 401–05.

28. Seed.

29. Konetzke, III, 1, pp. 438–42.

30. I shall not analyze in detail the later evolution of marriage law nor its application. I have done so previously for the case of Cuba. See Martínez-Alier.

31. Cuba, one of the last Spanish colonies, in an economic boom through sugar production that depended on a rapidly growing slave population, became the privileged terrain for applying this matrimonial legislation.

Rereading the Past

William Bigelow

1992 has become a catalyst for coordinating . . . against continued racism, imperialism, and [the] exploitive mentality that gets taught in the educational system. —Jan Elliott, from "Christopher Columbus Is Alive and Well and Living in Washington, D.C.," unpublished work.

Most of my students have trouble with the idea that a book—especially a *textbook*—can lie. When I tell them that I want them to argue with, not just read, the printed word they're not sure what I mean. That's why I start my U.S. history class by stealing a student's purse.

As the year opens, my students may not know when the Civil War was fought, what James Madison or Frederick Douglass did or where the Underground Railroad went, but they do know that a brave fellow named Christopher Columbus discovered America. Okay, the Vikings may have actually *discovered* America, but students know it was Columbus who mapped it and *did* something with the place. Indeed, this bit of historical lore may be the only knowledge class members share in common.

What students don't know is that year after year their textbooks have, by omission or otherwise, lied to them on a grand scale. Some students learned that Columbus sailed on three ships and that his sailors worried whether they would ever see land again. Others know from readings and teachers that when the Admiral landed he was greeted by naked, reddish skinned people whom he called Indians. And still others may know Columbus gave these people little trinkets and returned to Spain with a few of the Indians to show King Ferdinand and Queen Isabella.

All this is true. What is also true is that Columbus took hundreds of Indian slaves and sent them back to Spain where most of them were sold and

Reprinted with permission from Language Arts, *Vol. 66, No. 6, October 1989. Copyright 1989 by the National Council of Teachers of English.*

subsequently died. What is also true is that in his quest for gold Columbus had the hands cut off any Indian who did not return with his or her three month quota. And what is also true is that on one island alone, Hispaniola, an entire race of people were wiped off the face of the earth in a mere 40 years of Spanish administration.

So I begin class by stealing a student's purse. I announce that the purse is mine, obviously, because look who has it. Most students are fair-minded. They saw me take the purse off the desk so they protest: "That's not yours, it's Nikki's. You took it, we saw you." I brush these objections aside and reiterate that it is, too, mine and to prove it I'll show all the things I have inside.

I unzip the bag and remove a brush or a comb, maybe a pair of dark glasses. A tube of lipstick works best: "This is my lipstick," I say. "There, that proves it *is* my purse." They do not buy it and, in fact, are mildly outraged that I would pry into someone's possessions with such utter disregard for her privacy. (I've alerted the student to the demonstration before the class, but no one else knows that.)

It's time to move on: "Ok, if it's Nikki's purse, how do you know? Why are you all so positive it's not my purse?" Different answers: We saw you take it; that's her lipstick, we know you don't wear lipstick; there is stuff in there with her name on it. To get the point across, I even offer to help in their effort to prove Nikki's possession: "If we had a test on the contents of the purse who would do better, Nikki or I?" "Whose labor earned the money that bought the things in the purse, mine or Nikki's?" Obvious questions, obvious answers.

I make one last try to keep Nikki's purse: "What if I said I *discovered* this purse, then would it be mine?" A little laughter is my reward, but I don't get any takers; they still think the purse is rightfully Nikki's.

"So," I ask, "Why do we say that Columbus discovered America?" Now they begin to see what I've been leading up to. I ask a series of rhetorical questions which implicitly make the link between Nikki's purse and the Indians' land: Were there people on the land before Columbus arrived? Who had been on the land longer, Columbus or the Indians? Who knew the land better? Who had put their labor into making the land produce? The students see where I'm going—it would be hard not to. "And yet," I continue, "What is the first thing that Columbus did when he arrived in the New World?" Right: he took possession of it. After all, he had discovered the place.

We talk about phrases other than "discovery" that textbooks could use to describe what Columbus did. Students start with the phrases they used to describe what I did to Nikki's purse: He stole it; he took it; he ripped it off. And others: He invaded it; he conquered it.

I want students to see that the word "discovery" is loaded. The word itself carries with it a perspective, a bias; it takes sides. "Discovery" is the phrase of the supposed discoverers. It's the conquerors, the invaders, masking their theft. And when the word gets repeated in textbooks those textbooks become, in the phrase of one historian, "the propaganda of the winners."

To prepare students to examine critically the textbooks of their past we begin with some alternative, and rather un-sentimental, explorations of Columbus's "enterprise," as he called it. The Admiral-to-be was not sailing for mere adventure and to prove the world was round, as my fourth grade teacher had informed her class, but to secure the tremendous profits that were to be made by reaching the Indies. From the beginning, Columbus's quest was wealth, both for Spain and for himself personally. He demanded a 10 percent cut of everything shipped to Spain via the western route — and not just for himself but for all his heirs in perpetuity. And he insisted he be pronounced governor of any new lands he found, a title which carried with it dictatorial powers.

Mostly I want the class to think about the human beings Columbus was to "discover" — and then destroy. I read to students from a letter Columbus wrote to Lord Raphael Sánchez, treasurer of Aragón and one of his patrons, dated March 14, 1493, during his return from the first voyage. He reports being enormously impressed by the indigenous people:

> As soon . . . as they see that they are safe and have laid aside all fear, they are very simple and honest and exceedingly liberal with all they have; none of them refusing anything he may possess when he is asked for it, but, on the contrary, inviting us to ask them. They exhibit great love toward all others in preference to themselves. They also give objects of great value for trifles, and content themselves with very little or nothing in return . . . I did not find, as some of us had expected, any cannibals among them, but, on the contrary, men of great deference and kindness.[1]

But, on an ominous note, Columbus writes in his log, ". . . should your Majesties command it, all the inhabitants could be taken away to Castile [Spain], or made slaves on the island. With 50 men we could subjugate them all and make them do whatever we want."[2]

I ask students if they remember from elementary school days what it was Columbus brought back with him from his travels in the New World. Together students recall that he brought back parrots, plants, some gold and a few of the people Columbus had taken to calling "Indians." This was Columbus's first expedition and it is also where most school textbook accounts of Columbus end — conveniently. Because the enterprise of Columbus was not to bring back exotic knickknacks, but riches, preferably gold. What about his second voyage?

I read to them a passage from Hans Koning's fine book, *Columbus: His Enterprise:*

We are now in February 1495. Time was short for sending back a good "dividend" on the supply ships getting ready for the return to Spain. Columbus therefore turned to a massive slave raid as a means for filling up these ships. The brothers [Columbus and his brothers, Bartolome and Diego] rounded up fifteen hundred Arawaks — men, women and children — and imprisoned them in pens in Isabela, guarded by men and dogs. The ships had room for no more than five hundred, and thus only the best specimens were loaded aboard. The Admiral then told the Spaniards they could help themselves from the remainder to as many slaves as they wanted. Those whom no one chose were simply kicked out of their pens. Such had been the terror of these prisoners that (in the description by Michele de Cuneo, one of the colonists) "they rushed in all directions like lunatics, women dropping and abandoning infants in the rush, running for miles without stopping, fleeing across mountains and rivers."

Of the five hundred slaves, three hundred arrived alive in Spain, where they were put up for sale in Seville by Don Juan de Fonseca, the archdeacon of the town. "As naked as the day they were born," the report of this excellent churchman says, *"but with no more embarrassment than animals...."*

The slave trade immediately turned out to be "unprofitable, for the slaves mostly died." Columbus decided to concentrate on gold, although he writes, "Let us *in the name of the Holy Trinity* go on sending all the slaves that can be sold" [emphasis in Koning].[3]

Certainly Columbus's fame should not be limited to the discovery of America: He also deserves credit for initiating the trans–Atlantic slave trade, albeit in the opposite direction than we're used to thinking of it.

Students and I role play a scene from Columbus's second voyage. Slavery is not producing the profit Columbus is seeking. He still believes there is gold in them thar hills and the Indians are selfishly holding out on him. Students play Columbus; I play the Indians: "Chris, we don't have any gold, honest. Can we go back to living our lives now and you can go back to wherever you came from?" I call on several students to respond to the Indians' plea. Columbus thinks the Indians are lying. How can he get his gold? Student responses range from sympathetic to ruthless: Okay, we'll go home; *please* bring us your gold; we'll lock you up in prison if you don't bring us your gold; we'll torture you if you don't fork it over, etc. After I have pleaded for awhile and the students-as–Columbus have threatened, I read aloud another passage from Koning's book describing the system Columbus arrived at for extracting gold from the Indians:

> Every man and woman, every boy or girl of 14 or older, in the province of Cibao (of the imaginary gold fields) had to collect gold for the Spaniards. As their measure, the Spaniards used ... hawks' bells.... Every three months, every Indian had to bring to

one of the forts a hawks' bell filled with gold dust. The chiefs had
to bring in about 10 times that amount. In the other provinces of
Hispaniola, 25 pounds of spun cotton took the place of gold.

Copper tokens were manufactured, and when an Indian had
brought his or her tribute to an armed post, he or she received such
a token, stamped with the month, to be hung around the neck.
With that they were safe for another three months while collecting
more gold.

Whoever was caught without a token was killed by having his
or her hands cut off. There are old Spanish prints . . . that show
this being done: The Indians stumble away, staring *with surprise* at
their arm stumps pulsing out blood.

There were no gold fields, and thus, once the Indians had handed
in whatever they still had in gold ornaments, their only hope was
to work all day in the streams, washing out gold dust from the peb-
bles. It was an impossible task, but those Indians who tried to flee
into the mountains were systematically hunted down with dogs
and killed, to set an example for the others to keep trying. . . .

Thus it was at this time that the mass suicides began: the Arawaks killed themselves with casaba poison.

During those two years of the administration of the brothers
Columbus, an estimated one half of the entire population of Hispaniola was killed or killed themselves. The estimates run from
125,000 to 500,000.[4]

It is important students not be shielded from the horror of what
"discovery" meant to its victims. The fuller they understand the consequences
of Columbus's invasion of America the better they will be equipped to critically
re-examine the innocent stories their textbooks have offered through the
years. The goal is not to titillate or stun, but to force the question: Why wasn't
I told this before?

Students' assignment is to find a textbook, preferably one they used in
elementary school, but any textbook will suffice, and write a critique of the
book's treatment of Columbus and the Indians. I distribute the following
handout to students and review the questions aloud. I don't want them to
merely answer the questions one by one, but to consider them as guidelines
in completing their critiques:

—How factually accurate was the account?

—What was omitted—left out—that in your judgment would be impor-
tant for a full understanding of Columbus? (For example, his treatment of the
Indians; slave taking; his method of getting gold; the overall effect on the
Indians.)

—What motives does the book give to Columbus? Compare those with
his real motives.

—Who does the book get you to root for, and how do they accomplish that? (For example, are the books horrified at the treatment of Indians or thrilled that Columbus makes it to the New World?)

— What function do pictures in the books play? What do they communicate about Columbus and his "enterprise"?

— In your opinion, *why* does the book portray the Columbus/Indian encounter the way it does?

— Can you think of any groups in our society who might have an interest in people having an inaccurate view of history?

I tell students that this last question is tough but crucial. Is the continual distortion of Columbus simply an accident, repeated innocently over and over, or are there groups in our society who could benefit from everyone having a false or limited understanding of the past? Whether or not students are able to answer the question effectively, it is still important they struggle with it before our group discussion of their critiques.

The subtext of the assignment is to teach students that text material, indeed all written material, should be read skeptically. I want students to explore the politics of print, that perspectives on history and social reality underlie the written word and that to read is both to comprehend what is written, but also to question *why* it is written. My intention is not to encourage an "I-don't-believe-anything" cynicism,[5] but rather to equip students to bring a writer's assumptions and values to the surface so students can decide what is useful and what is not in any particular work.

For practice, we look at some excerpts from a textbook that belonged to my brother in the fourth grade in California, *The Story of American Freedom*, published by Macmillan in 1964. Students and I read aloud and analyze several paragraphs. The arrival of Columbus and crew is especially revealing — and obnoxious. As is true in every book on the "discovery" I've ever encountered, the reader watches events from the Spaniards' point of view. We are told how Columbus and his men "fell upon their knees and gave thanks to God," a passage included in virtually all elementary school accounts of Columbus. "He then took possession of it [the island] in the name of King Ferdinand and Queen Isabella of Spain."[6] No question is raised of what right Columbus had to assume control over a land which was obviously already occupied by people. The account is so adoring, so respectful of the Admiral, that students can't help but sense the book is offering approval for what is, quite simply, an act of naked imperialism.

The book keeps us close to God and Church throughout its narrative. Upon returning from the New World, Columbus shows off his parrots and Indians (nowhere is there an admission that these people were kidnapped by Columbus), and immediately following the show, "the king and queen lead the way to a near-by church. There a song of praise and thanksgiving is sung."[7] Intended or not, the function of linking church and Columbus is to remove him and his actions still further from question and critique. My job, on the other hand, is to encourage students to pry beneath every phrase and illustration, to begin to train readers who can both understand the word and challenge it.

I give students a week before I ask them to bring in their written critiques. In small groups students share their papers with one another. I ask them to take notes towards what my co-teacher, Linda Christensen, and I call the "collective text": What themes seem to recur in the papers and what important differences emerge?

Here are some excerpts from papers written this year by students in the Literature and U.S. History course that Linda and I co-teach. Trey wrote his critique as a letter to Allyn and Bacon, publishers of *The American Spirit*:

> . . . I'll just pick one topic to keep it simple. How about Columbus. No, you didn't lie, but saying, "Though they had a keen interest in the peoples of the Caribbean, Columbus and his crews were never able to live peacefully among them," makes it seem as if Columbus did no wrong. The reason for not being able to live peacefully is that he and his crew took slaves, and killed thousands of Indians for not bringing enough gold. . . .
>
> If I were to only know the information given in this book, I would have such a sheltered viewpoint that many of my friends would think I was stupid. Later in life people could capitalize on my ignorance by comparing Columbus's voyage with something similar, but in our time. I wouldn't believe the ugly truths brought up by the opposition because it is just like Columbus, and he did no harm, I've known that since the eighth grade.

Keely chose the same book, which happens to be the text adopted by Portland Public Schools, where I teach:

> . . . I found that the facts left in were, in fact, facts. There was nothing made up. Only things left out. There was one sentence in the whole section where Indians were mentioned. And this was only to say why Columbus called them "Indians." Absolutely nothing was said about slaves or gold. . . .
>
> The book, as I said, doesn't mention the Indians really, so of course you're on Christopher's side. They say how he falls to his knees and thanks God for saving him and his crew and for making their voyage successful.

After students read and discuss their papers in small groups we ask them to reflect on the papers as a whole and write about our collective text: What did they discover about textbook treatments of Columbus? Here are some excerpts.

Matthew wrote:

> As people read their evaluations the same situations in these
> textbooks came out. Things were conveniently left out so that you
> sided with Columbus's quest to "boldly go where no man has gone
> before". . . . None of the harsh violent reality is confronted in these
> so-called true accounts.

Gina tried to account for why the books were so consistently rosy:

> It seemed to me as if the publishers had just printed up some
> "glory story" that was supposed to make us feel more patriotic
> about our country. In our group, we talked about the possibility
> of the government trying to protect young students from such vio-
> lence. We soon decided that that was probably one of the farthest
> things from their minds. They want us to look at our country as
> great, and powerful, and forever right. They want us to believe
> Columbus was a real hero. We're being fed lies. We don't question
> the facts, we just absorb information that is handed to us because
> we trust the role models that are handing it out.

Rebecca's collective text reflected the general tone of disillusion with the
official story of textbooks:

> Of course, the writers of the books probably think it's harmless
> enough — what does it matter who discovered America, really, and
> besides it makes them feel good about America. But the thought
> that I have been lied to all my life about this, and who knows what
> else, really makes me angry.

The reflections on the collective text became the basis for a class discussion of these and other issues. Again and again, students blasted their textbooks for consistently making choices which left readers with inadequate, and
ultimately untruthful, understandings. And while we did not press to arrive
at definitive explanations for the omissions and distortions, we did seek to
underscore the contemporary abuses of historical ignorance. If the books wax
romantic about Columbus planting the flag on island beaches and taking possession of land occupied by naked red-skinned Indians, what do young
readers learn from this about today's world? That white people have a right
to dominate peoples of color? That might — or wealth — makes right? That it's
justified to take people's land if you are more "civilized" or have a "better"
religion? Whatever the answers, the textbooks condition students to accept
some form of inequality; nowhere do the books suggest that the Indians were
sovereign peoples with a right to control their own lands. And, if Columbus's
motives for exploration are mystified or ignored then students are less apt to

look beyond today's pious explanations for U.S. involvements in, say, Central America or the Middle East. As Bobby, approaching his registration day for the military draft, pointed out in class: "If people thought they were going off to war to fight for profits maybe they wouldn't fight as well, or maybe they wouldn't go."

It's important to note that some students are left troubled from these myth-popping discussions. One student wrote that she was "left not knowing who to believe." Josh was the most articulate in his skepticism. He had begun to "read" our class from the same critical distance from which we hoped students would approach textbooks:

> I still wonder.... If we can't believe what our first grade
> teachers told us why should we believe you? If they lied to us why
> wouldn't you? If one book is wrong, why isn't another? What is
> your purpose in telling us about how awful Chris was? What in-
> terest do you have in telling us the truth? What is it you want from
> us?

What indeed? It was a wonderfully probing series of questions and Linda and I responded by reading them (anonymously) to the entire class. We asked students to take a few minutes to write additional questions and comments on the Columbus activities or to try to image our response as teachers—what *was* the point of our lessons?

We hoped students would see that the intent of the unit was to present a new way of reading, and ultimately, of experiencing the world. Textbooks fill students with information masquerading as final truth and then ask students to parrot back the information in end of the chapter "checkups." The Brazilian educator, Paulo Freire, calls it the "banking method": students are treated as empty vessels waiting for deposits of wisdom from textbooks and teachers.[8] We wanted to assert to students that they should not necessarily trust the "authorities" but instead needed to be active participants in their own learning, peering between lines for unstated assumptions and unasked questions. Meaning is something *they* need to create, individually and collectively.

Josh asked what our "interest" was in this approach. It is a vital question. Linda and I see teaching as political action: We want to equip students to build a truly democratic society. As Freire writes, to be an actor for social change one must "read the word and the world."[9] We hope that if a student is able to maintain a critical distance from the written word then it's possible to maintain the same distance from one's society: to stand back, look hard and ask, "why is it like this, how can I make it better?"

Postscript:

To complete our unit, Linda and I asked students to create a project that would reach beyond the classroom walls to educate others in the school or larger community. As a class we had uncovered multiple layers of a twisted and biased history. We worried that unless we offered students a chance to act on their new learning, our teaching would unintentionally yet effectively tell students that their role is to uncover injustice, not to do anything about it.

Students could choose the form of their projects. The only requirement was that each individual or group make a presentation outside the classroom. They took us at our word. One group of musicians produced a raucous rock video about the damming of the Columbia River which drowned the ancient fishing grounds of the Celilo Indians. Another group choreographed and performed for other classes a dance, at the same time bitter and humorous, on Columbus's "discovery" and search for gold. As some students danced/acted, one recited quotes from Columbus.

Several students interviewed local Northwest Indian tribal leaders about their struggle for fishing rights on the Columbia River. The group produced a videotape subsequently broadcast during the school's closed-circuit television news show.

One young woman, Nicole Smith-Leary, wrote and illustrated a children's book, *Chris*. In Nicole's story, a young boy named Christopher moves from his old Spain Street neighborhood to a new house on Salvadora Street. He's miserable and misses his old friends, Ferdie and Isie. While wandering the new neighborhood he spots a colorful playhouse and declares, "I claim this clubhouse in the name of me, and my best friends Ferdie and Isie." The rightful owners of the clubhouse soon return and confront Christopher who insists that the structure is now *his* because he "discovered" it.

"How can you come here and discover something that we built and really care about?" the boys demand.

The story ends happily when they agree to let Christopher share the clubhouse if he helps with the upkeep—a metaphorical twist that would have been nice 500 years earlier.

Nicole read her story to a number of classes at a local elementary school. She opened each session by asking if anyone had something to write with. When an unsuspecting youngster volunteered a pencil, Nicole thanked the student, then pocketed it. This elementary school version of purse-stealing gave Nicole a handy introduction to the theft-posing-as-discovery lesson in her short story.

Like Rebecca and many other students, Nicole was angry she had been lied to about Columbus and the genocide of indigenous people in the Caribbean. However, the final project assignment encouraged her to channel that anger in an activist direction. She became a teacher, offering the youngsters a framework in which to locate and question the romanticized textbook patter about "exploration" and "discovery." Nicole's story and lesson provided a kind of revenge: getting back at those who miseducated her so many years before. But as she taught she also learned—learned that the best way to address injustice is to work for change.

Chapter Notes

1. *The Annals of America, Volume 1: 1493–1754, Discovering a New World,* Encyclopaedia Britannica, Chicago, 1968, pp. 2, 4.

2. Quoted in Hans Koning, *Columbus: His Enterprise* (New York: Monthly Review Press, 1976), pp. 53–54. As Koning points out, none of the information included in his book is new. It is available in Columbus's own journals and letters and the writings of the Spanish priest, Bartolomé de las Casas. Even Columbus's adoring biographers admit the Admiral's outrages. For example, Pulitzer Prize winner Samuel Eliot Morison acknowledges that Columbus unleashed savage dogs on Indians, kidnapped Indian leaders and encouraged his sailors to rape Indian women. At one point Morison writes, "The cruel policy initiated by Columbus and pursued by his successors resulted in complete genocide" (Samuel Eliot Morison, *Christopher Columbus, Mariner,* New York: New American Library, 1942, p. 99). But the sharpness of this judgment is buried in Morison's syrupy admiration for Columbus's courage and navigational skills.

3. Koning, pp. 84–85.

4. Koning, pp. 85–87.

5. It's useful to keep in mind the distinction between cynicism and skepticism. As Norman Diamond writes, "In an important respect, the two are not even commensurable. Skepticism says, 'You'll have to show me, otherwise I'm dubious'; it is open to engagement and persuasion. . . . Cynicism is a removed perspective, a renunciation of any responsibility." See Norman Diamond "Against Cynicism in Politics and Culture," in *Monthly Review,* Vol. 28, No. 2, June, 1976, p. 40.

6. Edna McGuire, *The Story of American Freedom,* (New York: Macmillan, 1964), p. 24.

7. McGuire, p. 26.

8. See Paulo Freire, *Pedagogy of the Oppressed* (New York: Continuum, 1970). This banking method of education, Freire writes, ". . . turns [students] into 'receptacles' to be 'filled' by the teacher. . . .

"Education thus becomes an act of depositing, in which the students are depositories and the teacher is the depositor. Instead of communicating, the teacher issues communiques and makes deposits which the students patiently receive, memorize, and repeat. This is the 'banking' concept of education, in which the scope of action allowed to the students extends only as far as receiving, filing, and storing the deposits. They do, it is true, have the opportunity to become collectors or cataloguers of the things they store. But in the last analysis, it is men [people] themselves who are filed away through the lack of creativity, transformation, and knowledge in this (at best) misguided system."

9. Paulo Freire and Donaldo Macedo, *Literacy: Reading the Word and the World* (South Hadley, Mass.: Bergin and Garvey, 1987).

King Sugar

Eduardo Galeano

Vast, dark, unknown, the land lay flat for thousands of years, hardly used at all by men and women, for the few Indians never knew how to use it and never cared to learn. The wolf, the bear, the panther and the bison flourished and increased faster than people. The land waited for a master who did not come for a long, long time. — Gerald W. Johnson, from *America Is Born,* William Morrow, 1959.

Plantations, Latifundia, and Fate

Undoubtedly gold and silver were the main motivating force in the conquest, but Columbus on his second voyage brought the first sugarcane roots from the Canary Islands and planted them in what is now the Dominican Republic. To the Admiral's joy they took hold rapidly. Grown and refined on a small scale in Sicily, Madeira, and the Cape Verde islands, and purchased in the Orient at high prices, sugar was so precious to Europeans that it figured in the dowries of queens. It was sold in pharmacies, weighed out by the gram. For almost three centuries after the discovery of America no agricultural product had more importance for European commerce than the American sugar. Canefields were planted in the warm, damp littoral of Northeast Brazil; then in the Caribbean islands — Barbados, Jamaica, Haiti, Santo Domingo, Guadeloupe, Cuba, Puerto Rico — and in Veracruz and the Peruvian coast, which proved to be ideal terrain for the "white gold." Legions of slaves came from Africa to provide King Sugar with the prodigal, wageless labor force he required: human fuel for the burning. The land was devastated by this selfish plant which invaded the New World, felling forests, squandering natural fertility, and destroying accumulated soil humus. The long sugar cycle generated a prosperity as mortal as the prosperity generated by the silver and gold of Potosí, Ouro Prêto, Zacatecas and Guanajuato. At the same time, directly or indirectly but decisively, it spurred the growth of Dutch, French, English and United States industry.

The demand for sugar produced the plantation, an enterprise motivated by its proprietor's desire for profit and placed at the service of the international market Europe was organizing. Internally, however — since it was to a considerable extent self-sufficient — the plantation was feudal in many important aspects, and its labor force consisted mainly of slaves. Thus three distinct historical periods — mercantilism, feudalism, slavery — were combined in a single socio-economic unit. But in the constellation of power developed by the plantation system, the international market soon took the center of the stage.

Subordinated to foreign needs and often financed from abroad the colonial plantation evolved directly into the present-day latifundio, one of the bottlenecks that choke economic development and condemn the masses to poverty and a marginal existence in Latin America today. The latifundio as we know it has been sufficiently mechanized to multiply the labor surplus, and thus enjoys an ample reserve of cheap hands. It no longer depends on the importation of African slaves or on the *encomienda* of Indians; it merely needs to pay ridiculously low or in-kind wages, or to obtain labor for nothing in return for the laborer's use of a minute piece of land. It feeds upon the proliferation of minifundios — pocket-sized farms — resulting from its own expansion, and upon the constant internal migration of a legion of workers who, driven by hunger, move around to the rhythm of successive harvests.

The plantation was so structured as to make it, in effect, a sieve for the draining-off of natural wealth, and today the latifundio functions in the same way. Each region, once integrated into the world market, experiences a dynamic cycle; then decay sets in with the competition of substitute products, the exhaustion of the soil, or the development of other areas where conditions are better. The initial productive drive fades with the passing years into a culture of poverty, subsistence economy, and lethargy. The Northeast was Brazil's richest area and is now its poorest; in Barbados and Haiti human antheaps live condemned to penury; in Cuba sugar became the master key for United States domination, at the price of monoculture and the relentless impoverishment of the soil. And this has not been the role of sugar alone: the story has been the same with cacao, which made the fortunes of the Caracas oligarchy; with the spectacular rise and fall of cotton in Maranhão; with the Amazonian rubber plantations, which became the cemeteries of Northeastern workers recruited for a few pennies; with the devastated quebracho forests in northern Argentina and Paraguay; with Yucatán's henequen plantations, where Yaqui Indians were sent for extermination. It is also the story of coffee, which advances leaving deserts behind it, and of the fruit plantations in Brazil, Colombia, Ecuador, and the unhappy lands of Central

America. Each product has come to embody the fate of countries, regions and peoples; and mineral-producing communities have, of course, traveled the same melancholy road. The more a product is desired by the world market, the greater the misery it brings to the Latin American peoples whose sacrifice creates it. The area least affected by this iron law has been Río de la Plata, feeding the international market with its hides, meat and wool; yet even it has been unable to break out of the cage of underdevelopment.

How the Soil Was Ravaged in Northeast Brazil

Because they discovered precious metals first, the Spaniards only began raising sugar in their colonies — initially in Santo Domingo, then in Veracruz, Peru and Cuba — as a secondary activity. Brazil, on the other hand, became the world's largest sugar producer and remained so until the middle of the 17th century. Portugal's Latin American colony was also the chief market for slaves; native workers, always scarce, were rapidly killed off by the forced labor, and sugar needed thousands of hands to clear and prepare the ground, to plant, harvest, transport, grind, and refine the cane. Brazilian colonial society flourished in Bahía and Pernambuco as a subproduct of sugar until the discovery of gold moved its center to Minas Gerais.

The Portuguese Crown granted lands in usufruct to Brazil's first big land-lords. The feats of conquest proceeded in tandem with the organization of production. Twelve "captains" received by written grant the whole of the vast unexplored territory, to be exploited in the king's service. However, the business was mostly financed by Dutch capital and thus became more Flemish than Portuguese. Dutch entrepreneurs not only participated in establishing sugar estates and importing slaves; they also picked up the crude sugar in Lisbon, refined it, sold it in Europe, and pocketed a third of its value in profits. In 1630 the Dutch West India Company invaded and conquered the northeast coast of Brazil and took over direct control of sugar production. To multiply their profits, the sources of sugar had to be multiplied, and the company offered the British in Barbados all facilities to start massive production in the Antilles. It brought Caribbean colonists to Brazil to acquire technical and organization knowledge. When the Dutch were finally thrown out of the Brazilian Northeast in 1654, they had already laid the foundations for intense and ruinous competition by Barbados. They had taken slaves and cane roots there, set up sugar estates, and provided all the implements. Brazilian exports plummeted to half of what they had been, and sugar prices were halved by the end of the 17th century. Meanwhile, Barbados's black population increased tenfold in a few decades. The Antilles were nearer to the European market, and Barbados developed superior techniques and offered virgin land — while Brazilian soil was wearing out. The crisis in the sugar-growing

Northeast was also precipitated by serious slave revolts and by the gold boom to the south, which robbed the plantations of labor. The crisis was definitive: it has dragged itself painfully down the centuries into our time.

Sugar has destroyed the Northeast. The humid coastal fringe, well watered by rains, had a soil of great fertility, rich in humus and mineral salts and covered by forests from Bahía to Ceará. This region of tropical forests was turned into a region of savannas. Naturally fitted to produce food, it became a place of hunger. Where everything had bloomed exuberantly, the destructive and all-dominating latifundio left sterile rock, washed-out soil eroded lands. At first there had been orange and mango plantations, but these were left to their fate, or reduced to small orchards surrounding the sugarmill-owner's house, reserved exclusively for the family of the white planter. Fire was used to clear land for canefields, devastating the fauna along with the flora: deer, wild boar, tapir, rabbit, pacas and armadillo disappeared. All was sacrificed on the altar of sugarcane monoculture.

At the end of the 16th century Brazil had no less than 120 sugarmills worth some £2 million, but their masters, owners of the best lands, grew no food. They imported it, just as they imported an array of luxury articles from overseas with the slaves and bags of salt. Abundance and prosperity went hand in hand, as usual, with chronic malnutrition and misery for most of the population. Cattle were relegated to deserts far inland from the humid coastal zone to the *sertão* which, with two head of cattle to the square mile, supplied (and still supplies) tough, tasteless and always scarce meat.

A legacy of those colonial days which continues is the custom of eating dirt. Lack of iron produces anemia, and instinct leads Northeastern children to eat dirt to gain the mineral salts which are absent from their diet of manioc starch, beans and — with luck — dried meat. In former times this "African vice" was punished by putting muzzles on the children or by hanging them in willow baskets far above the ground.[1]

The Brazilian Northeast is today the most underdeveloped area in the Western hemisphere.[2] As a result of sugar monoculture it is a concentration camp for 30,000,000 people — on the same soil that produced the most lucrative business of the colonial agricultural economy in Latin America. Today less than a fifth of Pernambuco's humid zone is used for growing sugar; the rest is not used at all.[3] The big sugarmill owners, who are also the biggest planters of cane, permit themselves this luxury of waste. It is not in the Northeast's arid and semiarid interior that food conditions are worst, as is erroneously believed. The *sertão*, a desert of stones and sparse vegetation, has periods of hunger when the scorching sun produces drought and the semblance of a lunar landscape, forcing the people to flee and sowing crosses along the roadsides. But in the humid littoral — that coastal fringe still so ironically known as the "forest zone" in tribute to the remote past and to the pitiful remnants of forestation surviving from centuries of sugar — hunger is

endemic. Where opulence is most opulent, there — in this land of contradictions — misery is most miserable; the region nature chose to produce all foods,
denies all. The sugar latifundio, a structure built on waste, must still import
food from other areas, particularly from the center and south, at escalating
prices. The cost of living in Recife is the highest in Brazil, well above Rio de
Janeiro. Beans cost more in the Northeast than in Ipanema, the capital city's
most luxurious beach resort. The price of half a kilo of manioc starch equals
the wage an adult sugar-plantation worker receives for working from sunrise
to sunset: if he complains, the foreman summons the carpenter to measure
the man for the length and width of the boards that will be needed. In large
areas the owner's or administrator's "right of the first night" for each girl is
still effective. A third of Recife's population lives in miserable hovels; in one
district, Casa Amarela, more than half the babies die before they are a year
old. Child prostitution — girls of 10 or 12 sold by their parents — is common
in Northeastern cities. Some plantations pay less for a day's work than the
lowest wage in India. A United Nations Food and Agriculture Organization
(FAO) report in 1957 said that in the area of Victoria, near Recife, protein
deficiency in children produces a weight loss 40 percent worse than is generally
found in Africa. Many plantations still operate private prisons, but as René
Dumont notes, "those who are responsible for murder by undernourishment
are not locked inside, since they are the keepers of the keys."[4]

Pernambuco now produces less than half as much sugar as the state of
São Paulo, and has a far lower per hectare yield; but Pernambuco's inhabitants, densely concentrated in the humid zone, depend on sugar for their
livelihood, while São Paulo contains the greatest industrial center in Latin
America. In the Northeast not even progress is progressive, for it is in the
hands of a few owners. The food of the minority is the hunger of the majority.
Beginning in 1870 the sugar industry was substantially modernized as big
central mills were installed, and the absorption of land by latifundios progressed alarmingly, sharpening the hunger of the area. In the 1950s, booming
industrialization increased the consumption of sugar in Brazil itself. This
stimulated Northeastern production, but without causing any rise in the per
hectare yield. New lands of inferior quality were planted to cane, and sugar
devoured still more of the few food-producing areas. Turned into a wage-
worker, the peasant who had previously tilled his small plot experienced no
benefit, since he did not earn enough money to buy what he had once produced. As usual, the expansion expanded hunger.

The Devastation of the Caribbean

"You believe perhaps, gentlemen," said Karl Marx in 1848, "that the
production of coffee and sugar is the natural destiny of the West Indies. Two

centuries ago, nature, which does not trouble herself about commerce, had planted neither sugarcane nor coffee trees there."⁵ The international division of labor was not organized by the Holy Ghost but by men — more precisely, as a result of the world development of capitalism.

It was the fate of the "sugar islands" — Barbados, the Leewards, Trinidad-Tobago, Guadeloupe, Puerto Rico, Haiti and Santo Domingo — to be incorporated one by one into the world market and condemned to sugar until our day. Grown on a grand scale, sugar spreads its blight on a grand scale and today unemployment and poverty are these islands' permanent guests. Cuba also continues to depend on the sale of sugar, although the agrarian reforms of 1959 sparked an intensive diversification of the economy which has ended seasonal unemployment. Cubans no longer work only during the five or so months of the sugar harvest, but for 12 months in the continuous job of building a new society.

Barbados was, starting in 1641, the first Caribbean island where sugar was grown for bulk export, although the Spaniards had planted cane earlier in Santo Domingo and Cuba. It was, as we have seen, the Dutch who introduced sugar into the little British island; by 1666 Barbados had 800 plantations and over 80,000 slaves. Occupied vertically and horizontally by the developing latifundio, Barbados suffered no better fate than the Brazilian Northeast. It had previously produced a variety of crops on small holdings: cotton and tobacco, oranges, cows and pigs. Canefields devoured all this and devastated the dense forests in the name of a glorious illusion. The island soon found that its soil was exhausted, that it was unable to feed its population, and that it was producing sugar at uncompetitive prices.

By this time sugar cultivation had spread to the Leeward Islands, to Jamaica, and to the Guianas on the South American mainland. Jamaica entered the 18th century with ten times more slaves than white colonists. Its soil too was soon exhausted. In the second half of the century the world's best sugar was being raised on the spongy coastal plains of Haiti, a French colony then known as Saint Domingue. Northern and western Haiti became a human antheap: sugar needed hands and more hands. In 1786 the colony brought in 27,000 slaves; in the following year 40,000. Revolution broke out in the fall of 1791 and in one month, September, 200 sugar plantations went up in flames; fires and battles were continuous as the rebel slaves pushed France's armies to the sea. Ships sailed containing ever more Frenchmen and ever less sugar. The war spilt rivers of blood, wrecked the plantations, and paralyzed the country, and by the end of the century production had fallen to almost nothing. By November 1803 almost all of the once flourishing colony was in ashes and ruins. The Haitian revolution had coincided — and not only in time — with the French Revolution, and Haiti bore its share of the international coalition's blockade against France: England controlled the seas. Later, as its independence became inevitable, Haiti also had to suffer blockade *by*

France. The United States Congress, yielding to French pressure, banned trade with Haiti in 1806. In 1825 France recognized its former colony's independence, but only in exchange for a huge cash indemnity. General Leclerc had written to his brother-in-law Napoleon in 1802, soon after taking prisoner the slave armies' leader Toussaint L'Ouverture, "here is my opinion about this country: all the blacks in the mountains, men and women, must be suppressed, keeping only the children under 12; half the blacks in the plains must be exterminated, and not a single mulatto with epaulets must be left in the colony."[6] The tropics took their revenge on Leclerc: "Gripped by the black vomit" and despite the magical incantations of Pauline Bonaparte, he died without carrying out his plan.[7] But the cash indemnity was a millstone around the necks of those independent Haitians who survived the bloodbaths of the successive military expeditions against them. The country was born in ruins and never recovered: today it is the poorest in Latin America.

Chapter Notes

1. An English traveler, Henry Koster, attributed this custom to the contact the white children had with little blacks "who infect them with this African vice."

2. In various ways the Northeast is the victim of internal colonialism for the benefit of the industrialized south. Within the Northeast, the *sertão* region is subordinated to the sugarbelt with it supplies, and the latifundios in their turn are subordinated to processing plants that industrialize sugar production. The ancient institution of the individually owned sugar estate is in crisis: the central mills have devoured the plantations.

3. According to investigations by Pernambuco's Instituto Joaquim Nabuco de Pesquisas Socials, cited by Kit Sims Taylor, "Brazil's Northeast: Sugar and Surplus Value," *Monthly Review,* March 1969.

4. René Dumont, *Lands Alive* (New York: Monthly Review Press, 1965), p. 34.

5. Karl Marx, "On the Question of Free Trade," in *The Poverty of Philosophy* (New York: International Publishers, 1963), p. 223.

6. As quoted in Tadcusz Lepkowski, *Haití* (Havana, 1968), vol. I.

7. Alejo Carpentier has written a fine novel about this fascinating period of Haitian history, *The Kingdom of This World* (1957). It contains a perfect recreation of the Caribbean adventures of Pauline and her husband.

Misguided Development

Luis Guillermo Lumbreras

After several days, the dying man does not smell the stench of his own body. If you continue polluting your bed, one night you will die suffocated by your own wastes. — Eduardo Galeano, in *Blue Tiger and the Promised Land,* quoting Chief Seattle.

Five hundred years ago, through the mountains of what today are Argentina, Bolivia, Peru and Chile, merchant caravans with hundreds of llamas trooped along broad and well-tended roads. From Atacama in northern Chile to the Bolivian altiplano around Lake Titicaca, they carried the precious chañar wood — soft when newly cut, hardening as it dries, making it perfect for fashioning dinnerware and adornments. From the desert, they carried copper and semiprecious stones; from the tropical forests, brilliantly colored feathers and hard woods; from the cold seas, salted fish. Charki (dehydrated llama or guanaco meat), chuño (dehydrated potatoes) and many varieties of corn were traded back and forth from west to east, north to south.[1]

At the time the Spaniards arrived, in Francisco Pizarro's fateful expedition of 1531, Andean society had reached a stage of development comparable to that of Europe in the times of classical Greece and Rome. Tawantinsuyu, the great Inka[2] empire extending through the Andes from Colombia to Chile, was a sophisticated urban society.[3] On its edges were simpler societies of horticulturalists and hunters and gatherers — whom the Inkas considered "barbarians." But even these simpler societies were learning new tricks for survival in the rugged Andean conditions.

The victorious Spaniards introduced an alien technology, which had been developed through thousands of years of experimentation, from the Old

World's Paleolithic Age to the Renaissance. It had served Europe well, but in a very different ecosystem. Convinced that the same techniques would work anywhere, the newcomers scorned those of native societies and set out to make the New World like the Old. Much of our continent's economic weakness and dependency can be traced to that fateful decision.

In the Andes, where the great Inka Empire and its predecessors had achieved economic success on entirely different principles, the consequences were disastrous. Our fields became filled with new plants and animals, displacing those better adapted to the environment. New cities and a productive infrastructure were faithfully copied from Europe, at great expense: the same food, the same clothing, the same social and productive organization. We Andeans began to measure our success by an "index of modernity" which meant nothing other than how close our systems were to those of Europe. Aboriginal customs and people were segregated and marginalized, and anything "Indian" became stigmatized.

Human settlement began in all parts of the Andes at about the same time, more than 12,000 years ago. These earliest Andeans all started out as hunters and gatherers. Over thousands of years, Andean societies became highly diversified, pursuing different ways of mastering their resources, each according to its circumstances.

Such unequal development has usually been interpreted linearly, as though everyone were traveling the same development path, on which the Europeans (as they saw it) had advanced the farthest. In reality, they were on separate paths, because they were confronting very different problems and had to invent very different types of solutions.

It is generally thought that agriculture in the Andes was discovered in the moist forests of northern and eastern Peru. If so, this was not the only place. Agriculture in the region goes back to the eighth or ninth millennium B.C., probably with such plants as yucca, sweet potato, and peanuts, which reproduce easily in the humid tropical climate and do not require complex methods of cultivation.

As long as cultivation was confined to a few gardens for minor consumption, people could take advantage of a few natural clearings. Once they began seeking larger harvests, however, they had to clear and prepare fields. Gradually, Andeans learned to rotate their crops, to program the productive cycles and to maintain quality. In the process, they discovered new plant species, increasing the food supply, and this in turn supported a population increase, as evidenced by the larger size of villages.

In those areas that were constantly inundated from heavy rains, the ancient Andeans learned to build elevated fields, now called "camellones," separated by deep furrows. Abandoned for nearly five centuries, their vestiges have been discovered in Colombia, Ecuador, Peru and Bolivia. They look like fields plowed by giants, with furrows one to four meters wide and deep separating broad flat lands. Recent experiments show that these lands, today barren and absolutely unusable in times of flooding, must at one time have been highly productive.[4]

Where agriculture was impossible, as in the Chocó region in western Colombia, hunters and gatherers perfected their techniques, for example by developing traps for burrowing animals.

In the puna, the high, barren plateau at the summit of the central and southern Andes, there were very successful societies of hunters of camelids — the camel-like llamas, vicuñas and guanacos. Living from this meat, plus the tubers and wild grasses they gathered, these societies not only survived but grew. Thousands of years after their formation, descendants of these societies began to domesticate the animals and plants. Probably by selective breeding of llamas, they developed the wool-bearing subspecies, the alpaca. The plants they sowed included potato, olluco (with tuberous roots like a small new potato), quinoa ("pigweed," an annual plant, the seeds of which are ground as cereal and the leaves eaten like spinach), and caniwa or cananhua (a food grass similar to millet).

During the second millennium B.C., people domesticated all the Andean species of plants and animals possible. This era is sometimes referred to as the Andes's "neolithic" age, comparable in its accomplishments to the neolithic age of the Old World (which began around 10,000 B.C. in the Mideast, later in other areas).

In Cuzco, the Inkas had established experimental agricultural centers, which still functioned when the Spaniards arrived in the 1500s. There they tested the adaptability of plants to different ecosystems and improved their qualities and their productivity. Naturally, they also called on the experience and knowledge of the "amautas," or wise elders. There must have been similar experimentation, at a much earlier time, that led to the production of the alpaca.

The domestication of plants and animals is only the first level in the advance of humans' transformation of their natural environment. The next step was to use this new knowledge in ways that furthered the reproduction and growth of the human species.

In this regard, the Andean "neolithic" period was successful in very diverse zones. In the forest areas, domestication soon led to the formation of villages that engaged in cultivation along with hunting, fishing and gathering. Their populations grew, even though they had to move from place to place in pursuit of the various sources of subsistence. In the western forests, near the rivers from Ecuador to Chile, material cultures became quite sophisticated. The Valdivia culture of central Chile flourished around 3000 B.C., and Chorrera on the coast of Ecuador around 1500 B.C. The first to make ceramics were on the Atlantic coast of Colombia, followed by those in the Guayas region in Ecuador. The copper alloy "tumbaga" was developed through a chemical process, using natural vegetable acids, which makes the copper look like gold.[5] Communities in the tropical forest seem to have begun making cloth around 3000 B.C., as well as producing ceramics.

Thus, there was a nascent manufacturing in these areas, including pottery-making, basket-making, wood-working, and the use of animal parts and plants to make polychrome feathered cloths, headpieces, musical instruments and so on.[6]

In the coastal desert of Peru, plants were first domesticated around the sixth millennium B.C. Cotton, used mainly by fishermen for nets and cords, turned out to be a superior fiber to anything they had known previously for binding the gourds they used as floaters and as containers. But before plant cultivation could have the transforming effect it had in other areas, coastal peoples had to conquer the desert. This led to another kind of technological breakthrough: the control of water.

In the desert, the rivers that come down from the mountains leave cones of deposits in the form of irregular deltas. Because of the steepness of the slopes, the waters are torrential and flow rapidly toward the sea, easily changing their course each summer when the rains fall in the highlands. In addition, some years the waters do not come down at all and the rivers dry up, and other years the waters pour forth in great quantities at any time of the summer. When there is water, it is distributed unevenly, moistening only those areas near the riverbed and leaving the edges extremely arid. This greatly accelerates desertification and sanding of the surrounding area. In those conditions, agriculture cannot develop without a very complex irrigation infrastructure.

The fishing societies' growing experience in weather prediction, and their increasing population — giving them more labor power — made it possible for them to develop irrigation to "domesticate" water via irrigation. They also undertook costly (in labor power) projects of clearing and leveling the lands. This in turn permitted a great expansion of agriculture in the second millennium B.C. Although the coastal people continued fishing and shellfish gathering, agriculture soon became their main means of subsistence.

Causeways were built to channel water beyond the area of the alluvial deposits, forming artificial valleys. These channels also permitted the rationalization of water consumption and the drainage of excess. Pre-colonial canals extended kilometer after kilometer, to supply precisely measured levels and amounts of water. When they crossed the desert hills that surround these artificial valleys, water would seep from one canal into another, creating a moist interstice on the hillside where people grew crops. In the desert landscape these must have looked like hanging gardens 12 to 15 meters long, amidst the hills. Today, uncultivated and barren, they look like a long necklace with rectangular pendants of varying widths and lengths, attached to a very straight line crossing the sand-covered hills.[7]

The coastal people were very careful not to destroy what they had so laboriously constructed, because agricultural land is very scarce in Peru. For that reason they never invaded the agricultural lands for urban projects. They used barren lands for their cities, some of which eventually grew to great size and complexity. Chan Chan in northern Peru, where the valleys of Moche and Chicama intersect at the edge of the cultivated fields and close to the sea, was six kilometers long in the 15th century. Sufficient water was carried to the city via canals, complemented by a system of wells — "haucha-ques" — that drew waters from the subsoil.

Today, the cities have invaded the valleys, so that the desert area has widened, cement being added to sand. River water carries off the urban waste which is deposited on the beaches, infecting marine flora and fauna in the proximity. The old canals are lost in the desert, and those parts that remain are taken as examples of the impenetrable mysticism of the Indians, with no thought about how they might be used. The new hydraulic projects, designed with dams built according to the Western tradition, bring water to the valleys but remove the natural nutrients that come down with the annual turbulences, and in their course impoverish the fauna and flora of the coast.

In the heights of Arequipa, beyond Pocsi, there are hundreds of hectares of lands prepared by building stone-walled terraces known as "andenes." Though abandoned, they, and the canals that brought them water, are still part of the desert landscape. Below them, in a little valley, lie exquisite gardens of fruits, pastures for thoroughbred European cattle and crops that have enough water to thrive. The terraces had doubled the cultivable area of the little valley. But they were not practical for pasture for Arequipa's dairy industry, and so were left to die.

The andenes represented a productive strategy for maximum utilization of the scarce water resources of the central Andes. They made it possible to prepare lands on the slopes for sowing without serious dangers of erosion. When the Spaniards arrived, evidence shows, they were under construction in many parts of Tawantinsuyu.[8]

In the Andes such terracing was a momentous discovery, which our Western mentality has yet to appreciate. As with the "camellones" to counter flooding, or the great canals of the desert, the West did not know what to do with the terraces and classified them as "primitive." We froze them, turning those that existed into ruins and curiosities and taking no heed of any possibility of turning to them and using them creatively.[9]

The West became our paradigm; no time or resources would be invested in developing or reproducing the methods of the indigenous world, considered the antithesis of development and modernization. The pursuit of such "modernity" came at a high cost, because our tropical and mountainous lands were not necessarily suited for the procedures of the prairies and cold forests. Very early on, colonial societies had to rely on the importation of capital and consumer goods to satisfy the Old World paradigm. "High technology" industry would arrive in our lands as long as we had the means to pay; when we fell behind in our payments the technology grew ever more difficult and costly to acquire, and our status as poor "Westerners" grew worse, distancing us ever more from the model countries.

A thousand rich Indians paid tribute to Spain with products of their stock-raising in Chucuito in the 16th century. They were truly rich, all of them owners of thousands of head of camelids. These were only 1,000 among many thousands of indigenous taxpayers who maintained, even in the early colonial period, a stock of native animals which today we cannot even imagine. From the south of Colombia to the beginnings of the Chilean archipelago in Chiloé, livestock was used for transport, meat, wool and hides. Today the native livestock is unknown in all the north — except for certain limited areas — and in the south is important only in traditional Andean communities. In Lima the sale of llama or guanaco meat is punished the same as the selling of the meat of dogs. Few people living have had the opportunity to eat roast alpaca or llama "charki." Instead, the West has brought sheep and beef, devastating existing pastures and demanding preparation of special lands for them. This sacrificed the cultivation of foodstuffs, but bestowed the seal of modernity.

The great projects of Andean antiquity were abandoned because of Western arrogance and the limitations of Western experience, which did not include having to produce food in the desert. The "neolithic" age of the Europeans had provided them with plants suitable for well-watered lands; their "metal" age had given them access to instruments for plowing lands hardened by the winter cold and for cutting down the trees of the cold forests. None of this knowledge was of use here in the desert. Sowing of plants of European origin in many cases was done at the cost of abandoning immense areas of native cultivation, given the demand for water that agriculture for Western taste required.

In the 500 years since the arrival of the Europeans, nothing new has been done in the direction of developing our own unique ecological resources. The ancestral experiments remain frozen. The forests are used only for the exploitation of their wood, frequently causing irreversible devastation. Having in their culture procedures for dealing with the humid evergreen forests of America, the Europeans and their imitators have applied methods suitable for the cold leaf-shedding forests of Europe, with disastrous results.

We are still blind to the misdirection of our development. The Andean world remains impoverished because we are unable to see except through colonial lenses. As the pre-European technical development of the Andes demonstrates, our impoverishment is not explained by race or geography, as has often been assumed — that is, it is not due to any technical incapacity of our Indian and mestizo people, nor to the special difficulties of our terrain.

Rather, it is a question of recovering the knowledge of our ancestors, and of sovereignty—the capacity to make use of that knowledge. It is not we who have failed; our underdevelopment is the product of a historic failure of the West, whose own patrimony prevented it from perceiving the limits of its power.

Chapter Notes

1. Lautaro A. Núñez and Tom Dillehay, *Movilidad Giratoria, Harmonia Social y Desarrollo en los Andes Meridionales: Patrones de Tráfico e Interacción Económica* (Antofagasta, Chile: Universidad del Norte, 1978).

2. John Hyslop, *The Inka Road System* (New York: Academic Press, 1984). The spelling "Inka" is preferred (over the older "Inca") by modern anthropologists to distinguish a "k" sound in Quechua which is distinct from the Spanish or English hard "c."

3. Frank Salomon, *Los Señores Étnicos de Quito en la Época de los Incas* (Cambridge, England: University Press).

4. Marc J. Dourojeanni, *Amazonía: ¿Qué Hacer?* (Iquitos, Peru: Estudios Teológicos de la Amazonía, 1990).

5. From the Malayan word for copper, used by Europeans to refer to various copper alloys.

6. Today there are indigenous communities here and there throughout the Andes who have resisted assimilation and have continued to produce their handicrafts, which are often highly prized by collectors. But unfortunately these crafts have not continued to develop.

7. Paul Kosok, *Life, Land and Water in Ancient Peru* (Brooklyn, N. Y.: Long Island University Press, 1965).

8. There is also evidence of experiments with them in places such as the so-called "amphitheaters" of Moray near Cuzco.

9. John Murra, *The Economic Organization of the Inca State* (Greenwich, Conn.: JAI Press: 1980): García Diez de San Miguel, *Visita Hecha a la Provincia de Chucuito por García Diez de San Miguel en el Ano 1567* (Lima: La Casa de la Cultura del Perú 1964).

Columbus in High School

James Loewen

What passes for identity in America is a series of myths about one's heroic ancestors. — James Baldwin, from "A Talk to Teachers," *Saturday Review,* December 21, 1963.

The history books make Columbus the first great hero in American history. I surveyed 12 American history textbooks used in high schools in the United States.[1] They grant him 800 words — two and a half pages including pictures and a map. However, what we learn in high school is not what he did in history.

Textbooks begin by trying to explain why Europe responded differently to Columbus than to Leif Eriksson or explorers to the Americas before Eriksson. The following composite account of the ensuing changes in Europe is drawn verbatim from the texts.

> "Life in Europe is slow paced." "Curiosity about the rest of the world was at a low point." Then, "people's horizons gradually widened, and they became more curious about the world beyond their own localities." "Many Europeans were filled with burning curiosity. They were living in a period called the Renaissance." "What started Europeans thinking new thoughts and dreaming new dreams? A series of wars called the Crusades were partly responsible." "The Crusades caused great changes in the ways that Europeans thought and acted." "The desire for more trade quickly spread."

Although these accounts of changes in Europe are much longer than I have indicated, their level of scholarship is discouragingly low. They provide

---

"Columbus in High School" is condensed from the forthcoming book, Lies My Teacher Told Me *(New York: The New Press, 1992).*

no causal explanations for the age of European exploration. Instead, they argue for Europe's greatness in transparently psychological terms — "people grew more curious" and the like — using words that veer suspiciously close to "national character."

Some texts do describe the rise of nation-states under monarchies. Otherwise, they do a poor job telling of the changes in Europe that led to the Age of Exploration. Some cite the Protestant Reformation, even though inconveniently it began 25 years *after* 1492. Some make vague or nearly tautogical statements like this one, from *The American Tradition:* "Interest in practical matters and the world outside Europe led to advances in shipbuilding and navigation."

What is occurring here? We must pay attention to what the texts are telling us and what they are not telling us. The topic could hardly be more important. Texts are discussing the changes in Europe that not only prompted Columbus's 1492 voyage and the probable contemporaneous trips to America by Portuguese, Basque and Bristol fishermen,[2] but then led to Europe's domination of the world.

Progress in things military was no doubt the most portentous single development in Europe. Beginning in about 1400, Europe's incessant wars gave rise to an arms race, including developments in shipboard guns, archery, drill and siege warfare. Other developments included bureaucracy, double-entry bookkeeping, and printing. Theology played a role: amassing wealth became seen as a key means of winning esteem on earth and even in the Hereafter. A final development causing the reaction to Columbus's reports about Hispaniola to be radically different from the reactions to earlier expeditions was Europe's recent success in taking over and exploiting or exterminating other island societies.

Why don't textbooks mention arms as a cause of exploration and domination? Why don't they tell us of Europe's prior experiments with colonization on Malta and the Canaries? Why don't they treat *any* of the foregoing factors? Because they aren't nice? Because they reflect on us, in a way? We must admit that these qualities are less endearing than "the Renaissance," "curiosity about the world," or "humanism," cited by American history texts as causes of European expansion.

Columbus's enterprise was epoch-making precisely because Europe was now ready to react differently. High school students don't usually think about the rise of Europe to world domination. It's not presented as a question. It seems natural, a given, rather than something to be explained. American history textbooks reinforce rather than challenge this tendency not to think about it.

The textbooks do concede that Columbus didn't start from scratch. Every textbook account of the European exploration of the Americas begins with Prince Henry the Navigator, of Portugal, between 1415 and 1460. Henry is seen as discovering Madeira and the Azores and sending out ships to circumnavigate Africa for the first time. The authors seem unaware that ancient Phoenicians and Egyptians reached Madeira, the Azores, Ireland, traded with the aboriginal inhabitants of the Canary Islands, and circumnavigated Africa more than 600 years before Christ. The omission is ironic, because Prince Henry's knowledge of the Afro-Phoenicians inspired him to replicate them.[3] But this information clashes with a social archetype: our culture views technology as a European development. Texts depict Henry as inventing navigation because they implicitly assume that before Europe there was nothing, at least nothing modern. In fact, Henry was mostly collecting ideas that were already known in the ancient Mediterranean and had been developed further in Arabia, North Africa and China.[4] But our histories imply Europe did it all by itself. Not only did Henry have to develop new instruments, according to *The American Way,* but "people didn't know how to build seagoing ships, either." We are left to wonder how, without Europe's aid, American Indians ever reached Easter Island, Polynesians Madagascar, or Afro-Phoenicians the Canaries. By "people" *Way* of course means Europeans — a textbook example of Eurocentrism.

Nonetheless, long before Christopher Columbus reached America, people from Africa, Asia and Europe almost surely reached our shores. Native Americans also crossed the Atlantic to Europe.[5] The famous 1492 expedition looks to have been the last in a series of voyages to and from the Americas. A chronological list of trips to America given on page 93 includes the first trip for which we have any confirmation down to Columbus, with comments on the quality of the available evidence.

The evidence for each of these journeys offers us fascinating glimpses into the societies and cultures that existed on both sides of the Atlantic and in Asia before 1492. They also reveal controversies among those who study the distant past. Unfortunately for students, however, hypotheses are incompatible with the style of writing found in history textbooks. Textbooks seem locked into a rhetoric of certainty. Therefore textbooks do a ghastly job of introducing students to the issues in pre–Columbian exploration.

Eight of the 12 history texts I studied do tell of Leif Eriksson and the Norse,[18] but the books do much worse in discussing possible explorations by non–Europeans. Although seafarers from Africa and Asia probably sailed to the Americas, they never sailed into the history books. The most famous are the voyages of Afro-Phoenicians, probably launched from Morocco but ultimately from Egypt, that may have ended up on the Atlantic coast of Mexico in about 750 B.C. Moderately good evidence suggests that 2,000 years after the Afro-Phoenicians, West Africans were also a presence in the Americas. Perhaps the strongest proof comes from Columbus's 1492 voyage. When Columbus arrived in Hispaniola, he got from the Tainos some spear points made of "guanine." The Indians said they acquired them from black traders who

Expeditions to America

Year	From	To	Quality of Evidence
70,000? B.C. 12,000? B.C.	Siberia	Alaska	High: this was the first crossing and peopled the Americas
6000? B.C.	Indonesia (or other direction)	South America	Moderate: similarities in blow-guns, paper-making, etc.[6]
5000? B.C.	Japan	Ecuador	Moderate: similar pottery, fishing styles.[7]
1500? B.C.	Siberia	Canada, New Mexico	High: linguistic and cultural analysis
c.1000 B.C. to present	Siberia	Alaska	High: continuing contact by Inuits across Bering Sea[8]
1000 B.C.	China	Central America	Low: Chinese legend; cultural similarities[9]
1000 B.C.– A.D. 300	Afro-Phoenicia	Central America	Moderate: Negroid and Caucasoid likenesses in sculpture and ceramics, cultural similarities, etc.[10]
500 B.C.	Phoenicians, Celts	New Hampshire, etc.	Low: megaliths, perhaps writing, linguistics[11]
A.D. 600	Ireland, via Iceland	Newfoundland? West Indies?	Low: legends of St. Brendan, written c.A.D. 850 confirmed by Norse sagas.[12]
1000– 1300	Greenland, Iceland	Labrador, Baffin Land, Newfoundland, Nova Scotia, possibly Cape Cod and further south	High: oral sagas, confirmed by archaeology on Newfoundland[13]
c.1460	W. Africa	Hispaniola, Panama, possibly Brazil	Moderate: Portuguese in West Africa, Columbus on Hispaniola, Balboa in Panama[14]
c.1460	Portugal	Newfoundland? Brazil?	Low: inference from Portuguese sources and actions[15]
1375? –1491	Basque Spain	Newfoundland coast	Low: cryptic historical sources[16]
1481–91	Bristol, England	Newfoundland coast	Low: cryptic historical sources[17]
1492	Spain	Caribbean, including Hispaniola	High: historical sources

came from the south and east. Guanine proved to be an alloy made of gold, silver and copper, identical to the gold alloy preferred by West Africans, who also called it guanine.[19] Of the 12 texts reviewed here, only two even mention the possibility of African or Phoenician exploration, and one of these, *A History of the Republic*, mentions these possibilities only to assure us that we need not concern ourselves with them. By way of contrast, five texts tell of a possible voyage by the fabulous Irish monk, St. Brendan, in perhaps A.D. 600. Such unequal treatment smacks of Eurocentrism: an Irish possibility merits telling while African ones do not.

We come now to the last "discoverer." In all the Americas, admiration for Christopher Columbus is most concentrated in the United States. In the words of President George Bush, "Christopher Columbus not only opened the door to a New World, but also set an example for us all. . . ."[20] Textbooks seem to need to present this hero without embarrassment. To make a better myth, Columbus and Western Europe must appear unprecedented. Hence, as we have seen, American histories downplay previous explorers, especially African ones. Pre-Columbian explorers are embarrassing to the "Columbus as great man" legend. While leaving out the predecessors, American history texts add detail after detail to heighten our appreciation of Columbus's daring and worthiness. The heroic collective account they tell goes like this:

> *Born* in Genoa, of humble parents, *Christopher Columbus became an experienced seafarer, venturing as far as Iceland and Guinea.* His experiences convinced him that the world must be round and that the fabled riches of the East — spices and gold — could be had by sailing west, superceding the overland routes which the Turks had closed off to commerce. *To get funding for his enterprise, he beseeched monarch after monarch in Western Europe.* Finally, after being dismissed once more by Ferdinand and Isabella of Spain, Columbus got his chance. *Isabella decided to underwrite a* modest *expedition. He outfitted three* pitifully small *ships, the Niña, the Pinta, and the Santa María, and set forth from Spain. After an* arduous *journey* of more than two months, during which his mutinous crew almost threw him overboard, he discovered the West Indies on *October 12, 1492.* Unfortunately, although *he made three more voyages to America,* he never knew he had discovered a New World. *Columbus died* in obscurity, unappreciated and penniless. Nevertheless, without his daring, American history would have been different, for in a sense he made it all possible.

Almost everything in this traditional account is either wrong or unknowable. I have italicized everything in it that we know probably to be true. Notice that we don't even know whether Columbus thought he was going to Japan and Indonesia or was trying to reach "new" lands to the west. After reviewing the evidence, Columbus's recent biographer, Kirkpatrick Sale, concluded "we will likely never know for sure." But Sale noted that such a conclusion is "not very satisfactory for those who demand certainty in their historical tales."[21] Predictably, all our textbooks are of this type. Thus they deny their readers an opportunity to realize that historians *don't* know all the answers, hence history *isn't* just a process of memorizing them.

Our texts do omit one tradition our culture still retains: the flat earth legend. To make a better myth, American culture has perpetuated the picture of Columbus boldly forging ahead, although the conventional wisdom and even his own crew imagined the world was flat. If his contemporaries thought that the world was flat, then Columbus's feat becomes still more daring. In truth, most Europeans knew the world to be round, as did most Native Americans. The American novelist Washington Irving wins credit for popularizing the flat earth fable in 1828.[22] It turns Columbus into a man of science who corrected our faulty geography and uplifts his voyages from mere passages for plunder into scientific expeditions.

Intense debunking of the flat earth legend by historians has made an impact. Not one of our textbooks retells this ancient fiction. They choose wholly ineffectual words to counter it, however. *Triumph of the American Nation* exemplifies the problem: "Convinced that the earth was round, a knowledge shared by many informed people of the day, Columbus believed that if he sailed far enough to the west he would reach Asia." Although the minor subordinate clause quietly notes that not everyone believed in flat earth geography, the main subordinate clause and the primary clause announce Columbus's belief that the earth is round and he therefore could reach Asia by sailing west. The sentence is nonsensical unless the reader infers that this belief set Columbus apart and was unusual.

Skipping ahead to the end of his life, having Columbus come to a tragic finish, sick, poor and ignorant of his great accomplishment, seems to make for a better story. "Columbus's discoveries were not immediately appreciated by the Spanish government," according to *The American Adventure*. "He died in neglect in 1506." The facts are opposite. Columbus died well off. Money from the Americas continued to flow in to him in Spain. Moreover, evidence from his last two voyages shows that he did know he had reached a "new" continent, South America — new at least to Europe.[23] Some archetypal need must impel textbook historians to write the converse. Plainly the drama of the great man dying not knowing what he wrought is supposed to grieve us.

Various textbooks embellish the standard Columbus legend. Some details are harmless, such as the fabrication about Isabella's sending a messenger galloping after Columbus and pawning her own jewels to pay for the expedition.[24] Though false, they make for a better story, I suppose; certainly they magnify Columbus's perseverance. All of the enhancements humanize Columbus so as to induce readers to identify with him and his accomplishments. Here is part of the treatment in *Land of Promise*:

> It is October, 1492. Three small, storm-battered ships are lost as sea, sailing into an unknown ocean. A frightened crew has been threatening to throw their stubborn captain overboard, turn the ships around, and make for the safety of familiar shores.

> Then a miracle: The sailors see some green branches floating on
> the water. Land birds fly overhead. From high in the ship's rigging
> the lookout cries, "Land, land ahead!" Fears turn to joy. Soon the
> grateful captain wades ashore and gives thanks to God.

Now, really. The *Niña, Pinta* and *Santa María* were not "storm-battered."
To make a better myth, these authors want the trip to seem harder than it
was, so they invent bad weather. Columbus's journal tells of seas so calm that
for days at a time, sailors were able to converse from one ship to another. Indeed, the only day they experienced even moderately high seas was the last,
when they knew they were near land.

To make a better myth, most of these books overlook Columbus's stop-
over in the Canary Islands, making the trip seem longer than it was. His
voyage across the unknown Atlantic took one month, not two.

To make a better myth, the texts make the ships tiny and inefficient,
when actually "these three vessels were fully suited to his purpose," as naval
author Pietro Barozzi has pointed out.[25]

To make a better myth, 6 of 12 texts exaggerate his crew's complaints into
a near-mutiny, complete with threats to throw Columbus overboard. After
studying the matter, Samuel Eliot Morison reduced the sailors' complaints to
mere griping: "The people began to mutter and grumble.... They were all
getting on each other's nerves, as happens even nowadays."[26] So much for the
threat of being thrown overboard. This exaggeration is not just a harmless
dramatic detail, however. Another archetype lurks below its surface: that
those who direct social enterprises are more intelligent than those who carry
them out.[27]

To make a better myth, all of these books find space for many other hu-
manizing particulars. They have the lookout cry "tierra!" Most tell us that
Columbus's first act after going ashore was "thanking God for leading them
safely across the sea." Many tell of Columbus's three later voyages to the
Americas. But they do not tell us what he did with the lands and peoples he
"discovered."

What set Columbus's voyages apart from all previous voyages to the
Americas was what Europe was to do with them. Christopher Columbus introduced the two great processes of race relations that have transformed the
modern world: the taking of land, wealth, and labor from indigenous peoples,
and the trans–Atlantic slave trade. The gruesome facts of his administration
of the "Indies," presented elsewhere in this book, are available in primary
source material — letters by Columbus and others and the fiery condemna-
tions of Bartolomé de las Casas, the Catholic priest who fought desperately
for more humane treatment of the Indians. Most texts use no primary
sources; a few select extracts that reveal nothing unseemly about the Great
Navigator. Not one uses primary sources to tell us how Columbus, his

relatives, and other successors cut off Indians' hands, forced Indians to work in the mines, introduced diseases new to the Indians, demoralized them, and pushed them to infanticide, suicide and flight.

A census of Hispaniola's adult population by Bartolomé Columbus in 1496 counted 1,100,000; a complete count would probably have totalled 3,000,000. By 1542 fewer than 200 Indians remained alive.[28] Thus nasty details like cutting off hands have somewhat greater historical importance than nice touches like "tierra!" Hispaniola under the Spanish is one of the major genocides in all human history. Nonetheless, only 1 of our 12 texts, *American Past and Present,* even mentions the extermination.

Columbus not only sent the first slaves across the Atlantic, he also sent more slaves — about 5,000 — than any other individual, mostly to the Canaries. Queen Isabella opposed outright enslavement and returned some Indians to the Caribbean. But other nations rushed to emulate Columbus. In 1501, the Portuguese began to depopulate Labrador. After the British established beachheads on the Atlantic coast of North America, they encouraged coastal Indian tribes to capture more distant tribes. Pilgrims and Puritans sold the Pequots into slavery in Bermuda in 1637. Charleston, South Carolina, became a major port for exporting Indian slaves. The French shipped virtually the entire Natchez nation in chains to the West Indies in 1731.[29] The slave trade wrecked whole Indian nations. The first genocide, the Tainos on Hispaniola, led to the second, on the Bahamas, which "are now deserted," in the words of Spanish historian Peter Martyr [de Anglería] reporting in 1516, because "the wretched islanders were transported to the gold mines of Hispaniola."[30] Puerto Rico and Cuba were next. Because the Indians died, Indian slavery then led to the massive slave trade the other way across the Atlantic, from Africa. This trade also happened first on Hispaniola, started by Columbus's son in 1505. Predictably, Hispaniola then had the first large-scale slave revolt, blacks and Indians together, beginning in 1519 and finally smashed by the Spanish in the 1530s.[31]

Of our 12 histories, only 6 even mention that the Spanish enslaved or exploited the Indians anywhere in the Americas; of these only four verge on mentioning that Columbus started it. *A History of the Republic* places its treatment under the heading "The Fate of Columbus," not the fate of the Indians! "Some Spaniards who had come to the Americas had begun to enslave and kill the original Americans. Authorities in Spain held Columbus responsible for the atrocities." Note that *A History* takes pains to isolate Columbus from the slaving charge — *other* Spaniards are misbehaving. Only *The American Adventure* clearly connects Columbus with the subject, although in *American History* John Garraty levels a vague charge: "Columbus was a great sailor and a brave and determined man. But he was not good at politics or business." The other eight books simply adore him.

Columbus's discoveries caused almost as much change in Europe as in the

Americas. Although they enriched Europe's most Catholic monarchy, they also shook Europe's religious uniformity, for how were these new peoples to be explained? By no stretch of the imagination were they in the Bible. They simply didn't fit within Christianity's explanation of the moral universe. The animals, too, posed a religious challenge: since Eden and Mt. Ararat were both in the Near East, where could these new American species have come from? Perhaps the Bible didn't know everything. Such questioning contributed to the Reformation which can be dated to Luther's 95 theses in 1517.[32]

Politically, reports of American Indian societies transformed European thinking, beginning in 1516 with Thomas More's *Utopia*. Based on an account of the Incan empire, More's work challenged European social organization by suggesting a more equal and superior alternative. Other philosophers seized upon the Indians as living examples of Europe's primordial past, which is what John Locke meant by his famous phrase, "In the beginning, all the world was America." Depending upon their political persuasion, some Europeans glorified Indian societies as examples of simpler better societies, from which Europe had slipped, while others maligned them as showing primitive underdevelopment. In either case, from Montaigne, Montesquieu and Rousseau down to Marx and Engels, Europeans were stunned to learn of societies like the Tainos — without monarchs, without much hierarchy, with democratically selected leadership. Sale believes the ideas of political liberty and equality really began here. Even more broadly, as *Larousse* puts it, before the discovery of America, "Europe was virtually incapable of self-criticism."[33]

Economically, exploiting the Americas transformed Europe, enriching first Spain, then through trade and piracy, other nations. Columbus's gold finds on Hispaniola were soon dwarfed by discoveries of gold and silver in Mexico and the Andes. Some authors hold that this wealth led to the rise of capitalism and eventually to the industrial revolution.[34] Muslim nations had rivaled Europe, but the new wealth undermined Islamic power. Africa suffered: the trans–Saharan trade collapsed, because the Americas supplied more gold and silver than the Gold Coast ever could. African traders now had only one commodity that Europe wanted: slaves. "Africans thus became victims of the discovery of America as surely as did the American Indians," in anthropologist Jack Weatherford's words.[35] Agriculture was also transformed. Adding corn and potatoes to European diets helped cause the population to explode in the 1500s and 1600s, which led in turn to the rapid European settlement of the Americas and Australia. The new crops also helped cause the northern countries of Britain, Germany, and finally Russia to become dominant European powers.[36]

One might expect our Eurocentric texts to give considerable attention to the effect on Europe of Columbus's "discovery" of the Americas. Alas, they do not. Three of the 12 credit Indians for developing important crops. Otherwise, the west-to-east flow of ideas goes unnoticed. Eurocentrism blinds authors to contributions *to* Europe, whether by Arab instruments, African navigators, or American Indian social structure. Recognizing that Europeans often learned from Indians, rather than just presenting the fruits of a higher civilization to them, might call into question the "story line" of the entire colonial enterprise. The conquerors did not recognize much of value in the Taino society they were destroying. By accepting the conquerors' limited viewpoint, our American histories rob us of the chance to appreciate how important America has been in the development of the modern world.

Our texts treat Columbus as an origin myth: he was good and so are we. They can say nothing bad about Columbus without reflecting badly on us, so they omit any untoward detail, no matter how important, that might undermine the moral and technical superiority of Europeans. I am not proposing the opposite: that he was *bad* and so are we. Neither morality nor immorality can simply be conferred upon us by history. History is more ambiguous than that.

Furthermore, we must consider, who are "we"? Columbus is no hero in Mexico, even though Mexico is much more Spanish in culture than the United States and might be expected to take pride in this hero of Spanish history. Why not? Because Mexico is also much more *Indian* than the United States. Mexicans see Columbus as white and European, which is why they don't celebrate him. So do we, which may explain why we *do* celebrate him, and why we leave out all the bad parts. Thus cherishing Columbus is characteristic of white history, not American history. No wonder people of color in this country are demanding new textbooks: right from the start, our history books are biased.

Columbus's conquest of Hispaniola can be seen as an amazing feat of courage by the first of many brave empire builders. It can also be understood as a bloody atrocity that left a legacy of genocide and slavery that endures in some degree to this day. Both views of Columbus are valid; indeed, both are necessary to understand his significance. He exemplifies both meanings of the word "exploit"—a remarkable deed and a taking advantage of. Columbus's "rightness" should no more be guaranteed by our texts' inclusions and exclusions than his "wrongness." The worshipful biographical vignettes of Columbus that today's texts supply merely indoctrinate students into a mindless identification with colonialism. In the words of historian Michael Wallace, the Columbus myth "allows us to accept the contemporary division of the world into developed and underdeveloped spheres as natural and given, rather than a historical product issuing from a process that began with Columbus's first voyage."[37]

Our histories still struggle with the issue of colonialist history, trying to move beyond Eurocentric language. *Land of Promise* states, "If Columbus had not discovered the New World, others soon would have." Three sentences

later, the authors try to take back the word: "As is often pointed out, Columbus did not really 'discover' America. When he arrived on this side of the
Atlantic there were perhaps 20 or more million people already here." Taking
back the words is ineffectual, however. *Promise*'s whole approach is of whites
discovering nonwhites rather than a mutual multicultural encounter. The
point isn't idle. Words are important — they influence or at least rationalize
policy. *Promise* reminds us of the usage of Chief Justice John Marshall, who
decreed in 1823 that Cherokees had rights to their land in Georgia by dint of
their occupancy but whites had superior rights owing to their "discovery."
How Indians managed to occupy Georgia without previously discovering it
he neglected to tell.[38]

The process of exploration has itself typically been multiracial and
multicultural. African pilots helped Prince Henry's ship captains learn their
way down the coast of Africa. On Christmas Day, 1492, Columbus needed
assistance: the *Santa María* had run aground off Hispaniola. Columbus sent
for help to the nearest Taino town, and "all the people of the town" responded,
"with very big and many canoes."[39] Native Americans cured Cartier's men
of scurvy near Montreal in 1535. They repaired Francis Drake's *Golden Hind*
in California so he could complete his round the world voyage in 1579. When
Admiral Peary discovered the North Pole, the first person there was probably
not the European American Peary, nor even the African American Matthew
Henson, his assistant, but their four Inuit guides, male and female, on whom
the entire expedition relied.[40] Our histories omit this assistance. We seem to
have a cultural need for heroic European archetypes who did it all on their
own.

So long as our texts hide from us the roles people of color have played
in exploration, from at least 6000 B.C. down to now, they encourage us to look
to Europe and its extensions as the seat of knowledge. So long as our texts
simply celebrate Columbus, rather than teaching both sides of his exploit,
they encourage us to identify with white Western exploitation, rather than
study it. Such texts prevent us from celebrating or even understanding the
lives of people like las Casas, who argued for humane treatment of the peoples
the Europeans met. They push us toward identifying only with the oppressor.
Thus they present a history that is even narrower than Eurocentric, for they
withhold from us not only Native viewpoints, but also those of Europeans and
white Americans whose perspective, deeds, words and heritage were other
than that of the exploiting "discoverer."

Chapter Notes

1. Nancy Bauer, *The American Way* (New York: Holt, Rinehart and Winston,
1979). Carol Berkin and Leonard Wood, *Land of Promise* (Glenview, Ill.: Scott,

Foresman, 1983). James West Davidson and Mark H. Lytle, *The United States—A History of the Republic* (Englewood Cliffs, N.J.: Prentice-Hall, 1981). Robert A. Divine, T.H. Breen, George M. Frederickson and R. Hal Williams, *America Past and Present* (Glenview, Ill.: Scott, Foresman, 1987). John A. Garraty, *American History* (New York: Harcourt Brace Jovanovich, 1982). Robert Green, Laura L. Becker and Robert E. Coviello, *The American Tradition* (Columbus: Charles E. Merrill, 1984). Allan O. Kownslar, and Donald B. Frizzle, *Discovering American History* (New York: Holt, Rinehart and Winston, 1974). Ira Peck, Steven Jantzen and Daniel Rosen, *American Adventurers* (Austin: Steck-Vaughn, 1987). Philip Roden, Robynn Greer, Bruce Kraig, and Betty Bivins, *Life and Liberty* (Glenview: Scott, Foresman, 1984). Robert Sobel, Roger LaRaus, Linda Ann De Leon, and Harry P. Morris, *The Challenge of Freedom* (River Forest, Ill.: Laidlaw, 1982). Social Science Staff of the Educational Research Council of America, *The American Adventure* (Boston: Allyn and Bacon, 1975). Paul Lewis Todd and Merle Curti, *Triumph of the American Nation* (Orlando: Harcourt Brace Jovanovich, 1982).

2. Jack Forbes, *Black Africans and Native Americans* (Oxford: Basil Blackwell, 1988), p. 20. David Quinn, *England and the Discovery of America, 1481-1620* (New York: Knopf, 1974), pp. 5-105.

3. Constance Irwin, *Fair Gods and Stone Faces* (New York: St. Martin's, 1963), pp. 193-211, 217, 241. Cyrus Gordon, *Before Columbus* (New York: Crown, 1971), pp. 119-125. Geoffrey Ashe, et al., *The Quest for America* (London: Pall Mall, 1971), pp. 78-79.

4. Richard Eaton, *Islamic History as Global History* (Washington: American Historical Association, 1990), p. 17.

5. Jack Forbes, *op. cit.*, pp. 7-14; Ivan Van Sertima, *They Came Before Columbus* (New York: Random House, 1976), chapter 12.

6. Stephen C. Jett, "The Development and Distribution of the Blowgun," *Annals of the Association of American Geographers* (Davis: University of California, 12/70). Paul Tolstoy, University of Montreal; Time-Life editors: *Feats and Wisdom of the Ancients* (Alexandria, Vir.: Time-Life, 1990), p. 122. Cf. Carroll Riley, et al., *Man Across the Sea* (Austin: University of Texas Press, 1971), especially article by Jett.

7. Betty J. Meggers, "Did Japanese Fishermen Really Reach Ecuador 5000 Years Ago?" *Early Man*, 1980, Vol. 2, pp. 15-19. Meggers, "Contacts from Asia," pp. 239-259 of Geoffrey Ashe, *op. cit.* Time-Life editors, *op. cit.*, p. 124.

8. William Fitzhugh, "Crossroads of Continents: Review and Prospect," in Fitzhugh and V. Chaussonet, eds., *Proceedings of the Crossroads Symposium* (Washington: Smithsonian Institution Press, forthcoming). Ian Stevenson, *Twenty Cases Suggestive of Reincarnation* (Charlottesville: University of Virginia Press, 1974), pp. 218-219.

9. Paul Shao, *The Origins of Ancient American Culture* (Ames: Iowa State University Press, 1983). Time-Life editors: *op. cit.*, p. 121. Ian Stevenson, *op. cit.*, pp. 218-219. Constance Irwin, *op. cit.*, pp. 249-251.

10. Alexander von Wuthenau, *The Art of Terracotta Pottery in Pre-Columbian Central and South America* (New York: Crown, 1970); *Unexpected Faces in Ancient America* (New York: Crown, 1975). Ivan von Sertima, *op. cit.* Thor Heyerdahl, "The Bearded Gods Speak," pp. 199-238 of Geoffrey Ashe, et al., *op. cit.* Time-Life editors: *op. cit.*, p. 123. Constance Irwin, *op. cit.*, pp. 67-71, 89-96, 122-145, 176-186. Kenneth Feder attacks Von Sertima's evidence in *Frauds, Myths and Mysteries* (Mountain View, Calif.: Mayfield, 1990), pp. 75-77.

11. Barry Fell, *America BC* (New York: Quadrangle, 1976). *Saga America* (New York: Times Books, 1980).

12. Geoffrey Ashe, et al., *op. cit.*, pp. 24-48, concludes the evidence for Irish voyage(s) is weak.

13. Erik Wahlgren, *The Vikings and America* (New York: Thames and Hudson, 1986), offers a readable and balanced summary of the evidence.

14. Samuel Marble, *Before Columbus* (Cranbury, N. J.: A. S. Barnes, 1980), pp. 22-25. Von Sertima, *They Came Before Columbus.* Arthur E. Morgan, *Nowhere Was Somewhere,* p. 198, citing Leo Wiener. Pathe Diagne, "Du Centenaire de la Découverte du Nouveau Monde par Bakari II, en 1312, et Christopher Colomb, en 1492" (Dakar?: privately printed, 1990). Michael Anderson Bradley, *Dawn Voyage* (Toronto: Summer Hill Press, 1987).

15. Samuel Marble, *Ibid.* Von Sertima, *op. cit.,* Arthur E. Morgan, *op. cit.,* p. 197; Geoffrey Ashe, *et al., op. cit.,* pp. 265-66; David Quinn, *England and the Discovery of America, 1481-1620* (New York: Knopf, 1974), pp. 41-43, 85-86.

16. Jack Forbes, *op. cit.,* p. 20.

17. David Quinn, *op. cit.,* pp. 5-105. Robert Blow, *Abroad in America* (New York: Continuum, 1990), p. 17.

18. Bauer, Berkin, Davidson, Divine, Garraty, Green, Sobel and Todd. Roden includes the Vikings on his map but does not mention them in the text.

19. Frederick Pohl, *Amerigo Vespucci* (New York: Columbia University Press, 1944), p. 230. Von Sertima, pp. 1, 11. Marble, *op. cit.,* pp. 23-25. Forbes, *op. cit.,* p. 15, doubts that guanine came from Africa.

20. Quoted in *huracán* (PO Box 7591, Minneapolis, 55407).

21. Sale, *op. cit.* New York: Knopf, 1990, pp. 23-26.

22. *Ibid.,* p. 344.

23. *Ibid.,* pp. 171, 185, 204-214, 362.

24. Hans Koning, *Columbus: His Enterprise* (New York: Monthly Review Press, 1976), pp. 39-40; Sale, *Ibid.,* p. 238.

25. Pietro Barozzi, "Navigation and Ships in the Age of Columbus," *Italian Journal,* 5, 4 (1990), pp. 38-41, p. 38.

26. Morison, *The Great Explorers.* New York: Oxford University Press, 1978, pp. 397- 398. Elsewhere, Morison gives talk of revolt a bit more credence, but Koning (*ibid.,* p. 50) pooh-poohs the mutiny. The best source for the trip, Columbus's journal, now lost but summarized by Bartolomé de las Casas, gives this account:

> Here [October 10] the men could bear no more and complained of
> the length of the voyage. But the Admiral encouraged them in the
> best way he could, giving them hope of the advantage [riches] they
> might gain from it. He added that however much they might com-
> plain, having come so far, he had nothing to do but go to the In-
> dies, and he would go on until he found them.

Columbus's most recent biographer gives the story little historical credibility (Sale, *op. cit.,* p. 60). By October 9, they were following large flocks of birds, which they believed (correctly) would take them toward land, making an October 10 mutiny threat quite unlikely.

27. Bill Bigelow, "Once Upon a Genocide...," in *Rethinking Schools,* Vol. 5, #1 (October-November 1990), pp. 7-8.

28. Benjamin Keen, "Black Legend," in *The Christopher Columbus Encyclopedia* (New York: Simon and Schuster, 1991). Sale, *op. cit.,* pp. 160-161. Cf. Alfred W. Crosby, Jr., *The Columbian Exchange: Biological and Cultural Consequences of 1492* (Westport, Conn.: Greenwood, 1972), pp. 11-12. *Columbian Exchange.*

29. J. Leitch Wright, Jr., *The Only Land They Knew* (New York: Free Press, 1981), p. 128. Jack Forbes, *op. cit.,* p. 28. Morison, *The Great Explorers,* p. 78. James W.

Loewen and Charles Sallis, *Mississippi: Conflict and Change* (New York: Pantheon, 1980), p. 40. Warren Lowes, *Indian Giver* (Penticton, BC: Theytus Books, 1986), p. 32, says Labrador means "place to get cheap labor."

30. Ronald Sanders, *Lost Tribes and Promised Lands: The Origins of American Racism* (Boston: Little-Brown, 1978), p. 131, also quoting and paraphrasing Peter Martyr [de Anglería], *De Orbe Novo* (1516).

31. Maria Norlander-Martinez, "Christopher Columbus: The Man, the Myth, and the Slave Trade," *Adventures of the Incredible Librarian*, 4/90, p. 17. Sale, p. 156. Ronald Sanders, *Lost Tribes and Promised Lands: The Origins of American Racism* (Boston: Little-Brown, 1978), p. 169; Galeano, *Memory of Fire*, p. 72; Troy Floyd, *The Columbus Dynasty in the Caribbean* (Albuquerque: University of New Mexico Press, 1973), pp. 75, 222.

32. Crosby, *op. cit.*, pp. 11–12. Cf. Angus Calder, *Revolutionary Empire* (New York: Dutton, 1981), pp. 13–14. Marcel Dunan, ed., *Larousse Encyclopedia of Modern History* (New York: Crescent, 1987), p. 40.

33. Arthur E. Morgan, *Nowhere Was Somewhere*. University of North Carolina Press, 1946; reprint, Westport, Conn.: Greenwood, 1976. Marble, *op. cit.*, pp. 73–75. Angus Calder, *Revolutionary Empire* (New York: Dutton, 1981), p. 13. Warren Lowes, *Indian Giver* (Penticton, BC: Theytus Books, 1986), p. 82 re Montaigne. Also Ronald Sanders, *op. cit.*, pp. 208–209. Note influence of L.H. Morgan on Marx and Engels. Sale, *op. cit.* Larousse, *op. cit.*, p. 67.

34. Cf. Eric E. Williams, ed., *Documents of West Indian History, V. I, 1492–1655,* p. xxxi. Karl Marx and Friedrich Engels, "Communist Manifesto," in Robert C. Tucker, ed., *The Marx-Engels Reader* (New York: Norton, 1978), p. 474. Jack Weatherford, *Indian Givers* (New York: Ballantine Fawcett, 1988), pp. 43, 58, argues that long-staple American cotton, more useful for making cloth than Old World varieties, prompted the industrial revolution; he also considers the early production of coins in Bolivia and sugar in the Caribbean to amount to proto-factories that spurred the Industrial Revolution in Europe.

35. Weatherford, *op. cit.*, pp. 12, 15–17; Larousse, *op. cit.*, p. 69; Sale, *op. cit.*, p. 236.

36. Half of all major crops grown throughout the world are of American origin. Cf. Crosby, *op. cit.*, p. 124 and chapter 5. Warren Lowes, *op. cit.*, pp. 59–60. William Langer, "American Foods and Europe's Population Growth, 1750–1850," *Journal of Social History, v. 8* (winter 1975), 51–66. Weatherford, *op. cit.*, 65–71. Another American export was probably syphilis, which began to plague Spain and Italy shortly after the return of ships from Columbus's second voyage. On the other hand, more than 200 drugs derive from plants whose pharmacological uses were first discovered by the Indians.

37. Michael Wallace, "The Politics of Public History," in Jo Blatti, ed., *Past Meets Present* (Washington: Smithsonian Institution Press, 1987), pp. 41–42.

38. *Johnson v. M'Intosh*; see Robert K. Faulkner, *The Jurisprudence of John Marshall* (Princeton, N. J.: Princeton University Press, 1968), p. 53.

39. Columbus quoted in Sale, *op. cit.*, p. 116. Cf. p. 201.

40. Virgel Vogel, *This Country Was Ours* (New York: Harper and Row, 1972), p. 38, re Cartier. Jack Weatherford, *op. cit.*, p. 30 re Drake.

Libraries and the Quincentennial

Chris Dodge

The first order of business is to stop the wounding that is going on today. Only when the wounding has stopped can the healing begin. —Ricardo Levins Morales, from *huracán*, Summer, 1991.

Members attending a mass meeting at the American Library Association's (ALA) 1990 conference considered a provocative resolution. The issue at hand was a call for libraries to "provide Columbus Quincentennial programs and materials which examine the event from an authentic Native American perspective, dealing directly with topics like cultural imperialism, colonialism, and the Native American Holocaust." An indication perhaps of librarians' tendency toward fair-mindedness, the measure was voted upon and passed after an amendment was defeated which would have removed the word "Holocaust." A similar resolution proposed at that year's Minnesota Library Association (MLA) conference produced stiffer opposition. In Minnesota, a number of librarians had difficulty accepting a document filled with such scary and potentially volatile words as "piracy," "brutality," "slave trading," "murder," "disease," "conquest" and "ethnocide." One dissenter even called into question the historical veracity of the Native American Holocaust.[1] And an amendment was narrowly defeated which would have totally excised the supposedly incendiary passages and changed the "Be It Resolved" clause to read simply: "To provide Columbus Quincentennial programs and materials which examine the event from all perspectives." So much for "radical" librarians.

Originally drafted by members of the Minnesota Library Association's Social Responsibilities Round Table (MSRRT) in late 1989, both the Quincentennial resolutions were intended to be consciousness-raising tools, if nothing else. But heading into 1992, it was apparent that a good deal of library consciousness still needed raising. A case in point was the lack of critical response to a Pizza Hut–sponsored BOOK IT! National Reading Incentive Program effort. That Quincentennial-piggybacked endeavor intended to further children's knowledge of geography was announced to the world with a celebratory press release using Eurocentric terms like "New World" and "Old World." Ironically, even the newsletter of the ALA Office for Library Outreach Services—the one body within ALA expressly intended to deal with minority concerns—reproduced the BOOK IT! press release information without the slightest hint of criticism. Likewise, no institutional concern was voiced in 1991 when the Children's Book Council—a nonprofit organization with which the ALA maintains official relations—issued a crassly Eurocentric "Discovery of America Display Kit," featuring a Columbus mobile ("Boldly depicts Columbus's undertaking") and a "New World" bookmark set. What was done about it? The independent Minnesota Library Workers for Peace and Justice (MLWPJ) responded with a letter to BOOK IT! and the Children's Book Council. Beyond that: silence. The library press didn't even trouble to report either of the two protests.[2]

What has been done by libraries and library workers to counter the omissions, half-truths and myths about Columbus? The activities of individuals like Peter McDonald are certainly notable. While working as Native American bibliographer at New York City Public Library, McDonald was instrumental in organizing Columbus in Context (CIC), a New York–based coalition of "counter–Quincentenary" activists. At its 1990 conference, held in conjunction with the 25th National Assembly of Clergy and Laity Concerned, CIC presented over half a dozen programs featuring such panelists and speakers as author Hans Koning, scholar John Mohawk, and Cherokee activist Jan Elliott.

McDonald has also been involved in the latter's efforts with the Committee for American Indian History to put together a Quincentennial conference in Florida which would target librarians, educators, and museum officials, as well as the general public. With displays and bibliographies expected to be an integral part of libraries' recognition of the 1992 commemoration, McDonald envisions compiling a resource guide for libraries, one which would feature both graphic and written materials representing the views of American Indians, African Americans and other people of color whose voices are all-too-typically ignored.

Institutional response to the Quincentennial has generally perpetuated the glorification of Columbus as hero. Take, for example, the January 29, 1990, issue of *Library of Congress Information Bulletin* which spoke blandly of the 1492 "discovery" as being "based on the enriching process of encounter, transculturation, syncretism, and the intermix of races . . . [a] process [which] continues to enrich our Hemisphere." A curator of the Library's 1992 "Old World/New World: the Worlds of Columbus" exhibit did acknowledge in the *Bulletin* that "Even such a term as 'the New World' is a loaded one that may bring with it a definite and controversial perspective." One wonders, then, why the term was used in the exhibit's title in the first place. The issue goes on to detail the Library's schedule of Quincentennial events, which range from the presentation of a specially-commissioned musical composition to a "Columbus Goes to the Movies" retrospective.

Nationwide, library professional associations have been similarly guilty of using the Quincentenary as a marketing gimmick. It was only thanks to several concerned library workers in Washington State that the theme of the 1992 Washington Library Association conference was changed from "Discover New Worlds" (complete with ship logo) to "Innovations." And when the motto, "Rediscover Libraries: Exploring New Worlds of Information," was chosen for the Midwest Federation of Library Associations' 1991 meeting, only an initial ship logo (replete with computer disk sails) gave way — the conference title itself remained. In counterpoint to this, small library organizations like MLWPJ have made it evident that they are willing and able to confront business-as-usual attitudes about the Quincentennial. When General Mills hopped on the Columbus bandwagon, covering Cheerios boxes with such claptrap as a sign reading "Welcome to America," the notion that Columbus and crew "celebrated with . . . Honey Nut Cheerios," and the depiction of a grinning native astride a horse (a beast which had not yet been introduced in the Western hemisphere), they heard protest. Citing the ALA resolution which warned against using the 1992 commemoration as a time of celebration, MLWPJ conveners appealed to General Mills to "correct or remove such hurtful, inaccurate images and texts" from their cereal boxes. And, to impart further leverage, they sent copies of their letter — along with the ALA resolution and the Cheerios version of Columbus's log — to selected members of the library and Native American press, U.S. Representative Ben Nighthorse Campbell, and organizations like the Minnesota Council for the Social Studies. Library media again ignored this action.

The prime locus of library/Quincentennial activity has apparently been Minnesota. Besides the organizational effort previously described, the efforts of catalogers at Minnesota's Hennepin County Library (HCL) are worth noting. As part of an ongoing effort to provide fairer and more accurate subject headings than those provided by the Library of Congress, HCL catalogers have, for example, replaced the subdivision *"Discovery and Exploration"* with *"Exploration,"* so that material once assigned the heading *North America — Discovery and Exploration* is now simply assigned *North America — Exploration.* Catalogers at HCL have also established specific subject headings like *"Conquistadors," "Trail of Broken Treaties, 1972," "Native American Holocaust (1492-1900),"* and *"Jews, Spanish — History — Expulsion, 1492";* converted inauthentic terms like *Eskimos to Native people's self-preferred names, in this case Inuit,* and recast "Summary" notes for children's Columbus books into non-celebratory language.

Librarians in Minnesota have also participated in initial efforts to seek legislation that would rename Columbus Day, working alongside members of the Native American community, Minnesota Peace and Justice Coalition and others. And MSRRT has been involved in organizing Quincentennial-related programs. One of them, "The Columbus Quincentennial: Is There Anything to Celebrate," held at the 1990 MLA conference, examined "What the Columbus legacy has meant, especially to Native Americans and Afro Americans, and how we ought to respond or participate in the Quincentennial itself." Topics like the commercial thrust of the anniversary, the library community's participation in the hoopla, and the need to acknowledge the less savory aspects of U.S. history were all presented at the program, moderated by Sanford Berman. Fervent networkers, Berman and a number of his Minnesota colleagues have epitomized activist librarianship, exchanging information both on an ad hoc and ongoing basis with an international array of organizations and individuals working on counter–Quincentennial activities. One such individual, Joe Grant, traced the beginnings of Columbus misinformation to biographer Washington Irving ("An author in search of a hero"), detailed Columbus's slave-trading, and provided "questions to discuss with your friends" and lists of critical information sources, all in his sampler April 1990 comic book, *Adventures of the Incredible Librarian.* [3]

"The Columbus Administration is still in office," states artist Ricardo Levins Morales. Where do libraries exist in that administration? Have they been a complicit part of the tradition which values gold and wealth more than people? For some grassroots social activists, peace and justice cannot possibly exist until all — libraries included — recognize and acknowledge the full truth about their heritage. As Levins Morales puts it, 1992 presents an ideal opportunity to begin healing the wounds of colonialism and oppression, but the wounding must first cease before the body can heal. Along with schools, museums and churches, libraries are an integral place to begin this effort.

Chapter Notes

1. According to Russell Thornton (*American Indian Holocaust and Survival: A Population History Since 1492,* Norman: University of Oklahoma Press, 1987) a population of over 5,000,000 American Indians in the land area which is now the United States declined to about 250,000 by the last decade of the 19th century.

2. When the fall 1991 catalog of Upstart ("A division of Freline, Inc.") urged libraries and elementary schools to "celebrate Columbus's anniversary" by purchasing a selection of celebratory "Discover" posters, bookmarks, display items, and the like, MLWPJ wrote to the company calling for a more sensitive and even-handed treatment

of the Quincentenary. In part, the letter noted, "Your 'Discover' items not only over-look the Columbian impact upon Native Americans, but actually render them invisi-ble, repeatedly invoking the myths of 'discovery' and a 'New World' as though no other peoples (or surely none of any consequence) had ever lived here before Europeans ar-rived."

   3. *Adventure of the Incredible Librarian,* Sampler issue/April 1990, p. 17.

Once Upon a Genocide: Columbus in Children's Literature

William Bigelow

On Columbus Day, we pause as a Nation to honor the skilled and courageous navigator who discovered the Americas and, in so doing, brought to our ancestors the promise of the New World. In honoring Christopher Columbus, we also pay tribute to the generations of brave and bold Americas who, like him, have overcome great odds in order to chart the unknown. —President George Bush.

Christopher Columbus. Gleiter, Jan and Kathleen Thompson. Ideals (Great Tales Series), 1985. 32 pp. 3rd grade.

Christopher Columbus. Monchieri, Lino (Grisanti, Mary Lee, trans.) Silver Burdett, 1985. 62 pp. Upper elementary.

Christopher Columbus: Admiral of the Ocean Sea. Osborne, Mary Pope. Dell, 1987. 90 pp. Upper elementary/middle school.

Christopher Columbus: The Intrepid Mariner. Dolan, Sean J. Fawcett Columbine (Great Lives Series), 1989. 117 pp. Middle school.

Christopher Columbus and His Voyage to the New World. Young, Robert. Silver Press (Let's Celebrate Series), 1990. 32 pp. 2nd grade.

Columbus. D'Aulaire, Ingri and Edgar Parin. Doubleday, 1955. 59 pp. 5th grade.

Meet Christopher Columbus. de Kay, James T. Random House, 1989. 72 pp. 2nd grade.

Where Do You Think You're Going, Christopher Columbus? Fritz, Jean. G.P. Putnam's Sons, 1980. 80 pp. Upper elementary.

This article originally appeared in Rethinking Schools, *Vol. V, No. 1. Reprinted with permission from Rethinking Schools, Ltd., 1001 E. Keefe Avenue, Milwaukee, WI 53212.*

Children's biographies of Christopher Columbus function as primers on racism and imperialism. They teach youngsters to accept the right of white people to rule over people of color, of powerful nations to dominate weaker nations. And because the Columbus myth is so pervasive — Columbus's "discovery" is probably the *only* historical episode with which all my students at Jefferson High School are familiar — it is vital that educators analyze how this myth inhibits children from developing democratic, multi-cultural and anti-racist attitudes.

Almost without exception, children's biographies of Columbus depict the journey to the New World as a "great adventure" led by "probably the greatest sailor of his time." It's a story of courage and superhuman tenacity. Columbus is brave, smart and determined.

But behind this romanticized portrayal is a gruesome reality. For Columbus, land was real estate and it didn't matter to him that other people were already living there; if he "discovered" it he took it. If he needed guides or translators he kidnapped them. If his men wanted women he captured sex slaves. If the indigenous people resisted he countered with vicious dogs, hangings and mutilations.

On his second voyage, desperate to show his royal patrons a return on their investment, Columbus rounded up some 1,500 Taino Indians on the island of Hispaniola and chose 500 as slaves to be sold in Spain. Slavery did not show a profit as almost all the Tainos died en route to Spain or soon after their arrival. Nonetheless, Columbus wrote, "Let us in the name of the Holy Trinity go on sending all the slaves that can be sold" (Koning, 1976, p. 85).

Columbus decided to concentrate on the search for gold. He ordered every Taino 14 years and older to deliver a regular quota. Those who failed had their hands chopped off. In two years of the Columbus regime perhaps a quarter of a million people died (see las Casas, 1971; Keen, 1959; Koning, 1976; Meltzer, 1990; Morison, 1942; Sale, 1990; Zinn, 1980).

None of these facts is based on new or controversial research. Some of the most horrifying details of Columbus's reign in the Indies come from biographers like Samuel Eliot Morison who are great admirers of the Admiral (1942).

This article follows Columbus as he sails through children's biographies, comparing the books with the historical record, then analyzing how these accounts may influence young readers. I especially focus on portrayals of Columbus's relationship to Native Americans and how these accounts justify racism and other social inequalities. I conclude with an examination of the pedagogy implicit in these books and a discussion of more appropriate ways to teach Columbus.

Portrait of Columbus:
The Books vs. the Historical Record

Columbus's Motives

Why did Columbus want to sail west to get to the Indies? The answer offered children in today's books hasn't changed much since I was in fourth grade. I remember my teacher, Mrs. O'Neill, asking our class this question. As usual, I didn't have a clue, but up went Jimmy Martin's hand. "Why do men want to go to the moon?" he said triumphantly. Mrs. O'Neill was delighted and told us all how smart Jimmy was because he had answered a question with a question. In other words: just because — because he was curious, because he loved adventure, because he wanted to prove he could do it — just because. And for years I accepted this explanation (and envied Jimmy Martin).

In reality, Columbus wanted to become rich. It was no easy task convincing Queen Isabella and King Ferdinand to finance this highly questionable journey to the Indies, partly because his terms were pretty outrageous. Columbus demanded 10 percent of all the wealth returned to Europe along the new trade route to Asia (where Columbus *thought* he was headed) — that's 10 percent of the riches brought back by *everyone,* not just by himself. And he wanted this guaranteed *forever,* for him, for his children, for their children, in perpetuity. He demanded that he be granted the titles, "Viceroy" and "Admiral of the Ocean Sea." He was to be governor of all new territories found; the "Admiral" title was hereditary and would give him a share in proceeds from naval booty.

As for Queen Isabella and King Ferdinand, curiosity, adventure and "exploration" were the last things on their minds. They wanted the tremendous profits that could be secured by finding a western passage to the Indies as well as the riches that might be plundered from new-found lands.

The books acknowledge — and even endorse — Columbus's demands and readily admit that securing "gold and spices" was an objective to the Enterprise. "Of course [Columbus] wanted a lot! What was wrong with that?" James de Kay's *Meet Christopher Columbus* (1989) tells second graders. But this quest for wealth is downplayed in favor of adventure. "Exploration" meant going to "strange cities" were "many wonderful things" could be seen (de Kay, 1989). Travel was exciting: Columbus "felt the heady call of the open sea. 'I love the taste of salt spray in my face,' he told a friend, 'and the feel of a deck rising and falling under my feet...'" (Monchieri, 1985).

According to these eight biographies, the major reason Columbus wants to sail west is because of his deep faith in God. Columbus thought

that the Lord had chosen him to sail west across the sea to find the
riches of the East for himself and to carry the Christian faith to the
heathens. His name was Christopher. Had not the Lord chosen his
name-saint, Saint Christopher, to carry the Christ Child across the
dark water of a river? [D'Aulaire, 1955]

Uncritically using a term like "heathens" to denote the indigenous peoples of
America is a problem shared by most of the books.

Children's miseducation in international affairs begins with the factors
each book emphasizes to explain Columbus's Enterprise. Religion, curiosity,
adventure — Columbus books prefer these motives. But each of these explanations pales before the Spanish empire's quest for wealth and power. In bury-
ing these more fundamental material forces, the Columbus books encourage
students to misunderstand the roots of today's foreign policy exploits. Thus
students are more likely to accept platitudes — "We're involved in Latin
America for freedom and democracy" — than to look for less altruistic explanations.

The Kind and Noble Columbus

None of the biographies I evaluated — all in print and widely available —
disputes the ugly facts about Columbus and the Spanish conquest of the
Caribbean. Yet the sad irony is that all encourage children to root for Columbus. "It was lucky that Christopher Columbus was born where he was or he
might never have gone to sea" (Fritz, 1980). "There once was a boy who loved
the salty sea" (D'Aulaire, 1955). Some of the books, particularly those for
younger readers, refer to Columbus affectionately, using his first name.
Unlike the people he will later exterminate, Columbus is treated as a real
human being, one with thoughts and feelings. "When Christopher Columbus
was a child, he always wanted to be like Saint Christopher. He wanted to sail
to faraway places and spread the word of Christianity" (Osborne, 1987).
Gleiter and Thompson's *Christopher Columbus* (1985) is structured as a conver-
sation between Columbus and his son, Fernando. The Admiral of the Ocean
Sea is good and kind. In illustrations he has perfect teeth and a strong chin.
The series title of Robert Young's *Christopher Columbus and His Voyage to the New
World* (1990) sums up the stance of every biographer: "Let's Celebrate."

The books cheer Columbus on towards the Indians. Each step on the road
to "discovery" is told from his point of view. When Columbus is delayed, this
is the "most unhappy part of his great adventure" (de Kay, 1989). Every successful step towards realizing the Enterprise is rewarded with exclamation
marks: "Yes, [the Queen] would help Columbus!" (Osborne, 1987). "After all
these years, Columbus would get his ships!" (de Kay, 1989).

Columbus's devout Christianity is a theme in all the books — and is never questioned. The most insistent of these, and the worst of the lot in almost every respect, is Sean J. Dolan's *Christopher Columbus: The Intrepid Mariner* (1989). Already by the second page of Dolan's reverent volume we're reading about Columbus's attachment to his leather-bound Bible. Dolan continually dips us into the Admiral's thoughts; and these meditations run deep and pious: "[He] believed that the awe-inspiring beauty that surrounded him could only be the handiwork of the one true God, and he felt secure in his Lord and Savior's protection. If only my crewmen shared my belief, Columbus thought" (Dolan, 1989). And this is only on the third page — Dolan's narrative goes on like this for 114 more. The reader is practically strangled by Columbus's halo.

Jean Fritz's *Where Do You Think You're Going, Christopher Columbus?* (1980) is the only book which takes a somewhat skeptical tone about religion as a motive. Fritz tells her readers that Queen Isabella

> was such an enthusiastic Christian that she insisted everyone in Spain be a Christian too. . . . Indeed, she was so religious that if she even found Christians who were not sincere Christians, she had them burned at the stake. (Choir boys sang during the burning so Isabella wouldn't have to hear the screams.)

This is pretty strong stuff, but the implied critique would likely be lost on the book's targeted readers, upper elementary students.

The close association between Jesus, God and Columbus in all the books, with the possible exception of Jean Fritz's, discourages children from criticizing Columbus. "Columbus marveled at how God had arranged everything for the best," the D'Aulaires write (1955). Well, if God arranged everything, who are we, the insignificant readers, to question?

Moreover, no book even hints that the Indians believed in their own God or gods who also watched over and cared about them. The Columbus expedition may be the first encounter between two peoples — Us and Them — where children will learn that "God is on *our* side."

Evils? Blame the Workers

Columbus's journey across the Atlantic was not easy, according to most of the books, because his crew was such a wretched bunch. The sailors are stupid, superstitious, cowardly and sometimes scheming. Columbus, on the other hand, is brave, wise and godly. These characterizations, repeated frequently in many of the books, protect the Columbus myth; anything bad that happens, like murder and slavery, can always be blamed on the men.

Columbus, the leader, is pure of heart; the rabble embodies everything wicked and selfish. (These negative portrayals are less pronounced in Monchieri's *Christopher Columbus* [1985]. The book depicts seamen as pliant and ignorant, but at least concedes that "almost all proved to be good sailors.")

Taken together, the books' portrayals serve as a kind of antiworking class, proboss polemic. "Soon [Columbus] rose above his shipmates, for he was clever and capable and could make others carry out his orders" (D'Aulaire, 1955). Evidently, ordinary seamen are not "clever and capable," and thus are good merely for carrying out the instructions of others. "Soon [Columbus] forgot that he was only the son of a humble weaver," the D'Aulaires write, as if a background as a worker were something to be ashamed of. The books encourage children to identify with Columbus's hardships, even though his men worked and slept in horrible conditions while the future Admiral slept under a canopy bed in his private cabin and had a personal servant. The lives of workers are simultaneously ignored and held in contempt.

The "Discovery"

The Indigenous Peoples as Non-humans

At the core of the Columbus myth — and repeated by all eight books — is the notion that Columbus "discovered" America. Indeed, it's almost as if the writer churned out one ever so slightly different version after another.

James T. de Kay describes the scene in *Meet Christopher Columbus* (1989):

> The sailors rowed Columbus to the shore. He stepped on the beach. He got on his knees and said a prayer of thanks.
> Columbus named the island San Salvador. He said it now belonged to Ferdinand and Isabella.
> He tried to talk to the people on San Salvador. But they could not understand him.

Of course *he* couldn't understand *them*, either. But de Kay attributes the inability to understand solely to the Indians. Is it these Indians' implied ignorance that allows heavily armed men to come onto their land and claim it in the name of a kingdom thousands of miles away? In *Christopher Columbus and His Voyage to the New World* (1990), Robert Young doesn't even tell his young readers of the *people* on these islands. Young's Columbus found "lands" but no people. In illustrations we see only palm trees and empty beaches.

Why don't any of the books prompt students to question what rightfully should be portrayed as an invasion? Naïvely, I kept waiting for some writer to insert just a trace of doubt: "Why do you think Columbus felt he could claim land for Spain when there were already people living there?" or "Columbus doesn't write in his journal why he felt entitled to steal other people's property. What do you think?"

This scene of Columbus's first encounter with the Indians — some version of which is read in school by virtually every child in the United States — constructs a powerful metaphor about relations between different countries and races. It is a lesson not just about the world 500 years ago, but about the world *today*. Clothed, armed, Christian, white men from a more technologically "advanced" nation arrive in a land peopled by darker skinned, naked, unarmed, non–Christians — and take over. Because no book indicates which characteristic of *either* group necessitates or excuses this kind of bullying, students are left alone to puzzle it out. Might makes right. Whites should rule over people who aren't white. Christians should control non–Christians. "Advanced" nations should dominate "backward" nations. Each and every answer a student might glean from the books' text and images invariably justifies imperialism and racism: it's acceptable for one people to determine the fate of another people; it's acceptable for white people to control people of color.

In Columbus's "New World adventures," the Indians are just background noise. Only one book, *Where Do You Think You're Going, Christopher Columbus?* (1980), tries to imagine what the Indians might have been thinking about the arrival of the Spaniards. Still, the point here seems more to gently poke fun at Columbus and crew than to seriously consider the Indians' point of view: ". . . if Spaniards were surprised to see naked natives, the natives were even more surprised to see dressed Spaniards. All that cloth over their bodies! What were they trying to hide? Tails, perhaps?" Jean Fritz's interior monologue for the Indians makes fun of the explorers but in the process trivializes the Indians' concerns.

Not a single Columbus biography ever asks children: "What might the Indians have thought about the actions of Columbus and his men?" According to Mary Pope Osborne, Columbus "thought [the Indians] could easily be brought under control and that they had no religion of their own. He wrote that they would make 'good Christians and good servants'" (1987). But Osborne doesn't prompt children to wonder what the Indians would have thought about Columbus's plans.

The silent Indians in Columbus stories promote a contemporary consequence. Children absorb the message that white people in developed societies have consciousness and voice, but Third World people are thoughtless and voiceless objects. The text and images rehearse students to look at the world from the assumption: *they* are not like *us*. A corollary is that *we* are more competent than *they* in determining the conditions of their lives: their social and economic systems, their political alliances and so on. Intervention in Vietnam, subversion of Salvador Allende's government in Chile, the invasions of Grenada and Panama, the attempted overthrow by proxy of the Nicaraguan and Angolan governments: *our* right to decide what's best for *them* is basic to the conduct of this nation's foreign policy. The Columbus myth, as most children's first exposure to "foreign policy," helps condition young people to accept the unequal distribution of power in the world.

Theft, Slavery and Murder Justified

Columbus's genocidal policies towards the Indians were initiated during his second journey to the New World. The three books aimed at children in early elementary grades, Gleiter and Thompson's *Christopher Columbus* (1985), de Kay's *Meet Christopher Columbus* (1989) and Young's *Christopher Columbus and His Voyage to the New World* (1990), conveniently stop the story after his first journey. The Columbus myth can take root in young minds without the complication of the slavery and mass murder to come.

Columbus returned to a hero's welcome in Spain after his first trip. He also arrived telling all kinds of lies about gold mines and spices and unlimited amounts of wealth to be had for the taking. The admiral needed royal backing for a second trip, and had to convince his sponsors that the islands contained more than parrots and naked heathens.

During this second voyage, in February of 1495, Columbus launched the slave raids against the Taino Indians of Hispaniola. Four of the eight books I examined — the ones aimed at older children — admit that Columbus took Indians as slaves (Dolan, 1989; Fritz, 1980; Monchieri, 1985; and Osborne, 1987). However, the books' critique is muted. No account tells children what slavery meant for its victims. One of the books, Monchieri's *Christopher Columbus* (1985), says that taking slaves was "a great failing of Columbus.... He saw nothing wrong with enslaving the American Indians and making them work for Spanish masters.... Missionaries protested against this policy, but they were not listened to." End of discussion. Mary Pope Osborne in *Christopher Columbus: Admiral of the Ocean Sea* (1987), writes that "this terrible treatment of the Indians was Columbus's real downfall." However, Osborne is unable to offer even this minimal criticism of the admiral without at the same time justifying his actions: "Since Columbus felt despair and disappointment about not finding gold in the Indies, he decided to be like the African explorers and try to sell these Indians as slaves" (Osborne, 1987). Neither book ever describes the character of slave life — or slave death.

The other two biographies simply offer Columbus's justifications for taking slaves: "African explorers were always sending Africans back to Spanish slave markets, Columbus told himself. Besides, the natives were all heathens. It wasn't as if he were selling Christians into slavery" (Fritz, 1980). "Because the Indians were not Christians, Columbus believed that they could be enslaved and converted without the Spanish feeling any guilt" (Dolan, 1989).

Dolan later blames slave-taking all on the men: "Given the attitude of the men at large, however, [Columbus] had little choice but to give his approval to the slaving sorties."

Imagine, if you will, Nazi war crimes described in this way — nothing about the suffering of the victims, tepid criticism of the perpetrators — their crimes explained through the justifications of Hitler and his generals. How long would these books last in our schools?

From the beginning, locating gold was Columbus's primary objective. In one passage, not included in any of the children's books, Columbus writes: "Gold is a wonderful thing! Whoever owns it is lord of all he wants. With gold it is even possible to open for souls the way to paradise" (Johansen and Maestas, 1979, p. 16). Two of the eight books, those by Fritz and Dolan, describe Columbus's system for attempting to extract gold from the Indians. Dolan writes that Columbus instituted "a system of forced tribute: each Indian was to provide a certain amount of gold each year. Penalties for failure to comply with this rule included flogging, enslavement or death" (1989). Nothing here about cutting people's hands off, which is what Columbus did, but still the description is pretty explicit. Fritz writes simply that Indians who didn't deliver enough gold "were punished." She concludes that "between 1494 and 1496 one-third of the native population of Hispaniola was killed, sold, or scared away" (1980).

The passive voice in Fritz's version — "*was* killed, sold, or scared away" — protects the perpetrators: exactly who caused these deaths? More significantly, these accounts fail to recognize the Indians' humanity. The books' descriptions are clinical and factual, like those of a coroner. What kind of suffering must these people have gone through? How did it feel to have their civilization completely destroyed in just a few years? What of the children who watched their parents butchered by the Spanish gold-seekers? These books show no passion or outrage — at Columbus, at the social and economic system he represented, or at school textbooks for hiding this inhumanity for so many years. This devastation happened to human beings, several hundred thousand of them, maybe more. Why don't the writers of these books get angry?

I find the most "honest" books about Columbus's Enterprise — those that admit slavery and other atrocities — the most distressing. They lay out the facts, describe the deaths, and then it's on to the next paragraph with no look back. These books foster a callousness towards human suffering — or is it simply a callousness toward people of color? Apparently students are supposed to value bravery, cunning and perseverance over a people's right to life and self-determination. The stories prepare young people to watch without outrage the abstract nightly news accounts — a quick segment about an army massacre in El Salvador followed by a commercial for Chrysler Le Baron.

Contempt for Native Resistance

Given that Columbus biographies scarcely consider Indians as human beings, it's not surprising that native resistance to the Spaniards' atrocities is either barely acknowledged or treated with hostility. Gleiter and Thompson's *Christopher Columbus* (1985) notes that in future trips Columbus "fought with the natives." In a sentence, Lino Monchieri writes, "The Indians became rebellious because [Columbus] compelled them to hand over their gold" (1985). At least here the author credits the Indians with what might be a legitimate cause for revolt, though offering no further details. Mary Pope Osborne buries the cause of resistance in nonexplanatory, bland, victimless prose: "But the settlers had run into trouble with the Indians, and there had been a lot of fighting" (1987).

Some writers choose to portray Indian resistance not as self-defense, but as originating from the indigenous people's inherently violent nature. In *Meet Christopher Columbus,* "unfriendly Indians" surprise innocent Spaniards: "Suddenly more than 50 Indians jumped out from behind the trees. They had bows and arrows. They attacked the men. The men fought back" (de Kay, 1989). Thus, Indian resistance to the Spaniards' invasion and land grab is not termed "freedom fighting," but instead is considered "unfriendly." Ironically, this story portrays the Spaniards' violence as self-defense. Note that in this quote the Spaniards are "men," the Indians are, well, just Indians.

The books which bother to differentiate between distinct groups of Indians single out the Caribs for special contempt. Caribs are presented as cannibals, even though no historical evidence exists to corroborate such a claim (Carew, 1988; las Casas, 1971; Sale, 1990). The Caribs lived on islands "so wild and steep, it seemed as if the waterfalls came tumbling out of the clouds. The Indians who lived there were wild too. They were cannibals who ate their enemies" (D'Aulaire, 1955). In Dolan's *Christopher Columbus: The Intrepid Mariner* (1989), Columbus sends an armed contingent to "explore" the island that today is St. Croix. Because Caribs attack the Spaniards, Dolan considers this resistance sufficient to label the Caribs as ferocious. In fact, according to the account of Dr. Diego Alvarez Chanca, an eyewitness, the Indians only attacked when the Spaniards trapped them in a cove (Morison, 1942, pp. 416–417). In today's parlance, the Caribs were the "radicals" and "extremists"—in other words, they tenaciously defended their land and freedom.

The books condition young people to reject the right of the oppressed to rebel. We have a right to own "Their" land, and "They" should not protest—at least not violently. Those who do resist will be slapped with a pejorative descriptor—cannibal, savage, communist, militant, radical, hard-liner, extremist—and subdued. Black South Africans' fight against apartheid, the Palestinians' intifada, Honduran peasants organizing for land redistribution, the United Farm Workers' quest for union recognition: the Columbus biographies implicitly discourage students from paying serious attention to these and other contemporary movements for social justice. Obviously, they leave children similarly ill-prepared to recognize and respect current Indian struggles for land and fishing rights.

Columbus's Legacy

I expected each book to end with at least some reflection on the meaning of Columbus's voyages. None did. In fact, only one book, *Meet Christopher Columbus* (1989), even suggests that today's world has anything to do with Columbus: Thanks to the Admiral, "Thousands of people crossed the ocean to America. This 'new world' became new countries: the United States, Canada, Mexico, Brazil and many others."

It's much simpler for the authors to ignore both short- and long-term consequences of Columbus's Enterprise. Instead of linking the nature of 15th and 16th century Spain to 20th century America, each book functions as a kind of secular Book of Genesis: In the beginning there was Columbus — he was good and so are we.

This is a grave distortion. In addition to the genocide of native peoples in the Caribbean, the most immediate effect of Columbus's voyages was the initiation of the Atlantic slave trade between Africa and America. The Spanish monarchs issued the first laws governing this slave trade as early as 1501, and by 1510 shiploads of slaves were transported to America for sale (Davidson, 1961). As historian Basil Davidson writes, "Throughout the years that followed it was to be the searing brand of this trade that it would consider its victims, not as servants or domestic slaves who deserved respect in spite of their servile condition, but as chattel slaves, commodities that could and should be sold at whim or will" (1961, p. 46).

Colonialism and slavery: This was the new world Columbus did not so much discover as helped to invent. In the emerging commercial ethos of his society, human beings were commodities whose value was measured largely in monetary terms. The natural environment was likewise cherished not for its integrity or beauty but for the wealth that could be extracted. Columbus's Enterprise and the plunder that ensued contributed mightily to the growth of the nascent mercantile capitalism of Europe. His lasting contribution was to augment a social order that confronts the world in commercial terms: How much is it *worth*?

Why are Columbus biographies characterized by such bias and omission? I doubt any writers, publishers or teachers consciously set out to poison the minds of the young. The Columbus story teaches important values, some would argue. Here was a young man who, despite tremendous adversity, maintained and finally achieved his objectives. Fear and narrow-mindedness kept others from that which he finally accomplished.

But in the Columbus biographies, these decent values intermingle with biases against working class people, people of color and Third World nations. The blindness of writers and educators to these biases may be an indication of how pervasive they are in the broader society. The seeds of imperialism, exploitation and racism were planted with Columbus's first trans–Atlantic Enterprise — and these seeds have taken root. Without doubt, ours is a very different world than 15th and 16th century Spanish America, but there is a lingering inheritance: the tendency for powerful groups to value profit over humanity, racial and cultural differences used to justify exploitation and inequality, vast disparities in living conditions for different social classes, economically and militarily strong nations attempting to control the fates of weaker nations. Hence, life amidst injustice in today's United States inures many of us to the injustices of 500 years earlier. Characteristics that appear to someone as natural and inevitable in the 20th century will likely appear as natural and inevitable in descriptions of the world five centuries ago.

The Pedagogy of Columbus Biographies

The Columbus stories encourage a passive relationship between reader and text. They never pose choices or dilemmas for children to think through. Did Columbus have a right to claim Indian land in the name of the Spanish Crown? Were those Indians who resisted violently justified in doing so? Why does the United States commemorate a Columbus Day instead of a Genocide Day? Each biography is structured as a lecture, not as a dialogue of problem posing. The narratives require readers merely to listen, not to think. The text is everything, the reader nothing. Not only are young readers conditioned to accept social hierarchy — colonialism and racism — they are also rehearsed in an authoritarian mode of learning.

By implication, I've tried in this review essay to suggest the outlines of a more truthful history of Columbus and the "discovery" of America. First, the indigenous peoples of America must be accorded the status of full human beings with inalienable rights to self-determination. The tale of "discovery" needs to be told from their perspective as well as from Europeans'. Although there is little documentation of how the Tainos interpreted the Spaniards' arrival and conquest, readers could be encouraged to think about these events from the native point of view. Columbus's interior monologue should not be the only set of thoughts represented in the story.

A more accurate tale of Columbus would not simply probe his personal history but would also analyze the social and economic system he represented. And children might be asked to think about how today's world was shaped by events begun in 1492. Above all, young readers must be invited to think and critique, not simply required to passively absorb others' historical interpretations. Such a book is waiting to be written.

Until we create humane and truthful materials, teachers may decide to boycott the entire Columbus canon. The problem with this approach is that the distortions and inadequacies characterizing this literature are also found throughout other children's books.

A better solution is to equip students to read critically these and other stories—inviting children to become detectives, interrogating their biographies, novels and textbooks for bias (see Christensen, 1991; Dorfman, 1983). In fact, because the Columbus books are *so* bad, they make perfect classroom resources to learn how to read for social as well as for literal meaning. After students have been introduced to a critical history of Columbus, they could probe materials for accuracy. Do the books lie outright? What is omitted from the accounts that would be necessary for a more complete understanding of Columbus and his encounters with native cultures? What motives are given Columbus and how do those compare with the actual objectives of the admiral and the Spanish monarchs? Whom does the book "root" for and how is this accomplished? What role do illustrations play in shaping an image of Columbus? *Why* do the books tell the story as they do? Who in our society benefits and who is hurt from these presentations? (Bigelow, 1989).

Teachers could assign children to write their own Columbus biographies—and some of these could be told from *Indians'* points of view. Or youngsters might take issues from their own lives suggested by the European invasion of America—fighting, fairness, stealing, racism—and write stories drawn from these themes. One of my students at Jefferson High School in Portland, Nicole Smith-Leary, wrote and illustrated a book about a young boy named Chris, who moves to a new neighborhood and "discovers" a clubhouse built by three other boys. ("'How can you come here and discover something that we built and really care about?' the boys demand.") Nicole took her story, which ends more happily than the one after which it's patterned, and read it to children in several elementary schools.

Encouraging students to ask critical questions in their reading directly challenges the passivity promoted by the Columbus biographers. Instead of merely absorbing the authors' words, children can begin to argue with them. Significantly, to invite students to question the injustices embedded in text material is implicitly to invite them to question the injustices embedded in the society itself. Isn't it about time we used the Columbus myth to allow students to begin discovering the truth?*

Thanks to Linda Christensen, Martha Bigelow, Jeff Edmundson, Bill Resnick, Norm Diamond, Maria Sweeney and Cynthia Ellwood for valuable comments on this article.

Epilogue: Dear Diary . . .

I, Columbus: My Journal — 1492-3. Roop, Peter and Connie, eds. Illustrated
by Peter E. Hanson. Walker and Co., 1990. 57 pp.

Diaries are a seductive form of literature. "This is the real thing," we
imagine as we sit down to read. As we begin, we strike a silent bargain with
the writer: You let me into your private thoughts and I'll try to look at the
world through your eyes.

This is the danger of the Roops's book. *I, Columbus* invites children into
the colonialist mind. And leaves them there. The very structure of the book
encourages children to view colonial conquest from the standpoint of the
white European conqueror. Youngsters buddy-up to Columbus and ride
along on his "voyage to the unknown," as the Roops call it.

Clearly the book is intended to foster an admiration for Columbus. The
Roops write in their acknowledgments: "Most of all we express our awe of
Columbus himself, a man with a vision and the determination to accomplish
it."

Perhaps in the zeal to enlist children in their Columbus fan club, the
Roops selected passages from his journal that portray him at his most appeal-
ing. Indeed the Roops's Columbus is more saint than conqueror. For example, on first encounter with the indigenous people of Guanahaní, the Roops's
Columbus is strict with his crew and kind to the Indians: "I warned my men
to take nothing from the people without giving something in exchange" (pp.
31–32). They neglect to include a passage from Columbus's journal that
foreshadows his massive slave raids: "They [the Indians] should be good servants and of quick intelligence, since I see that they very soon say all that is
said to them. . ." (Jane, p. 24).

The Roops's October 14 diary entry does acknowledge that Columbus
"captured" Indians, but fails to include a later passage from the diary on that
same day that places this act in a broader context. Columbus wrote: ". . . I
caused [the Indians] to be taken in order to carry them off that they may learn
our language and return. However, when Your Highnesses so command,
they can all be carried off to Castile or held captive in the island itself, since
with 50 men they would be all kept in subjection and forced to do whatever
may be wished" (Jane, p. 28). Columbus's captives resist, by attempting to
escape, sometimes successfully. The Roops edit this native resistance out of
their book, as they also omit Columbus's further kidnappings. For example,
on November 12, Columbus describes the kidnap of "seven head of women,
small and large, and three children" (Jane, p. 57).

Oddly, the real Columbus seems much more appreciative of Taino Indian culture and humanity than the Roops let on. On October 29, Columbus

enters Taino homes which "were well swept and clean, and their furnishing very well arranged; all were made of very beautiful palm branches" (Jane, p. 48). None of this in the Roop edition. On November 6, Columbus describes the Tainos as "a people very free from wickedness and unwarlike..." (Jane, p. 57). And on December 16 writes: "They are the best people in the world and beyond all the mildest..." (Jane, p. 100). None of this in the Roop edition. Columbus even refers to some of the Indian leaders, like the Hispaniola cacique (leader), Guacanagarí, by their given names. The Roops's Indians have no names.

Right up to the final page of the book, the Roop diary encourages readers to empathize with Columbus and ignore the Indians. Columbus hits stormy weather on his return to Spain. On February 14, 1493, he writes: "The wind increased last night and the waves were frightful, coming in opposite directions.... I am comforted by the favors God has bestowed upon me.... Therefore I ought not to fear this storm. But my weakness and anxiety will not allow my mind to be reassured."

"I also feel great anxiety because of the two sons I have in Córdoba at school, if I leave them orphaned." Every reader can empathize with Columbus-the-father's worries about his children left at home. However, the diary narrative prevents readers from feeling this same empathy for the Taino Indians Columbus has carried off to Spain, or for the orphans *they've* left at home.

I, Columbus follows the same pattern as other biographies. It's one more piece of propaganda for the powerful that miseducates children. However, unlike other biographical accounts, the choice of the journal structure more easily excuses the Roops from prompting students to question the myth. We're only letting Columbus tell his own story, they can claim. Even more effectively than other biographies, the Roops's diary silences the perspectives of the "discovered."

Sources

Bigelow, W. "Discovering Columbus: Rereading the Past." *Language Arts,* 66 (1989), 635–643.

Carew, J. *Fulcrums of Change: The Origins of Racism in the Americas and Other Essays.* Trenton, N. J.: Africa World Press, 1988.

Christensen, L. "Unlearning the Myths That Bind Us." *Rethinking Schools,* May/June 1991, 1–17.

Davidson, B. *The African Slave Trade: Precolonial History 1450–1850.* Boston: Little, Brown, 1961.

Dorfman, A. *The Empire's Old Clothes: What the Lone Ranger, Babar and Other Innocent Heroes Do to Our Minds.* New York: Pantheon, 1983.

Jane, C. *The Journal of Christopher Columbus.* New York: Bramhall House, 1960.

Johansen, B. and R. Maestas. *Wasi'chu: The Continuing Indian Wars*. New York: Monthly Review Press, 1979.

Keen, B., trans. and ed. *The Life of the Admiral Christopher Columbus by His Son Ferdinand*. New Brunswick, N. J.: Rutgers University Press, 1959.

Koning, H. *Columbus: His Enterprise*. New York: Monthly Review Press, 1976.

las Casas, B. de, *History of the Indies*, A. Collard, trans. and ed. New York: Harper and Row, 1971.

Meltzer, M. *Columbus and the World Around Him*. New York: Franklin Watts, 1990.

Morison, S.E. *Admiral of the Ocean Sea: A Life of Christopher Columbus*. Boston: Little, Brown, 1942.

Sale, K. *The Conquest of Paradise: Christopher Columbus and the Columbian Legacy*. New York: Alfred A. Knopf, 1990.

Zinn, H. *A People's History of the United States*. New York: Harper and Row, 1980.

Exhibiting Ideology

Jan Elliott

The process of creating and entrenching highly selective, reshaped or completely fabricated memories is what we call "indoctrination" or "propaganda" when it is conducted by official enemies, and "education," "moral instruction" or "character building" when we do it ourselves. It's a valuable mechanism of control since it effectively blocks any understanding of what is happening in the world. One crucial goal of successful education is to deflect attention elsewhere . . . where our problems allegedly lie and away from our institutions and their systematic functioning and behavior, the real source of a great deal of violence and suffering in the world. It is crucially important to prevent understanding and to divert attention from the sources of our own conduct, so that elite groups can act without popular constraints to achieve their goals, which are called "the national interest" in academic theology. . . .

For those who stubbornly seek freedom, there can be no more urgent task than to come to understand the mechanism and practices of indoctrination. These are easy to perceive in the totalitarian societies, much less so in the system of "brainwashing under freedom" to which we are subjected and which all too often we serve as witting or unwitting instruments. — Noam Chomsky, from *The Manufacture of Consent.*

A Review of First Encounters: Spanish Explorations in the Caribbean and the United States, 1492–1570

The Florida Museum of Natural History (FMNH) has an exhibit recounting the first eight decades of Spain's "exploration and settlement of the Caribbean and the United States" (sic). This exhibit was partially funded by the National Endowment for the Humanities. It was on display until January 2, 1990, and then was to tour major cities of the United States for three years. This exhibit is an early sign of the mania we can expect to see as the nation prepares for the

---

Earlier versions of "Exhibiting Ideology" appeared in The Gainesville Sun *(December 1989) as a guest editorial and in* Akwasasne Notes *(January 1990).*

quincentennial celebration of Christopher Columbus's invasion of the "New World." The phrases "New World" and "Old World" will be seen frequently throughout this exhibit. The producers of the exhibit do not enclose the two phrases in quotation marks to show that these were colonialist expressions. They are, in fact, used in a colonialist attitude throughout. This is only one of the many very subtle and pervasive examples of the institutionalized racism and cultural insensitivity on which this country, and this exhibit, was built.

On Friday, November 24, 1989, a demonstration was organized outside of the museum (see epilogue, p. 132). Among the protesters were Indians from many different tribes, including a Taino Indian from Puerto Rico, Hector Rosa. The exhibit says that the Taino are extinct, but Hector didn't know that, so we let him stay. The overall implication of the exhibit is that "Indians" no longer exist except as a part of our colorful past. Unfortunately, mainstream national thinking reflects this belief. But the Indians are here and you will be seeing more of them as groups organize to protest both the continued celebration of Columbus Day as a national holiday and the upcoming Quincentenary of the 1492 invasion.

As we carried our signs in protest a woman came out of the museum and approached Russell Means, leader of the American Indian Movement. She began to berate him and the other protesters for spoiling the children's enjoyment of the exhibit, for which she and others had worked many hours. She said that they had tried to present a "balanced" view. Russell asked how she thought the Jewish communities in America would react if the Nazis put together an exhibit presenting a balanced view of the Holocaust and then forced everyone to observe Hitler Day as a national celebration. When the racist and colonialist attitudes of the dominant few become so institutionalized that the historically oppressed peoples themselves fail to recognize these views as racist, this becomes another form of enslavement. I would like to point out the way that this exhibit contributes to that enslavement.

One of the last frames of the exhibit reveals its major failing. A frame entitled "The Native Perspective" reads, "Native American views of the first encounters are elusive. We have the Spanish accounts but not those of the Native People. At times the Spaniards did record what they thought were native reactions, but their interpretations were probably hindered by the language barrier."

Since this is to be a national exhibit, viewed by thousands of school children and adults from all segments of the culture, there could have been some effort made to give a more complete account by including a "Native American Perspective." Though cultural language barriers still exist, this could have been more than just another European interpretation of history.

The first frame of the exhibit reads, "On the Eve of Discovery." The word "Discovery" used here should be enclosed in quotation marks to indicate that we are a little more enlightened today than to think that this was an uninhabited continent just waiting to be "discovered." The civilizations that the Europeans encountered and discounted were civilizations based upon thousands of years of wisdom and understanding of this land and the peoples' place on it.

A few frames down it reads, "Columbus's primary goal was to convert the natives to Catholicism." The word "natives" used here to refer to highly individualized groups such as the Taino and the Arawak is demeaning. "His logs suggest that he had other ideas like using the Native Peoples for laborers and finding gold and wealth." The word "laborers" here suggests in a very subtle way that Columbus intended to pay for their work. It should read "slaves" to accurately indicate the intentions.

Quoting from *The Journal of Christopher Columbus* (Clarkson N. Potter, New York, 1960), Columbus says, "So tractable, so peaceable, are these people that I swear there is not in the world a better nation. They love their neighbors as themselves, and their discourse is ever sweet and gentle, and accompanied with a smile; and though it is true that they are naked, yet their manners are decorous and praiseworthy." Then he adds that he is sure that these people can be "made to work, sow and do all that is necessary and to adopt our ways." Columbus took these characteristics to indicate weakness. In less than a decade after Columbus's arrival in the "New World," hundreds of thousands of people were killed. Sometimes entire villages were wiped out, or shipped to Europe and sold as slaves. The historical and scholarly documentation of the atrocities committed against the original peoples of this continent by the Europeans is massive. Yet those non–Indians gathered outside the museum on the first day of protest were horrified when Russell Means said, "Columbus makes Hitler look like a juvenile delinquent." Educational propaganda has become so inculcated that those who try to present a truly "balanced" view are labeled troublemakers.

Under the Taino exhibit it reads, "He first encountered the Lucayans of the Bahamas who had little gold and an unsophisticated material culture." By European standards, a murderous, barbaric people who have a sophisticated material culture are more highly evolved than those who practice consciousness development through the medicine wheel and devalue the accumulation of material goods.

We are told by the exhibit that the "First Settlement," La Navidad, was built in the village of Chief Guacanagarí. Was this then the "First settlement"? I once visited St. Augustine with a Papago friend, Floyd Flores and a Hopi friend, Thomas Banyacya, where we encountered endless signs reading "oldest settlement," "oldest schoolhouse," "oldest jail," etc. We will have to yield the one on the "oldest jail" because we didn't have jails before the advent of the white man and private property. The oldest continuously settled village on the North American continent is Old Oraibi located on Hopi Land in Arizona. Indians are frequently accused of having a culture based on myth rather than fact like the scientific culture of the Europeans. Indians are taught their myths and know what they are supposed to learn from them. Non-Indians are given theirs, such as Thanksgiving, Christmas, Columbus Day, Vietnam, and "oldest city," and they don't even know that they are myths.

Another frame reads, "By 1503, the island's [Hispaniola] governor, Nicholas de Ovando, had drawn up a plan for founding 15 perimeter towns in order to *subdue* the native inhabitants and control the island." We object here to the words "native" as explained above and to the word "subdue," which implies friendly white people encountering savages.

A frame on the Cuenca Artifacts at Nueva Cádiz, Venezuela, reads "Aboriginal materials include shell beads (28), Precolumbian jade (29) and Cobova-ware, made by Indians living in the Spanish Settlement." This implies that certain Indians were friendlier than others and freely chose to live with the Spanish. Is free choice ever possible when one group holds all the power and the other group holds none?

Under a frame "Early Explorations of La Florida" it reads, "In 1517 after hostile encounters with the Maya of Yucatan, Cordoba's expedition took refuge in La Florida." Nowhere in this exhibit will you see the words "hostile" or "savage" applied to the Europeans. This exhibit is still justifying the murder of Indians by "peaceable CHRISTIAN" people.

A later frame that deals with the failed expedition of Panfilodo Narváez reads, "Many of the army, including Narvaez, were lost at sea. Others managed to land on the Texas coast, where they were enslaved by natives. Only four members of the expedition escaped the Indian captors." In the interest of balance, why are the words "made to labor" used in reference to Indians when they are being made to work and why is the word "enslaved" used to describe the situation of the murdering invaders when they are stopped by the Indians? Why is "enslaved" not used to describe Indians "living" in a Spanish settlement?

One frame shows a large picture of De Soto in relation to the small print caption of "cruelties in Florida." The easily overlooked picture shows the Spaniards cutting off hands and feet of Indians, and looting and burning a village. Under De Soto's picture it reads, "In return, he was to receive titles, lands, and a share of the colonies' profits." It does not say that the mercenary invaders were willing to kill any number of Indians in exchange for glory and money.

A frame that depicts the Tatham Mound of West Central Florida reads, "Studies of human remains from the site indicates that there was violent conflict with the Spaniards and, possibly, an epidemic that killed 74 natives who were found in a single mass burial." If there was violent conflict "with" the Spaniards, it implies that the violence was on the part of the natives, unidentified as a tribe. It also implies that the number of natives that were killed by an epidemic was a much larger proportion of the "natives" than were killed in the confrontation. In the interest of balance, exactly how many Indians encountered how many Europeans in this conflict and how many on each side died?

On a frame that depicts De Soto's crossing of the Mississippi it says, "For nearly the entire way, they were harassed by the Indians." Were the Japanese "harassed" by Americans after the bombing of Pearl Harbor on December 7th, 1941 or was that justifiable defense of one's homeland? The word "harassed" again places the Indians in an offensive rather than a defensive situation.

In the frame entitled "Pre-Columbia Taino" it says "In some cases Natives coveted European objects that resembled aboriginal artifacts." If they looked like ours, they probably were. On the day of the first protest at the Museum, it probably looked like we were "coveting" the objects of the Europeans as in the Taino exhibit, but we were only noticing how much it looked like "our stuff."

Another frame reads as though it might be a real concession to balance when it says, "Although the impact on native populations was largely negative, the expeditions did result in the first exploration of the Grand Canyon and the Rio Grande watershed." Any sentence that begins with "although" is an apologetic attempt. It also plays into the European idea that anything is expendable, even human life, in the quest for "knowledge." This same kind of imperialist thinking today is used to justify the expenditure on the space program rather than on social programs for the homeless, our children or our elders. In the European minds the quest for expansion, whether in the name of knowledge or land, justifies the expenditure of the many for the few.

Under a frame that reads "La Florida Is Settled" is a picture of a praying priest. Catholicism and priests are icons of the European and any destruction of the icons represents the "heathenism" of those doing the destroying. The caption reads, "Algonquian Indians from the northern area of La Florida murder Father Segura and his Jesuit companions in 1571." In the interest of balance, please remember that this resulted after a period of 79 years of murder and cultural destruction by the invaders. The implication throughout is that the Europeans are conquerors and the Indians are "murderers."

In the frame entitled "Effects of European Contact on Aboriginal Societies: Disease, Disjunction, Depopulation," it reads "Spanish exploration and settlement of the Caribbean and La Florida infected the Native Peoples with the Old World pathogens. During the two centuries following Columbus's first voyage, these diseases killed millions of aborigines. It is a horrible paradox that the early Spanish expeditions that provide us with our only views of native cultures at the time of European contact also first introduced the diseases that ultimately led to the demise of those same cultures. It is disheartening to learn that our society is built upon the graves of millions of Native Americans who lived in the New World in 1492." The apologetic wording here is particularly revealing. In effect it says that the Europeans didn't deliberately wipe out the Americans but that it was an unintended consequence due to the Americans' own susceptibility to disease. How were the Europeans to know that these sweet and gentle peoples had no immunity to their diseases, such as greed and power, mumps and typhoid? It also implies that once disease had wiped out the Indian populations, there was just vacant land waiting to be claimed by the European settlers. This kind of thinking is still fostered by the government today. If there are no more real Indians left then the government can take and use even the small amounts of land that had been given to the descendants of the "real" Indians. The blatant genocide practiced by the early invaders has become a more subtle form of genocide regulated by government policy. If explicitly stated the "horrible paradox" referred to here would say, "We were just getting to know these Indians and they just up and died." This is another disavowal of their role in the deliberate destruction of the Indians.

This frame also lists possible disease epidemics in Florida in 1512–1562: 1513–1515 malaria, 1519–1524 smallpox, 1528– measles or typhoid fever, 1535–1539 unidentified, 1545–1548 bubonic plague, 1549– typhus, 1550– mumps, 1559– influenza.

The information is taken from a book, called *Their Number Become Thinned* by Henry Dobyns (1983). It is curious that this book is used to validate the theory that the Indians just "died." This book has been reviewed by many since its publication, including Dr. Jerald T. Milanich, curator in archaeology at the Florida Museum of Natural History. In his review, Milanich says "Using bits and pieces of information from various sources, [Dobyns] records the years of the epidemics. But he assumes what needs to be proven, that epidemics were pan-continental and that the Native Americans failed to develop immunities for over three centuries." He adds, "[Dobyns] supports his statements with misinterpretations and misrepresentations of data," and concludes that "a scholarly press like the University of Tennessee should have had the volume better reviewed before publishing it" (see *Agriculture and Human Values,* Vol. II, No. 3, 1985, pp. 84–85). My intent here is not to evaluate anthropological debates but to ask what political purpose these debates serve. One is to deflect the focus from murder and genocide and the reparations which these acts would demand to disease as an unintended consequence. Another purpose is to deflect attention away from the social problems that the Indian peoples face today by emphasizing that most of the Indians died out by the 1600s.

Underneath a frame which depicts Indians killing themselves to avoid enslavement, the narrative reads, "Although the native people could and did resist the Europeans, they could not fight the silent killers, Old World diseases." Again, this is the same old song. "We didn't murder them, they just died, therefore we have no moral responsibility today."

Under a frame reading "Early Spanish shipwrecks," it says, "Between 1500 and 1650, more than 180 tons of gold and 1600 tons of silver reached Spain from the New World." Here again "New World" shows from which viewpoint history is seen and the remainder of this passage needs no comment.

Under a frame showing how Indians were perceived by Europeans of the day is an engraving by Vischer (circa 1500) depicting Indians engaging in cannibalism. The caption reads, "Like mindless and innocent animals they destroy each other, then roast the flesh as their usual fare." Think about what had been going on between 1492 and 1660, between Columbus's description of these sweet and gentle people and the mindless and innocent animals description of 1660. It is easier to justify the killing of subhuman mindless animals for the purpose of stealing gold, silver and land than it is to kill sweet and gentle people for the same reasons. A national ideology had to develop in order to justify the continued raping of America and the killing of its people. This exhibit is helping to perpetuate that ideology.

One of the greatest ironies of this exhibit is displayed in one of the final frames entitled "Archaeological Looting." Its caption reads, "Human skull and broken ceramic artifacts left behind by looters interested in treasure rather than history." The obvious message here is that archaeologists have the expertise and training for intelligent looting and therefore only they should be allowed to dig up America. As for those only interested in treasure, that is the history of America from the Indian point of view. Maybe if the archaeologists dug up the bones of their own ancestors, they could learn something about them that would explain to the Indian peoples of North and South America the nature of these violent, greedy and bloodthirsty Europeans who destroyed, not discovered, America.

The video that concludes the exhibit seems to be a sales pitch for archaeology as does the whole exhibit. For those interested in archaeology as a career it might have some value. For Indians who have been trying to stop the archaeological desacralization of our burial mounds, it offers new evidence that the practice is indeed ongoing. Indians in both hemispheres have been approaching the many museums known to have been engaged in grave robbing. Invariably, we are told that the museum in question is not currently in possession of any human remains.

This video begins with a discussion of a burial mound in Florida called Tatham Mound. The narrator, holding a bone in his hand, says, "The study of human skeletons is a cornerstone to our understanding of ancient life." Yet they seem to have learned almost nothing from history. For the archaeologists, the only good Indian is still a dead Indian. The live ones, they think, protest too much.

Epilogue

On the first day of the Gainesville protest, we asked to speak to the museum director and to the curators of this exhibit. They refused to meet with us or to discuss the omission of truth that their "official" history required. This was an impromptu demonstration, but the brusque response by the officials of the University of Florida and the FMNH to Indian demands that a Native perspective be included in the exhibit doubled our anger and frustration over the 500 years of exclusion from the history of this continent. We decided to stage an ongoing protest to begin on December 7, Pearl Harbor Day, a day that Indians recognize as the *second* invasion of America.

Our protest had a small beginning but quickly grew as students and visitors to the museum began to listen to our critique and read the literature we had assembled to provide a more balanced account of the first encounters. The literature included my review of the exhibit. Our demands to the museum were that the Committee for American Indian History (CAIH) be given 1,000 square feet of space and the time to create an addition to the exhibit that would balance the Eurocentric account presented. These demands were unheeded even when presented to the president of the University and the director of the museum by the American Civil Liberties Union and our cooperating attorney. Even though they granted that we had the right to freedom of speech, they would not give the protestors the freedom of access to the public that is always reserved for the official institutions of the state. These institutions carry a legitimacy that can't be attained by those carrying cardboard protest signs out on the sidewalks in front of their institutions. In the minds of the American public, the truth is whatever gets presented to them through their school texts, museums, media and academic institutions. It is no accident that native peoples have been excluded from these state controlled truth vaults for 500 years. Our only access to these minds was through the media that was interested in the fact that we were protesting. Our problem was to get the media to understand our message and to give it to the public. Because of the protest, the media around the state began to pay attention to our demands for inclusion. The *Gainesville Sun* allowed us to publish *Exhibiting Ideology* as a guest editorial so we could speak in our own words.

The protesters began a ten-day encampment outside the museum, which lasted until December 16th, graduation day at the University. Instead of functioning as an educational institution and using the protest as an occasion to foster dialogue about diverse points of view, the management mentality of the museum director led him to call in the police. During these ten days, the protesters were harassed by the university police and museum security. One police officer in plain clothes identified himself as a *Miami Herald* reporter and photographer while interviewing and photographing the protesters. The protest site in front of the museum began to look like a shanty town with sleeping bags, lawn chairs, food and extra clothing sharing the tables that were set up by the protesters for distributing their literature. During the night, the temperatures dropped into the low 20s and 30s, but we were allowed no heaters at the concrete entrance to the museum, nor were we allowed to use the outdoor electrical receptacle to plug in coffee pots, lights, or radios. The police said that while we were allowed to maintain our vigil, we were not allowed to sleep on public property. Therefore, police were stationed on the site around the clock to insure that any protester who dozed during the night would be promptly awakened. Constant efforts were made by the protesters to keep on good terms with the individual police officers and to educate them about the reason why the protest was being staged. All strategy planning meetings were held on the site with the police in hearing distance.

In spite of the rather harsh atmosphere of the overnight vigils, many students brought their school work with them and participated in the vigils while they were studying for their final examinations.

During the ten-day encampment, two students, Michelle Diamond and Paul Finkelstein were arrested. They were charged with trespassing, failing to obey a police officer and resisting arrest without violence. Michelle's arrest came when she participated in a demonstration staged on the replica of the *Niña*. The *Niña* was highlighted by the museum as the main attraction of the exhibit. Dressed in authentic costumes provided by the museum, visiting school children acted out the roles of explorers and conquerors. They were prepared for these roles by the education coordinator of the museum, whose job is to visit local schools with the official supplementary curricular material for teachers to use in preparing their students for the tour. On weekends, classes of children assumed the roles of conquistadors in staged enactments on the replica. The children stayed completely in character even during questions from other visitors. The curriculum supplements and the play-acting are designed to teach the children the excitement of discovery and conquest — conquest of the seas, the new lands, and the people "encountered." The visiting children were also able to purchase mementos of the exhibit from the museum gift shop, including a coloring book called *Columbus Discovers America*, with the implicit directions, "Color me conqueror!"

Protesters had been told that they were not allowed to carry protest signs inside the museum. The signs might be too thought-provoking! Instead, they carried the signs in under their shirts and once inside quickly pinned them to the outside of their clothing. Technically, they were "wearing," not carrying the signs. Once inside, the protestors quietly surrounded the ship, while Michelle Diamond climbed onto the stern of the ship and sat down wearing a sign that read, "Florida State Museum teaches racism to kids." There were no signs warning against trespassing on the ship. Children had routinely climbed aboard the ship during tours and during the scheduled theater hours. Michelle was the only protester actually on-board the ship. The police surrounded the protesters but no moves were made to arrest anyone. Everyone was standing still while the television cameras and the news photographers, who had been warned that something significant would occur, did their thing. The museum director walked onto the scene, saw Michelle on the boat and immediately ordered the police to arrest her. No five minute warning was given for her to vacate the ship, as is usual in trespass cases. The officers lifted Michelle and carried her away.

Following the arrest, the protest attracted more sympathizers, including the Hillel Jewish Student Center, the National Organization for Women, the Students for the Ethical Treatment of Animals, and the Florida Greens. Members of the Anthropology Graduate Students Association began to do research using our reading guides and then created panels using photographs and laser prints to depict the atrocities committed against native peoples as witnessed by Friar Bartolomé de las Casas in the 16th century. Protestor Paul Finkelstein was in the process of placing one of these panels on a column outside the museum during a press conference when police grabbed him, handcuffed his hands behind his back and carried him to the lobby of the museum, where they placed him on his knees and left him there for visitors to view during the rest of the press conference. They charged him with opposing an officer and resisting arrest without violence. He spent the night in jail.

As graduation day neared and parents and alumni began arriving on campus, the police and the university administration became more restrictive. On graduation day we were told that the museum and the O'Connel Center were now private property and that any protesters would be arrested without warning.

Blacks, Indigenous People and the Churches, 1992

Ending the Pain, Beginning the Hope

Jean Sindab

[A] noble man . . . was by the Spaniards burnt alive. While he was at the stake, there came to him a monk of St. Francis, who began to talk to him of God and the Articles of our Faith, telling him to make sure his salvation if he believed. Upon which words . . . [he] asked the monk if the door of Heaven was open to the Spaniards, who answered, Yes, to the good Spaniards. Then replied the other, Let me go to Hell that I may not come where they are. —Bartolomé de las Casas, from *History of the Indies.*

In 1992, the international community is set to observe the anniversary of an event that shaped the world as we know it today. It will mark 500 years since Christopher Columbus set sail for India and ended up in the Americas, setting in motion a pattern of unequaled exploitation and oppression which continues until today.

Most of the discussion about his momentous event focuses on its impact on indigenous peoples of the Americas. Indeed, the Spanish government is set to celebrate this anniversary as "an encounter between two worlds." But it was *not* just an encounter between two worlds — but between three worlds: Europe, the Americas, and Africa. The coming together of these three continents was a cataclysmic event which bound together the destinies of their people.

In this background paper, I will focus on how the events of 1492 affected blacks and indigenous peoples, how they gave rise to the phenomenon of racism, which has been the historic and present role of the church, and finally

Background paper for Continental Consultation on Racism in the Americas, Rio de Janerio, Brazil, September 23 to 29, 1990, by Jean Sindab, Ph.D., director of Economic, Environmental Justice and Hunger Concerns, National Council of Churches.

135

how we can move forward as black and indigenous people to engage the
church in ending the pain of the last 500 years and begin to move into the
21st century in a world of justice, peace and respect for the integrity of
creation.

Beginning of the Pain: Invasion of the Americas

Adam Smith, the father of capitalism, and Karl Marx, the father of
Marxism — two men who represented very opposing views of the world — were
united on one issue: that Christopher Columbus's invasion of the Americas
in 1492 and Vasco da Gama's sailing round the Cape of Good Hope in Africa
in 1498 were the two most important events in the growth and development
of the Western world. In fact, they changed the history of humankind. These
exploratory ventures gave a strong impetus to trade, commerce and industry
in Europe, and laid the foundation for the wealth and power of Europe and
the Americas. This was in fact the objective. Hosea Jaffe, a historian, informs
us that "Europe was driven outwards not by wealth but by poverty." It was
the need for gold bullion and other treasures not available in Europe which
drove the Europeans toward the Americas to find ways to make their life
easier.[1]

The Spanish monarchy invested in Columbus's invasion force on the condition that he would repay this investment with profit by bringing back gold,
spices and other tribute. Columbus was followed by other invaders with the
same objective. Francisco Pizarro, after invading Peru, returned to Europe
with enough gold to provide its main source of bullion during the next three
centuries. Motivated by material greed, justified by ambitions to strike down
the pagan religion and win souls for Christ, these invaders set out to destroy
and steal. Within three years of Cortés's invasion of Mexico the ancient civilization of the Aztecs lay in ruins, its gold and precious stones at his disposal.[2]

This plunder and theft also took place in Africa. Jaffe informs us that by
1500 Portugal alone had taken some 700 tons of gold out of Africa, which
amounted to a massive primary accumulation of capital for Europe.[3] This
brutal search for profits and wealth was accomplished to the detriment of
black and indigenous peoples. The invasion of the Americas resulted in the
raping, torturing and killing of indigenous peoples. Within four years of Columbus's arrival on Hispaniola his men had killed or exported one third of
the original indigenous population of 300,000. When Columbus arrived in
the Americas there was an estimated population of 100 million indigenous
people throughout the hemisphere. Today that figure has been reduced to 35
million. Elaine Potiguara, a Brazilian indigenous woman, notes:

> During the entire period of Spanish and Portuguese colonization
> the Indians were subjected to a slow and fatal genocide. Today we
> are hardly 180 nations of the original 900. We are a scattered
> 200,000 out of the original 5 million Indians.[4]

A genocidal policy by the invaders resulted in massacres and death by the diseases they brought with them to the Americas. In addition the great indigenous civilizations — their religion, language and culture — were almost totally destroyed. Their land was sequestrated and it was only the spirit of resistance, which persists until today, which prevented indigenous people from being totally wiped from the face of the earth. Sadly, in the Caribbean some indigenous groups, e.g., the Arawaks, were in fact totally killed off.[5]

Invasion of Africa

As the indigenous peoples in the Americas were exterminated, the invaders found themselves forced to locate an alternative labor force to continue the exploitation of the vast resources of the Americas. Their eyes fell upon the African continent.

It was not the invasion of the Americas, however, which began the slave trade in Africa. Slavery had existed in Europe and Africa previously but primarily for domestic service, since there were no existing plantation systems or mines which generated a demand for large numbers of slaves. The opening up of the Americas was the historic development which changed all of this and doomed Africa to be a supply base for slave labor. In describing this ensuing slave trade one writer informs us:

> In terms of total numbers, focus upon a particular place, and tragic
> brutality it had no parallel in human history. This new black slave
> trade was larger, crueler, more systematic than anything Europe
> had known before. In many ways it was the most inhuman aspect
> of European history. For the middle passage remained for cen-
> turies one of the most brutal experiences inflicted by men upon
> men.[6]

Basil Davidson, the African historian, informs us that in 1518 a Spanish ship carried its first cargo of Africans from the Guinea coast to the Americas. This opened a slave trade which was to endure for three and a half centuries; for not only were the Africans available in abundant supply they were also found to be skilled in farming and mining.[7]

The Goree curator in Senegal puts the total number of Africans who lost their lives during the middle passage, or before by resisting capture, at 200 million. The numbers of slaves who actually reached the Americas were in the tens of millions.[8] This forced outflow of millions of Africans depopulated the continent and the devastating impact is still being felt today. This was the result of the events of 1492 which shaped the futures of Blacks and indigenous peoples for the next 500 years by generating an economic system and an ideological system to sustain it.

The Emergence of Racism and Capitalism

The history of 1492 clearly shows us that the rise of today's rich and powerful nations in Europe and the Americas was predicated on the stealing of indigenous land and forced labor of African slaves. This double thievery provided the economic and political power which established, maintained and expanded the exploitative capitalist system which today continues to perpetuate racism and inequality. However, the accumulation of wealth does not take place in a political and ideological vacuum. It is vitally important to create a context in which continued exploitation can be maintained. It is within this context that the growth of capitalist wealth gave rise to the ideology of racism. As Louis Ruchames writes:

> With the increase of slavery and the slave trade, and more numerous encounters of Europeans with Indians and Negroes, European scholars began to give greater attention to race and race difference. It is significant to note that it was only during the modern period that the term "race" came into use.[9]

As wealth expanded in this "new world" so did the tendency to see the world in black and white. Bernard Magubane describes the genesis of racial thought:

> The ideology of racism called into life and fed by the exploitative socioeconomic relations of capitalist imperialism, became a permanent stimulus for the ordering of unequal and exploitative relations of production along "racial" lines, and further demanded justification of these relations. The seemingly "autonomous" existence of racism today does not lessen the fact that it was initiated by the needs of capitalist development or that these needs remain the dominant factor in racist societies.[10]

In addition to serving these critical purposes, the ideology of racism served several other important functions for the oppressors. It "was a means of conquest, domination and rule. It was a means to unite the conquerors and demoralize the resister to enslave by enthusing the slave mentality that ensures docility."[11]

The Church and the Legitimation of Racism

Developing an ideology of racism, however, was not enough. That ideology had to be legitimized and institutionalized so that it became locked into the social consciousness of the society at large. It had to become part of the collective psyche. The horrors that accompanied the plundering of the Americas and Africa had to have a justification. The power of the church was called upon to undertake this legitimizing task. This is not surprising given the fact that the church had been involved with the invaders from the very beginning. A historian writing about this period tells us "The church was an intimate co-partner with colonial power and privilege and was in fact part and parcel of the state."[12] The ships coming to the Americas carried soldiers, merchants and missionaries. The missionaries' role of pacifying and evangelizing the indigenous peoples in the Americas was indispensable. With this process completed, the seizure of the land and mineral wealth was made easier.

The churches were instructed by the Crown of Spain to ensure that the peoples encountered in the Americas worked hard and were converted to Christianity. "Heathen, pagans" increasingly were the words used to describe both Blacks and indigenous peoples, thus making it acceptable to cast aside all acceptable legal and ethical norms of behavior in dealing with them. Many Europeans were of the opinion that their encounter with these "peoples" was the unfolding of a divine purpose that took precedence over teachings of Christian compassion and provided the justification for exploitation and enslavement. A Jesuit missionary on the West African coast wrote "the conversion of these barbarians is not to be achieved through love but only after they have been subdued by force of arms."[13]

It is this history which cast a lingering shadow on the church's relationship with racially oppressed people. Today the church still stands accused of racist practices and policies. It stands accused of aligning itself with the rich and powerful instead of the downtrodden. The church like society at large has relegated the racially-oppressed to the fringes of the church community. Blacks and indigenous Christians still struggle for full participation in the life of the church. Those who are not Christian struggle for respect for their spiritual and religious beliefs. Their designation as outsiders in society is due to the influence of the church. Just as the church has been responsible for the justification and legitimization of racism, they must now take earnest steps to reverse the process. Their approach to 1992 can be a significant beginning.

Ending the Pain: Beginning the Hope

The alienation of the church from the racially oppressed is sadly reflected in the fact that some churches are planning to celebrate 1992 as "500 years of evangelism." There is no victory for the church in celebrating conversion to Christianity through coercion, threats and repression. Such conversions were based not on the holy word of God but on the greedy imperatives of the state, which used the church to sanctify the holocaust it unleashed on racially oppressed people. In 1992, the church must not only recall its conversions over the last 500 years, it must show signs of its repentance and reflection. It should be a time for governments and churches to come to terms with what the white penetration of the Americas and Africa has meant for their people.

How should churches prepare for 1992? What should be their role? While there are shameful parts of the church history, there have been times when it has also been among the first to challenge the state on its treatment of oppressed people. There are many individuals within church structures who are deeply committed to the church disengaging from any collusion with racism and racial practices. Because of their efforts, today there are increasing signs of hope that the church will live up to its potential as a united advocate for racial justice.

One of the challenges for the churches is to stand with indigenous and black people in solidarity as they define the significance of 1992 and the way in which it should be commemorated. The churches are making a good beginning towards this end. The National Council of Churches of Christ in the United States approved a resolution condemning Columbus's invasion of the New World because "it resulted in church-supported racism, enslavement of Indians and moral decadence." The proposer of the resolution, an indigenous cleric, declared "the only thing Columbus discovered was that he was lost." This resolution states that what some historians have termed a discovery was in reality "an invasion and colonization of the land that has led to their descendants' impoverished lives, and a deep level of institutional racism and moral decadence." The resolution then goes on to make a strong confessing statement that "theological justifications for destroying native religious beliefs while forcing conversion to European forms of Christianity demanded a submission from the newly converted that facilitated their total conquest and exploitation."[14]

At the UN Subcommission on Racial Discrimination, 25 nongovernmental organizations called on the UN to provide assurances that "indigenous peoples are not hidden from the world during 1992 to suffer further in ignominy the tragic distortion of their history . . . this anniversary marks the beginning of their impoverishment, oppression and in many cases their genocide." A number of ecumenically-related organizations signed this statement.[15]

The World Council of Churches (WCC), which consists of over 300 member churches, has also taken steps to demonstrate solidarity with the racially oppressed with regard to 1992.

WCC Seventh General Assembly

In March, 1990, the WCC convened a global consultation on Justice, Peace, and the Integrity of Creation, a theme of the churches for the past seven years intended to unite them to work together on these issues. For the first time at a WCC meeting, there were a large number of indigenous and black participants who exercised considerable influence on the meeting. A covenant on racism was issued which declared:

> We covenant together to use the occasion of the 500th anniversary of the invasion of the Americas, not for glorification, but for confession, reparation and repentance for the brutal genocide and exploitation of indigenous people; we convenant to join actively in the land rights struggles of indigenous people as they struggle against racist institutions and policies which rape the land and resources; we covenant to fight against the violence of racism done to people in the first world context.[16]

Yes, we can say these are just words, but they do in fact represent new words for the church. There are now some empowered Black and indigenous people within the church structures determined to make things happen in activities around 1992 and beyond. The 1990 covenants agreed upon in Seoul are going forward to the 7th General Assembly of the WCC at Canberra. The Assembly is a major event for the ecumenical community. It occurs every seven years and brings together Christians from all over the world to discuss issues of significance for the church and society. This Assembly will receive numerous reports and resolutions dealing with the issues of racism against Blacks and indigenous peoples, and land rights. There is no question but that these issues will have a strong impact on the proceedings and will result in setting forth an ecumenical agenda in which they will be earnestly addressed.

The theme for the Assembly is "Come, Holy Spirit, renew the whole Creation." This theme is a fitting one to challenge the churches not only for their assembly, but for their planned approach to 1992. The pursuance of this theme into 1992 and beyond will address the major issues confronting both Black and indigenous communities today.

The legacy of 1492 has been injustice, racism, oppression, war, poverty, illiteracy, the ill-health of millions and the destruction of the earth. The unemployment which is a dominate feature of these communities today can only be overcome by a determination on the part of all social institutions to adopt a program of radical transformation that is committed to justice. The church stands as one of the strongest and most important institutions to lead the way.

Blacks and Indigenous People Prepare for 1992

Clearly Blacks and indigenous people are not simply sitting back and waiting for the churches to take action on 1992. They have begun their own plans. Both groups view 1992 as an opportunity to remind the global community of the desperate plight that is a reality for so many of their peoples.

The large number of Blacks in Central and Latin America is one of the best kept secret legacies of the invasion of 1492. Blacks throughout the region have started to tear down this wall of invisibility and silence about the racism and injustice they face. A Pan-American African congress is to be convened in October 1992. It is being organized by Mundo Afro, an Uruguyan group which is concerned about "rekindling the cultural values of their ancestors, the labor situation of Blacks and lack of opportunities for black women." Mundo Afro is demanding that the Black presence and contribution to Uruguay be acknowledged. The fact is ignored, for instance, that Black battalions fought in the war of independence for Uruguay. Despite this contribution, 80 percent of the Blacks work in the service industry with 75 percent of black women employed as domestic workers. Young Blacks usually drop out of school at 14 or 15 to enter the unskilled labor force where they can be easily exploited. Less than 50 Blacks have earned a university degree.[17]

In Brazil, where you have the largest numbers of Blacks outside of Africa their condition of oppression is covered up with the myth of "racial democracy." We are told that the basic problem in Brazil is poverty. However, there is certainly a clear and strong correlation between poverty and racism when of 13 million children on the street, over half are Black. Blacks swell the ranks of the unemployed and uneducated. They are in the favellas, they suffer from bad housing, inadequate health care and discrimination. Their conditions are the same as Blacks throughout the Americas who unequivocally are victims of racism.

Lack of space does not permit us to give details for Blacks in other parts of the Americas, but a statistical profile of their situation is just as bleak. The women are triply oppressed, suffering from racism, sexism and classism. The only country in the Americas where there is an *acknowledged* exploited large black population is the United States. It is hoped that the activities around 1992 will change that. It is crucially important that Blacks not be left out of the programs around 1992, and that the racism they struggle against daily becomes visible to the global community. As yet, the churches have not spoken out on the significance of this year for Blacks in the Americas. They must join with Blacks in planning activities.

Indigenous peoples have been preparing for 1992 for a long time. The UN Working Group on Indigenous Peoples has endorsed a number of resolutions and action plans, to ensure that the significance of the year receives high visibility. Several continent-wide meetings were scheduled for the years leading up to 1992. In a paper prepared for one of these meetings, indigenous people declared:

> The conquest and the mentality of "Manifest Destiny" still prevails
> . . . thus October 12, 1992, presents a great opportunity not to celebrate, not to cry about our bad luck, but rather to reflect upon 500 years of the European invasion and to formulate alternatives for a better life, in harmony with nature and with Human dignity.[18]

Blacks and Indigenous Together

While we can cite examples of Blacks and indigenous people separately preparing for 1992, there are rare situations in which we find them working closely together in coalitions involved not only in the planning for 1992, but on a more general level of the social justice struggle. There are many historic reasons for this reality. The strategy of divide and rule by the oppressor has been effectively applied to both communities. Both groups often find themselves jockeying for recognition of the primacy of their struggle. We compete with each other for the highest "suffering index," each insisting that their situation is the worst and, therefore, more "deserving" of attention and resources, each attempting to legitimize their claims to the resources. For too long, we have viewed each other through the eyes of the oppressor and taken on some of the same prejudicial feelings and racist attitudes and actions exhibited by them. Their stereotypes have often become ours. Our relationship has almost been reduced to quarreling over the meager crumbs which fall from the oppressors' table.

Our meeting, unfortunately, will not stop such debates and arguments, but with hope, it will do one historic thing: it will bring us together in one room to discuss our common history and our common legacy and ways in which we may be able to come together in one movement. The extent to which we are successful toward that end will be the ultimate test of this meeting.

The uniting of Blacks and indigenous peoples should not be an impossible dream. We are bonded together by the fact that this land in the Americas has been soaked by the blood of both of our ancestors, watered by their tears, and made productive by the sweat of their brows. Yet, today, we reap nothing of their sacrifices. It is clear from the brief historical overview presented here that the destinies of Blacks and indigenous people are closely linked and intertwined. And yet that history has not generated contemporary strategic alliances that would be helpful in breaking the shackles of oppression. That was not always so. Our historic victimization which yoked us together for the past 500 years forces us into an alliance against a common enemy. History is replete with documented evidence of Blacks and indigenous peoples fighting side by side against the oppressor. Indigenous communities sheltered runaway slaves, and those slaves in turn helped those communities strengthen their resistance to the invaders.

However, the connection between our people did not start only at the initiation of the Europeans who threw our societies together. As a new school text informs us:

> Some scientists and historians believe that African sailors, merchants and explorers came to the Americas long before Columbus and other European explorers. They point to studies which have compared the languages of the Caribbean and the West African peoples and have found common words in the languages of the two regions. Many sculptures portraying African people have been found at sites in Mexico. African skeletons have been uncovered in the Caribbean.[19]

These are not new findings. They have been discussed for years, together with the information on sea crossings by Africans to the Americas. What is new is that school children are now being taught this in their curriculums. That is a very hopeful sign indeed.

At the same time, we have to acknowledge that there is also a basis for non-cooperation between the two peoples, reflecting a sad side to our history. In the United States, black cavalry soldiers pursued indigenous peoples together with the whites. Indigenous peoples, on the other hand, were also among the slave-owning population in the United States. The peaceful ties and alliances that once existed among our people have been broken. Yet reasons for our coming together have never been stronger. The 500 years event might perhaps be an opportunity for us to start to rebuild some of those ties of early solidarity.

We can begin in a very basic way, with the full acknowledgment that 1992 is just as significant for Blacks as for indigenous peoples in the Americas. We must challenge the attempts to obscure or omit the black involvement in 1992 activities.

We must also carefully examine terms that we use to define ourselves and our struggle. In a real sense the term Blacks and indigenous peoples is misleading. Blacks in the Americas are *also* indigenous people. They are indigenous to the African continent. Their bonding to their land was broken when they were stolen and brought to the Americas. A real beginning should be made to lay claim to their motherland which was broken when they were stolen and brought to the Americas. They must also lay claim to the motherland in a spiritual and cultural sense to provide them with the sense of being and belonging which is necessary to move our struggle forward, and be empowered by our ancestral roots. We are not just "black." That term simply describes a color, it does not provide an identity. We are African American people. That is one of the bases for our alliances. In addition, the intermixing between Blacks and indigenous people stretching back over the last 500 years provides a context for our renewed cooperation.

The calls for solidarity are being heard by both sides increasingly and in different parts of the Americas. They are based not simply on a desire for unity, but from a realistic understanding of the need for such unity. An African American brother from the United States, in addressing the ethnic communities of Canada, urged us forward, saying:

> From [this perspective], the necessity for solidarity between all peoples-of-colour with their many friends and supporters throughout the world, is not simply a philosophic imperative, but a survival imperative. For the political, economic and social "divide-and-conquer" ploys of the oppressor intensify with every gain peoples-of-colour achieve, whether on Native American reservations, or in the Black communities of the peoples of African descent throughout the world.[20]

The unity we seek, however, must be based on some common goal and objective. We still have to determine the aspects we need to jointly focus upon in raising our demands. The one area where we have wide agreement and where we experience our most harsh exploitation, remains in the economic sector. The same greedy drive for profit and the accumulation of capital which was the impetus for 1492 still shapes the political, economic, and social parameters of our existence. Together we suffer economic exploitation. The Reverend Antonio Santana of the Program to Combat Racism in the United Methodist Church in Brazil points this out, noting:

> These struggles are directed against State or Government economic policies when these aggravate the economic situation in our countries. The results of [these economic] policies affect primarily the oppressed sections of the population and, in the nature of things, doubly harm the Black and Indigenous peoples who suffer both oppression and discrimination. Equally important are the struggles against the regional economic strategies designed by the various governments which tend to exclude Black and Indian regions from development plans and programmes. By this attitude they increase still further the state of poverty of these regions.[21]

We must use 1992 as an opportunity to challenge the international community to stand in solidarity with us as we confront the exploitative systems which continue to oppress us. We must especially challenge the churches, to move beyond words to concrete actions of solidarity. The Program to Combat

Racism of the WCC was established to do just that. We have insisted that Blacks and indigenous people define the reality of 1992 for the churches. Not to allow that to happen is not only a racist act of the churches, but would be a disempowering one as well. We in PCR are encouraging the church to stretch out its hand in a genuine partnership. The church must move closer to the people. It must fulfill the gospel which calls for a renouncing of riches and wealth and for solidarity with the poor who are not poor because of God's will, but because of oppression and exploitation. The words of Emilio Castro, General Secretary of the WCC, are encouraging to us. In discussing the role of the church he asserts, "The place of the church is not in the corridors of power, but in the streets, alongside the people."[22] Is the church ready to attack the root causes of poverty? In the next 500 years, can we learn as well as teach, receive as well as give? That is the challenge for us in the church. We must together discover ways that we can empower our communities, to increase their visibility in relation to 1992.

Neither the church nor any other institution can be responsible for our liberation; we must liberate ourselves. What is the way forward for us? We must begin to define our reality and recognize our power. In many countries of the Americas we are considered minorities. Yet in several Central and South American countries, such as Peru, Ecuador, Bolivia and Guatemala, the majority of the population is indigenous. In the United States there are 30 million Blacks, in Brazil alone there are 50 million. We can be a powerful force for 1992 and beyond by shaping the political issues for the 21st century. We must remember that it has been *our* demands for justice which have stood at the center of the struggle for radical social change. Our demands for land, for equality, for peace, for justice have shaped liberation theology and infused the church with new purpose. Our resistance to oppression has been the catalyst for social change. This we have accomplished working separately. Our potential and our full power would be even more developed if we joined forces. There are some hopeful signs in that direction. We must build on them and strengthen the calls for unity against the exploitative and oppressive forces arrayed against us since 1492. We have to heed the calls for coalition and partnership coming from those people of vision within our communities.

An indigenous brother from the International Indian Treaty Council in the United States in responding to our invitation to this meeting, welcomed the initiative, declaring:

> At this moment peoples of color in the Americas can do much to organize and defend themselves against the onslaught of further destruction of their rainforests, mineral resource exploitation and the promotion of eurocentrism. It demands for all oppressed and people of color to join together in unity, and spiritual solidarity.

He suggested that it would be good for the Pope to receive "indigenous leaders from the whole continent" as a way to help understanding in connection with the 1992 anniversary.

What Is the Way Forward?

What can we do to bind our peoples together in a continental coalition to address the issues that confront and challenge our communities on a daily basis? This meeting is convened to help you find the answers to that question. However, I would like to conclude with some action suggestions:

1. We must search together for the common ground of our struggle, to form the basis for our coalition work.

2. We must become an inclusive movement for social change. Our situation is too desperate to exclude any parts of our communities from active participation in the struggle. We must include our women as full partners in the decision-making and all levels of our struggle. Women have much to contribute. We must ensure that ending women's oppression is a central and strong part of the movement for social justice.

3. We must begin an exchange of ideas between our communities by inviting each other to our meetings, conferences, etc. We must work together on all our planned activities for 1992.

4. We must urge the leadership of our communities to educate their constituencies about our common issues.

5. We must issue joint challenges to governments, international organizations, and churches on 1992.

Conclusion

Sisters and Brothers, let this meeting be the beginning of our joint efforts to challenge the racial oppression we suffer. This racism set in motion by Columbus's bad navigational skills continues to have an equal impact on indigenous and black peoples throughout the Americas. It is this racism that is one of the dominant issues to be addressed as we go forward. The activities planned around the 500 years invasion will point the way toward ending the pain of the last half millennium.

Chapter Notes

1. Hosea Jaffe, *A History of Africa* (London: Zed Press, 1985), p. 43.
2. Paul Gorden Lauren, *Power and Prejudice: The Politics and Diplomacy of Racial Discrimination* (Boulder: Westview Press, 1988), p. 12.

3. Jaffe, p. 44.

4. Elaine Potiguara, *Indigenous Peoples Speak Your History,* Geneva PCR Information, No. 24, 1988, p. 14.

5. Potiguara, p. 15.

6. Lauren, p. 13.

7. Basil Davidson, *Africa in History* (New York: Collier Books, 1968), p. 180.

8. Jaffe, p. 48.

9. Bernard Magubane, *The Political Economy of Race and Class in South Africa* (New York: Monthly Review Press, 1979), p. 4.

10. Magubane, p. 6.

11. Jaffe, p. 56.

12. H. McKennie Goodpasture, *Cross and Sword: An Eyewitness History of Christianity in Latin America* (New York: Orbis Books, 1989), p. 1.

13. Lauren, p. 14.

14. Resolution of National Council of Churches of Christ of the U.S.A., May 1990, General Secretariat Office, 475 Riverside Drive, New York, NY. Quotes in Lutheran World Information, No. 21. Geneva, Switzerland, 1990, p. 10.

15. Lutheran World Information, No. 42, Geneva, Switzerland, 1989, p. 15.

16. *Now Is the Time,* final document and other texts from World Convocation on Justice, Peace and Integrity of Creation, Seoul, Korea, 1990, p. 32.

17. *Latinamerica Press,* June 14, 1990, p. 7.

18. Background Paper: *500 Years of Indian Resistance Meeting,* Quito, Ecuador, July, 1990. CONAIE

19. Marta Bermudez, *History and Culture of Cuba,* Student Supplemental Text, Rochester City School District, 1989, pp. 12-13.

20. Statement by Robert Starling Pritchard, Chairman of Panamerican Panafrican Association, Inc. New York, July 1990.

21. Antonio Santana, *Blacks and Indians in Latin America and the Caribbean: Challenges for the Future,* WCC/PCR Paper, 1990, p. 3-4.

22. Ecumenical Press Service, Item 7, Geneva, Switzerland, August 1990.

Deconstructing the Columbus Myth

Ward Churchill

The Spaniards . . . never had any legal cause of quarrel against them, but only always an intention to exercise a fury on them greater than the most consuming and prodigal rage, that ever made the worst of tyrants infamous. — Bartolomé de las Casas, from *History of the Indies.*

Was the "Great Discoverer" Italian or Spanish, Nazi or Jew?

It is perhaps fair to say that our story opens at Alfred University, where, during the fall of 1990, I served as distinguished scholar of American Indian studies for a program funded by the National Endowment for the Humanities. Insofar as I was something of a curiosity in that primarily Euroamerican-staffed and attended institution, situated as it is within an area populated primarily by white folk, it followed naturally that I quickly became a magnet for local journalists seeking to inject a bit of color into their otherwise uniformly blanched columns and commentaries. Given our temporal proximity to the much-heralded quincentennial celebration of Christopher Columbus's late 15th century "discovery" of a "New World" and its inhabitants, and that I am construed as being in some part a direct descendant of those inhabitants, they were wont to query me as to my sentiments concerning the accomplishments of the Admiral of the Ocean Sea.

My response, at least in its short version, was (and remains) that celebration of Columbus and the European conquest of the Western Hemisphere he set off is greatly analogous to celebration of the glories of nazism and Heinrich Himmler. Publication of this remark in local newspapers around Rochester, New York, caused me to receive, among other things, a deluge of lengthy

Excerpted from Indigenous Thought *Vol. 1, No. 2/3, June 1991.*

and vociferously framed letters of protest, two of which I found worthy of remark.

The first of these was sent by a colleague at the university, an exchange faculty member from Germany, who informed me that while the human costs begat by Columbus's navigational experiment were "tragic and quite regrettable," comparisons between him and the Reichsführer SS were nonetheless unfounded. The distinction between Himmler and Columbus, his argument went, resided not only in differences in "the magnitude of the genocidal events in which each was involved," but the *ways* in which they were involved. Himmler, he said, was enmeshed as "a high-ranking and responsible official in the liquidation of entire human groups" as "a matter of formal state policy" guided by an explicitly "racialist" ideology. Furthermore, he said the enterprise Himmler created as the instrument of his genocidal ambitions incorporated, deliberately and intentionally, considerable economic benefit to the state in which service he acted. None of this pertained to Columbus, the good professor concluded, because the "Great Discoverer" was ultimately "little more than a gifted seaman," an individual who unwittingly set in motion processes over which he had little or no control, in which he played no direct part, and which might well have been beyond his imagination. My juxtaposition of the two men, he contended, therefore tended to "diminish understanding of the unique degree of evil" that should be associated with Himmler, and ultimately precluded "proper historical understandings of the Nazi phenomenon."

The second letter came from a member of the Jewish Defense League in Rochester. His argument ran that, unlike Columbus (whom he described as "little more than a bit player, without genuine authority or even much of a role, in the actual process of European civilization in the New World which his discovery made possible"), Himmler was a "responsible official in a formal state policy of exterminating an entire human group for both racial and economic reasons," and on a scale "unparalleled in all history." My analogy between the two, he said, served to "diminish public respect for the singular nature of the Jewish experience at the hands of the Nazis," as well as popular understanding of "the unique historical significance of the Holocaust." Finally, he added, undoubtedly as a crushing capstone to his position, "It is a measure of your antisemitism that you compare Himmler to Columbus" because "Columbus was, of course, himself a Jew."

I must confess that the last assertion struck me first, and only partly because I'd never before heard claims that Christopher Columbus was of Jewish ethnicity. "What possible difference could this make?" I asked in my letter of reply. "If Himmler himself were shown to have been of Jewish extraction, would it then suddenly become antisemitic to condemn him for the genocide he perpetrated against Jews, Gypsies, Slavs and others? Would his historical crimes then suddenly be unmentionable or even 'okay'?" To put it another way, I continued, "Simply because Meyer Lansky, Dutch Schultz, Bugsy

Siegel and Lepke were all Jewish 'by blood,' is it a gesture of antisemitism to refer to them as gangsters? Is it your contention that an individual's Jewish ethnicity somehow confers exemption from negative classification or criticism of his/her conduct? What are you saying?" The question of Columbus's possible Jewishness nonetheless remained intriguing, not because I held it to be especially important in its own right, but because I was (and am still) mystified as to why *any* ethnic group, especially one that has suffered genocide, might be avid to lay claim either to the man or to his legacy. I promised myself to investigate the matter further.

A Mythic Symbiosis

Meanwhile, I was captivated by certain commonalities of argument inherent to the positions advanced by my correspondents. Both men exhibited a near-total ignorance of the actualities of Columbus's career. Nor did they demonstrate any particular desire to correct the situation. Indeed, in their mutual need to separate the topic of their preoccupation from rational scrutiny, they appeared to have conceptually joined hands in a function composed more of faith than fact. The whole notion of the "uniqueness of the Holocaust" serves both psychic and political purposes for Jew and German alike, or so it seems. The two groups are bound to one another in a truly symbiotic relationship grounded in the mythic exclusivity of their experience: one half of the equation simply completes the other in a perverse sort of collaboration, with the result that each enjoys a tangible benefit.

For Jews, at least those who have adopted the zionist perspective, a "unique historical suffering" under nazism translates into fulfillment of a biblical prophecy that they are "the chosen," entitled by virtue of the destiny of a special persecution to assume a rarified status among — and to consequently enjoy preferential treatment from — the remainder of humanity. In essence, this translates into a demand that the Jewish segment of the Holocaust's victims must now be allowed to participate equally in the very system which once victimized them, and to receive an equitable share of the spoils accruing therefrom. To this end, zionist scholars such as Irving Louis Horowitz and Elie Wiesel have labored long and mightily, defining genocide in terms exclusively related to the forms it assumed under nazism. In their version of "truth," one must literally see smoke pouring from the chimneys of Auschwitz in order to apprehend that a genocide, *per se,* is occuring.[1] Conversely, they have coined terms such as "ethnocide" to encompass the fates inflicted upon other peoples throughout history.[2] Such semantics have served not as tools of understanding but as an expedient means of arbitrarily differentiating the experience of their people — both qualitatively and quantitatively — from that of any other. To approach things in any other fashion would, it must be admitted, tend to undercut ideas like the "moral right" of the Israeli settler state to impose itself directly atop the Palestinian Arab homeland.

For Germans to embrace a corresponding "unique historical guilt" because of what was done to the Jews during the 1940s, is to permanently absolve themselves of guilt concerning what they may be doing now. No matter how ugly things become in contemporary German society, or so the reasoning goes, it can *always* be (and is) argued that there has been a marked improvement over the "singular evil which was Nazism." Anything other than outright nazification is, by definition, "different," "better" and therefore "acceptable." ("Bad as they are, things could always be worse.") Business as usual — which is to say assertions of racial supremacy, domination and exploitation of "inferior" groups, and most of the rest of the nazi agenda — is thereby freed to continue in a manner essentially unhampered by serious stirrings of guilt among the German public so *long as it does not adopt the literal trappings of nazism.* Participating for profit and with gusto in the deliberate starvation of much of the Third World is no particular problem if one is careful not to goose step while one does it.

By extension, insofar as Germany is often seen (and usually sees itself) as exemplifying the crowning achievements of "Western Civilization," the same principle covers all European and Euro-derived societies. No matter what they do, it is never "really" what it seems unless it was done in precisely the fashion the nazis did it. Consequently, the nazi master plan of displacing or reducing by extermination the population of the western USSR and replacing it with settlers of "biologically superior German breeding stock" is roundly (and rightly) condemned as ghastly and inhuman. Meanwhile, people holding this view of nazi ambitions tend overwhelmingly to see consolidation and maintenance of Euro-dominated settler states in places like Australia, New Zealand, South Africa, Argentina, the United States, and Canada as "basically okay," or even as "progress." The "distinction" allowing this psychological phenomenon is that each of these states went about the intentional displacement and extermination of native populations, and their replacement, in a manner slightly different in its particulars from that employed by nazis attempting to accomplish exactly the same thing. Such technical differentiation is then magnified and used as a sort of all purpose veil, behind which almost anything can be hidden, so long as it is not openly adorned with a swastika.

Given the psychological, sociocultural, and political imperatives involved, neither correspondent, whether German or Jew, felt constrained to examine the factual basis of my analogy between Himmler and Columbus before denying the plausibility or appropriateness of the comparison. To the contrary, since the paradigm of their mutual understanding embodies the *a priori* presumption that there *must be no such analogy,* factual investigation is precluded from their posturing. It follows that any dissent on the "methods" involved in their arriving at their conclusions, never mind introduction of countervailing evidence, must be denied out of hand with accusations of "overstatement," "shoddy scholarship," "stridency" and or "antisemitism." To this litany have lately been added such new variations as "white bashing," "ethnic McCarthyism," "purveyor of political correctitude" and any other epithet deemed helpful in keeping a "canon of knowledge" fraught with distortion, deception and outright fraud from being "diluted."[3]

Columbus as Proto-Nazi

It is time to delve into the substance of my remark that Columbus and Himmler, nazi *Lebensraumpolitik* and the "settlement of the New World" bear more than casual resemblance to one another. It is not, as my two correspondents wished to believe, because of his "discovery." This does not mean that if this were "all" he had done he would be somehow innocent of what resulted from his find, no more than is the scientist who makes a career of accepting military funding to develop weapons in any way "blameless" when they are subsequently used against human targets. Columbus did not sally forth upon the Atlantic for reasons of "neutral science" or altruism. He went, as his own diaries, reports and letters make clear, fully expecting to encounter wealth belonging to others. It was his stated purpose to seize this wealth, by whatever means necessary and available, in order to enrich both his sponsors and himself.[4] Plainly, he prefigured, both in design and by intent, what came next. To this extent, he not only symbolizes the process of conquest and genocide that eventually consumed the indigenous peoples of America, but bears the personal responsibility of having participated in it. Still, if this were all there was to it, I might be inclined to dismiss him as a mere thug rather than branding him a counterpart to Himmler.

The 1492 "voyage of discovery" is, however, hardly all that is at issue. In 1493 Columbus returned with an invasion force of 17 ships, appointed at his own request by the Spanish Crown to install himself as "viceroy and governor of the Caribbean islands and the mainland" of America, a position he held until 1500.[5] Setting up shop on the large island he called Española (today Haiti and the Dominican Republic), he promptly instituted policies of slavery (*encomienda*) and systematic extermination against the native Taino population.[6] Columbus's programs reduced Taino numbers from as many as 8 million at the outset of his regime to about 3 million in 1496.[7] Perhaps 100,000 were left by the time of the governor's departure. His policies, however, remained, with the result that by 1514 the Spanish census of the island showed barely 22,000 Indians remaining alive. In 1542, only 200 were recorded.[8] Thereafter, they were considered extinct, as were Indians throughout the Caribbean Basin, an aggregate population which totalled more than 15 million at the point of first contact with the Admiral of the Ocean Sea, as Columbus was known.[9]

This, to be sure, constitutes an attrition of population in real numbers every bit as great as the toll of 12 to 15 million — about half of them Jewish — most commonly attributed to Himmler's slaughter mills. Moreover, the proportion of the indigenous Caribbean population destroyed by the Spanish in a single generation is, no matter how the figures are twisted, greater than the 75 percent of European Jews usually said to have been exterminated by the nazis.[10] Worst of all, these data apply *only* to the Caribbean Basin; the process of genocide in the Americas was only just beginning at the point such statistics become operant, not ending, as it was upon the fall of the Third Reich. All told, it is probable that more than 100 million native people were "eliminated" in the course of Europe's ongoing "civilization" of the Western Hemisphere.[11]

It has long been asserted by "responsible scholars" that this decimation of American Indians that accompanied the European invasion resulted primarily from disease rather than direct killing or conscious policy.[12] There is a certain truth to this, although starvation may have proven just as lethal in the end. It must be borne in mind when considering such facts that a considerable portion of those who perished in the nazi death camps died, not as the victims of bullets and gas, but from starvation, as well as epidemics of typhus, dysentery, and the like. Their keepers, who could not be said to have killed these people directly, were nonetheless found to have been culpable in their deaths by way of deliberately imposing the conditions that led to the proliferation of starvation and disease among them.[13] Certainly, the same can be said of Columbus's regime, under which the original residents were, as a first order of business, permanently dispossessed of their abundant cultivated fields while being converted into chattel, ultimately to be worked to death for the wealth and "glory" of Spain.[14]

Nor should more direct means of extermination be relegated to incidental status. As the matter is framed by Kirkpatrick Sale in his book, *The Conquest of Paradise:*

> The tribute system, instituted by the Governor sometime in 1495, was a simple and brutal way of fulfilling the Spanish lust for gold while acknowledging the Spanish distaste for labor. Every Taino over the age of 14 had to supply the rulers with a hawk's bell of gold every three months (or, in gold-deficient areas, 25 pounds of spun cotton); those who did were given a token to wear around their necks as proof that they had made their payment; those who did not were, as [Columbus's son] Fernando says discreetly "punished" — by having their hands cut off, as [the priest, Bartolomé de] Las Casas says less discreetly, and left to bleed to death.[15]

It is entirely likely that upwards of 10,000 Indians were killed in this way alone, on Española alone, as a matter of policy, during Columbus's tenure as governor. Las Casas's *Brevisima relación,* among other contemporaneous sources, is also replete with accounts of Spanish colonists (*hidalgos*) hanging Tainos *en masse*, roasting them on spits, or burning them at the stake (often a dozen or more at a time), hacking their children into pieces to be used as dog feed and so forth, all of it to instill in the natives a "proper attitude of respect" toward their Spanish "superiors."

> [The Spaniards] made bets as to who would slit a man in two, or cut off his head at one blow; or they opened up his bowels. They tore the babes from their mother's breast by their feet and dashed their heads against the rocks. . . . They spitted the bodies of other babes, together with their mothers and all who were before them, on their swords.[16]

No SS trooper could be expected to comport himself with a more unrelenting viciousness. And there is more. All of this was coupled to wholesale and persistent massacres:

> A Spaniard . . . suddenly drew his sword. Then the whole hundred drew theirs and began to rip open the bellies, to cut and kill [a group of Tainos assembled for this purpose] — men, women, children and old folk, all of whom were seated, off guard and frightened. . . . And within two credos, not a man of them there remains alive. The Spaniards enter the large house nearby, for this was happening at its door, and in the same way, with cuts and stabs, began to kill as many as were found there, so that a stream of blood was running, as if a great number of cows had perished.[17]

Elsewhere, las Casas went on to recount how:

> In this time, the greatest outrages and slaughterings of people were perpetrated, whole villages being depopulated. . . . The Indians saw that without any offense on their part they were despoiled of their kingdoms, their lands and liberties and of their lives, their wives and homes. As they saw themselves each day perishing by the cruel and inhuman treatment of the Spaniards, crushed to earth by the horses, cut in pieces by swords, eaten and torn by dogs, many buried alive and suffering all kinds of exquisite tortures . . . [many surrendered to their fate, while the survivors] fled to the mountains [to starve].[18]

The butchery continued until there were no Tainos left to butcher. One might well ask how a group of human beings, even those like the Spaniards of Columbus's day, maddened in a collective lust for wealth and prestige, might come to treat another with such unrestrained ferocity over a sustained

period. The answer, or some substantial portion of it, must lie in the fact that
the Indians were considered by the Spanish to be *Untermenschen,* subhumans.
That this was the conventional view is borne out beyond all question in the
recorded debates between las Casas and the nobleman, Francisco de
Sepúlveda, who argued for the majority of Spaniards that American Indians,
like African blacks and other "lower animals," lacked "souls." The Spaniards,
consequently, bore in Sepúlveda's estimation a holy obligation to enslave and
destroy them wherever they might be encountered.[19] The eugenics theories
of nazi "philosopher" Alfred Rosenberg, to which Heinrich Himmler more or
less subscribed, elaborated the mission of the SS in very much the same
terms.[20] It was upon such profoundly racist ideas that Christopher Columbus
grounded his policies as initial governor of the new Spanish empire in
America.[21]

In the end, all practical distinctions between Columbus and Himmler—
at least those not accounted for by differences in available technology and extent of socio-military organization—evaporate upon close inspection. They
are cut of the same cloth, fulfilling precisely the same function and for exactly
the same reasons, each in his own time and place. If there is one differentiation that may be valid, it is that while the specific enterprise Himmler represented ultimately failed and is now universally condemned, that
represented by Columbus did not and is not. Instead, as Sale has observed,
the model of colonialism and concomitant genocide Columbus pioneered
during his reign as governor of Española was to prove his "most enduring
legacy," carried as it was "by the conquistadors on their invasions of Mexico,
Peru and La Florida."[22] The Columbian process is ongoing, as is witnessed
by the fact that, today, his legacy is celebrated far and wide.

Chapter Notes

1. See, for example, Irving Louis Horowitz, *Genocide: State Power and Mass Murder*
(New Brunswick, N. J.: Transaction Books, 1976) and Elie Wiesel, *Legends of Our Time*
(New York: Holt, Rinehart and Winston, 1968). The theme is crystallized in Manvell,
Roger, and Heinrich Fraenkel, *Incomparable Crime; Mass Extermination in the 20th Cen-
tury: The Legacy of Guilt,* (London: Heinemann, 1967).
2. See, as examples, Richard Falk, "Ethnocide, Genocide, and the Nuremberg
Tradition of Moral Responsibility" (in Virginia Held, Sidney Morganbesser and
Thomas Nagel [eds.], *Philosophy, Morality, and International Affairs* [New York: Oxford
University Press,] 1974, pp. 123–37), Monroe C. Beardsley, "Reflections on
Genocide and Ethnocide" (in Richard Arens [ed.], *Genocide in Paraguay* [Philadelphia:
Temple University Press, 1976], pp. 85–101), and Robert Jaulin, *L'Ethnocide à travers
les Amériques* (Paris: Gallimard Publishers, 1972) and *La Décivilisation, Politique et Prati-
que de Ethnocide* (Paris: Presses Universitaires de France, 1974).
3. Assaults upon thinking deviating from Eurocentric mythology have been

published with increasing frequency in U.S. mass circulation publications such as *Time, Newsweek, U.S. News and World Report, Forbes, Commentary, Scientific American,* and the *Wall Street Journal* throughout 1990–91. A perfect illustration for our purposes here is Jeffrey Hart, "Discovering Columbus," *National Review,* October 15, 1990, pp. 56–7.

4. See Samuel Eliot Morison, (ed. and trans.), *Journals and Other Documents on the Life and Voyages of Christopher Columbus,* (New York: Heritage, 1963).

5. The letter of appointment to these positions, signed by Ferdinand and Isabella, and dated May 28, 1493, is quoted in full in Benjamin Keen (trans.), *The Life of the Admiral Christopher Columbus by His Son Ferdinand* (New Brunswick, N. J.: Rutgers University Press, 1959), pp. 105–6.

6. The best sources on Columbus's policies are Troy Floyd, *The Columbus Dynasty in the Caribbean, 1492–1526* (Albuquerque: University of New Mexico Press, 1973) and Stuart B. Schwartz, *The Iberian Mediterranean and Atlantic Traditions in the Formation of Columbus as a Colonizer* (Minneapolis: University of Minnesota Press, 1986).

7. Regarding the 8 million figure, see Sherburn F. Cook and Woodrow Borah, *Essays in Population History, Vol. 1,* (Berkeley: University of California Press, 1971), esp. Chap. VI. The 3 million figure pertaining to the year 1496 derives from a survey conducted by Bartolomé de las Casas in that year, covered in J.B. Thatcher, *Christopher Columbus, Vol. 2* (New York: Putnam's, 1903–1904), p. 348ff.

8. For summaries of the Spanish census records, see Lewis Hanke, *The Spanish Struggle for Justice in the Conquest of America* (Philadelphia: University of Pennsylvania Press, 1947), p. 200ff. Also see Salvador de Madariaga, *The Rise of the Spanish American Empire* (London: Hollis and Carter, 1947).

9. For aggregate estimates of the precontact indigenous population of the Caribbean Basin, see William Denevan (ed.), *The Native Population of the Americas in 1492* (Madison: University of Wisconsin Press, 1976), Henry Dobyns, *Their Numbers Become Thinned: Native American Population Dynamics in Eastern North America* (Knoxville: University of Tennessee Press, 1983) and Russell Thornton, *American Indian Holocaust and Survival: A Population History Since 1492* (Norman: University of Oklahoma Press, 1987). For additional information, see Dobyns's bibliographic *Native American Historical Demography* (Bloomington: Indiana University Press, Bloomington, 1976).

10. These figures are utilized in numerous studies. One of the more immediately accessible is Leo Kuper, *Genocide: Its Political Use in the Twentieth Century* (New Haven, Conn.: Yale University Press, 1981).

11. See Henry F. Dobyns, "Estimating American Aboriginal Population: An Appraisal of Techniques with a New Hemispheric Estimate," *Current Anthropology,* No. 7, pp. 395–416.

12. An overall pursuit of this theme will be found in P.M. Ashburn, *The Ranks of Death* (New York: Coward, 1947). Also see John Duffy, *Epidemics in Colonial America* (Baton Rouge: Louisiana State University Press, 1953). Broader and more sophisticated articulations of the same idea are embodied in Alfred W. Crosby, Jr., *The Columbian Exchange: Biological and Cultural Consequences of 1492* (Westport, Conn.: Greenwood, 1972) and *Ecological Imperialism: The Biological Expansion of Europe, 900–1900* (Melbourne, Australia: Cambridge University Press, 1986).

13. One of the more thoughtful elaborations on this theme may be found in Bradley F. Smith, *Reaching Judgement at Nuremberg* (New York: Basic Books, 1977).

14. See Tzvetan Todorov, *The Conquest of America* (New York: Harper and Row, 1984).

15. Kirkpatrick Sale, *The Conquest of Paradise: Christopher Columbus and the Columbian Legacy* (New York: Alfred A. Knopf, 1990), p. 155.

16. Bartolomé de las Casas, *The Spanish Colonie (Brevisima revación)*, University Microfilms reprint, 1966.

17. Bartolomé de las Casas, *Historia de las Indias, Vol. 3,* Augustin Millares Carlo and Lewis Hanke (eds.), Fondo de Cultura Económica, Mexico City, 1951: esp. Chap. 29.

18. las Casas, quoted in Thatcher, *op. cit.,* pp. 348ff.

19. See Lewis Hanke, *Aristotle and the American Indians: A Study in Race Prejudice in the Modern World* (Chicago: Henry Regnery, 1959). Also see Rob Williams, *The American Indian in Western Legal Thought: The Discourses of Conquest* (New York: Oxford University Press, 1989).

20. The most succinctly competent overview of this subject matter is probably Robert Cecil, *The Myth of the Master Race: Alfred Rosenberg and Nazi Ideology* (New York: Dodd and Mead, 1972).

21. The polemics of Columbus's strongest supporters among his contemporaries amplify this point. See, for example, Oviedo, *Historia General y Natural de las Indias* (Seville, 1535; Salamanca, 1547, 1549; Valladolid, 1557; Academia Historica, Madrid, 1851–55), esp. Chaps. 29, 30, 37.

22. Sale, *op. cit.,* p. 156.

Victims of an American Holocaust

Steve Charleston

Being thus broken with so many evils, afflicted with so many torments, and handled so ignominously, they began at length to believe that the Spaniards were not sent from Heaven. — Bartolomé de las Casas, from *History of the Indies.*

When it comes to interracial dialogues, Native People are often the last to be heard. We don't have the numbers. We don't have the economic or political muscle. When the subject is racism, we are never the first community of color to come to mind. And yet we have an absolutely fundamental experience that must be taken seriously.

The Native experience of racism is the foundational experience for all that has occurred in this hemisphere over almost 500 years. In 1992 we will mark 500 years of colonial rule in our homeland. That track record alone gives us a critical insight into the function of Western racism. We've endured it longer than anyone else. The wisdom of Native People on this subject is the key, the source for developing a strategy to overthrow both Western racism and Western colonialism.

The most virulent form of the disease of racism has been used against Native America. Like other oppressed people, we have known slavery, poverty and political conquest. We have also known something else — genocide. The greatest mass extermination of any race, any culture, any people happened here. It happened to us.

Western colonialism may speak of an American history. Native People speak of an American Holocaust. If racism is the mathematics of hate, then genocide is its ledger book. How many Native People died in the American

Reprinted with permission from Sojourners, *P.O. Box 29272 Washington, DC 20017.*

Holocaust? Thirty million? Forty million? Fifty million? How many were slaughtered? How many were sent to concentration camps? How many died of diseases they couldn't even name? The American Holocaust is our experience. It is our testimony.

The testimony of Native People to this genocide is rarely heard because Native People have been trivialized by Western propaganda. If all those millions perished in a Holocaust, why has so little ever been said about it? The answer is simple: You cannot have a crime if you do not have a victim. A concerted, intentional, methodical effort has been made by the West to erase the memory of Native America. As a people we have been the objects of one of the most successful racist propaganda campaigns in history.

From the very beginnings of Western colonial expansion right up to the present day, we have been trivialized. The dominant society has used every means at its disposal: the dime novel, the Wild West show, the Saturday matinée, the Western television serial, textbooks, the Sunday sermon, cartoons, the editorial page, the congressional record; they have all been pressed into service to denigrate and diminish our stature as witnesses to the truth of the Holocaust. This process of trivialization is not accidental. It is the intentional, racist process by which the nightmare of the American Holocaust is transformed into the reassuring image of the American Dream.

The trivialization of Native America through the medium of Western colonial propaganda replaces Native People with a pantheon of mythical colonial heroes. As the memory of the Holocaust is obscured, new images of the American Dream are pushed forward into the national consciousness: faithful Pilgrims; brave pioneers; founding fathers; gentle missionaries; a new world; a wilderness; exploration; discovery, and the *Niña*, the *Pinta* and the *Santa María*.

Racist propaganda always seeks to divert attention. All of us, Native and non–Native alike, who look the other way, who accept the myths of the dream without question, who endorse the assumptions laid before us by colonialism, are guilty of perpetuating Western racism. We give tacit approval to the myths of colonialism.

Think about Columbus Day. How many of us have been raised to accept the doctrine of discovery? Think about Thanksgiving. How many of us accept the image of smiling Indians surrounded by smiling Pilgrims? Smiling victims embracing their smiling executioners? In light of the Holocaust, it is a macabre image. In light of racist propaganda, it is a powerfully effective image. If we believe it, we are part of it. We are part of the dream.

The central purpose of diverting our attention is to keep us from focusing on the real reason for the American Holocaust. Western racist propaganda has told the American public that the conflict between Western colonialism and Native America was a conflict over "things"—land, gold, or furs. Western colonizers needed these "things," and Native People had them but were supposedly too primitive to use them. The struggle over possession of them was tragic but necessary, we are told.

This is the logic of racism, and it has been widely accepted as historical fact. In truth, however, the Holocaust was not carried out for the sake of "things." It was the result of the longest continuous religious war in human history. Native People were slaughtered because they did not share "the dream."

The West has conducted a capitalist *jihad* against Native America. It has sought to convert Native People to the doctrine that Western capitalism is the best of all possible worlds. In response, Native People have maintained a guerrilla war against their oppressors. They have resisted conversion and held fast to the traditional spiritual center of their own way of life. They have kept an alternative alive.

The alternative of Native America is the alternative of the tribe over against the capitalist state. It can be symbolized as the horizontal against the vertical. Native civilization in North America represented a political, social and economic system that radiated out from a religious center through the communal network of extended family and kinship.

In contrast, colonial capitalism represents a vertical hierarchy of economic and political privilege exclusive of spiritual values that places men and women in an artificial competition based on race, class and gender. The choice offered to Native People by capitalism was clear: convert or die. The grim statistics of the American Holocaust bear silent tribute to the decision made by generations of Native People.

The lesson to be learned from the Native experience is that all of us still have a choice. Native America still stands. It has survived the Holocaust. It has endured the propaganda. It continues to resist the American Dream state. The religious war goes on, and Native People are in it for the duration. As veterans of the struggle against colonialism, capitalism and racism, they are still in the field. Though few in number and often without allies, they represent an unbeaten alternative to business-as-usual in the great American technocracy.

When people of color gather to discuss racism, they should consider the men and women who have sacrificed so much to keep this alternative alive. Native People do not share the assumptions and mythologies of their oppressors. They do not simply want a higher place on the pyramid of capitalism; they do not want a bigger piece of action for themselves; they do not aspire to joining the middle class. They do not want *more*. As the tribe they want enough for all to share equally.

The tribe as a metaphor for community is dangerous. It is dangerous to colonial capitalism. It is dangerous to racism. It is dangerous because it is a symbol for the strength of the oppressed. It is an inclusive symbol for all men and women who want to wake up from the dream. It says to people of all colors and cultures: There is a better way. Let go of the myths and the images and the empty promises. Join hands in the strong bond of kinship. Become a tribe. Fight back. Let the victims be redeemed and the survivors set free. The struggle is 500 years old. Now is the time to decide.

Indian Issues and Romantic Solidarity

Robert Allen Warrior

On November 22, 1988, the United Nations General Assembly passed a resolution declaring the 1990s to be the International Decade for the Eradication of Colonialism. *The resolution passed with only the United States voting against.*

With the calendar now turned to 1991, lots of folks are making big plans for the Columbus Quincentenary in 1992: protest marches, media campaigns, seminars, prayer vigils, art shows, teach-ins, sit-ins, curricula reforms, discovery voyages to Spain, environmental symposia, street theater, and anything else to express rage at the hundreds of millions of dollars the U.S. and other governments (colonial and neo-) will be spending on self-congratulatory fêtes in the name of America's most celebrated immigrant-entrepreneur.

Progressive/radical/liberal groups think this might be the moment they have been waiting for to mobilize this America for some kind of sincere social action. We won't know until it's tried: It's a distinct possibility that no amount of street theater will do anything but fuel white backlash.

And, perhaps protests against the Quincentenary will be nothing more than a sideshow to a sideshow. Election Day comes just four weeks after Columbus Day 1992, and Europe will be concentrating in 1992 on its economic unification. The U.S. might also be engaged by then in World War III in Iraq or some other naughty, renegade country.

Reprinted with permission from the Feb. 4, 1991 issue of Christianity and Crisis. *Copyright 1991 by Christianity and Crisis, Inc.*

Lame Deer Liberation

Hope springs eternal on the left, however, and the planning continues. The situation begs, of course, for American Indian input and leadership. I have attended, or have been invited to, many 1992 planning meetings by non-native groups.

What strikes me about all these groups is their pervasive ignorance of contemporary American Indian political issues. They expect to hear about visionary environmental ethics, spiritual gurus, and guilt-inspiring revisionist history of atrocious massacres, and are disappointed and confused when I mention the nuts and bolts of federal policy, economic development and community organizing.

This ignorance is actually the unique and pernicious form of racism that those on the left inflict upon American Indian people. For example, someone from the United Church of Christ (UCC) called me recently. They are about to publish a pastoral letter on racism and are including an annotated resource guide along with the letter.

They were having trouble finding materials about racism and American Indians and wondered if I could point them to some books and articles. I asked what they already had, and they rattled off three books about American Indian religion and spirituality, nothing remotely related to the structural, violent realities of Indian-hating as practiced in this country.

The incident reminded me of when I came to Union Seminary in 1988 and audited a class with Dorothee Soelle on Liberation Theologies for North America. The class decided on several political issues for which working groups were to come up with concrete strategies. One group tried to develop a recycling program for the neighborhood, another did an analysis of homelessness on the Upper West Side. These groups gathered statistics, studied federal policy, analyzed economic factors, and thought of ways to respond. Not the stuff revolutions are made of, but important issues.

Another group, on Native American Spirituality, was led by a student who told the class he had spent the summer riding around the West on his motorcycle talking to old Indians and sitting on hillsides trying to be at one with the earth. The group was one of the most popular in the class. No one seemed to ask what reading *Black Elk Speaks* or *Lame Deer: Seeker of Visions* has to do with justice or liberation.

A major focus of American Indian organizing for 1992 has been on how we can protect ourselves from this kind of exploitation and culture-vulture, wannabe-ism by groups who claim to be our friends. When I say things like this at conferences and meetings, by the way, people tend to get highly defensive and tell me how sincere they are in wanting to learn about American Indian cultures.

That's all well and good, as long as they don't pretend it's going to do

Indian people any political good. I know of no other group that must "share" its culture to pay for solidarity and a commitment to justice from the left. Fortunately, we still have some time before the Quincentenary spectacle to overcome this racism.

Homework

Those who sincerely wish to stand in solidarity with American Indian people in 1992 and beyond will do some homework in the coming year and learn some of the complexities of what the struggle for justice and self-determination is all about. The four major issues of American Indian politics — *religious freedom, land claims, resource management* and *federal-tribal government relations* — are areas in which sincere and educated engagement by non–Indians can make a difference.

In 1990 the U.S. Congress and the Department of the Interior embarked on a major overhaul of the Bureau of Indian Affairs. The Bureau, which spends about three-quarters of its budget on self-perpetuation, is overdue for an overhaul, but Indian people at the local level want to make sure things get better rather than worse. Unfortunately, the process is becoming something of a more-of-the-same paternalistic nightmare for Indian Country. Few non–Indian groups or individuals are monitoring the situation and intervening with their representatives and senators.

In 1983, the National Tribal Chairperson's Association (NTCA), a highly moderate group that Richard Nixon created, drafted a restructuring proposal that makes some sense and which could be a solid starting point for sincere debate. The trouble is, people working on the restructuring keep promising to give a damn about Indian input, but are moving ahead in spite of criticisms from every level of Indian groups.

(If you want information, Secretary of the Interior Marshall Lujan and his assistant Eddie Brown are the major architects on the executive side. NTCA and National Congress of American Indians, both in Washington, D.C., are the major Indian lobby groups working on the issues. Senators Daniel Inouye, D-Hawaii, John McCain, R-Arizona, and Dennis DeConcini, D-Arizona, are the major congressional players).

The area of American Indian religious freedom is something every religious person in the U.S. who is not a fundamentalist ought to be watching. In April 1990, the U.S. Supreme Court upheld the State of Oregon's right to deny unemployment compensation to two American Indian men who lost their jobs as substance-abuse counselors because they use peyote in the Native American Church.

As Vine Deloria, Jr., wrote to me at the time, "After the peyote and Bible study group decisions by the Supreme Court, the question is really whether there can be any religious activity that varies from the fundamentalist norm. I suspect that even Indians don't understand the scope of this decision. It is the *balancing test*—church freedoms vs. state welfare interests—that is really at stake."

State interests, no matter how dubious, are carrying the day with the Court in almost every case of peyote use or state development of sacred sites. As this set of justices further entrenches itself in conservatism, these American Indian precedents can be the basis for repression of any religious group the U.S. wants to stamp out.

Land claims and resource management also connect with wider issues. Nearly all the uranium the U.S. uses for its nuclear arsenal comes from Indian land, yet American Indian nations have almost no control over mineral leases on their own land. The Secretary of the Interior holds the land in trust and does what he or she wants with the resources.

The feds use this ludicrous system to buy cut-rate uranium and lease Indian land to themselves, states or counties, for nuclear and toxic waste dumps. Environmental and antinuke groups often fail to intervene successfully in these situations because they do not understand that Indian control of resources and tribal sovereignty are central to making any significant progress.

These, of course, are quick sketches of complex historical and contemporary situations. Unless we can establish a stronger foundation in the substance of these issues and awaken our friends from their spiritual and cultural fantasies, efforts to achieve justice for American Indian people and communities will continue to be ineffective.

The Quincentenary will provide a time for well-informed non–Indians to help effect changes in the racist, paternalistic policies of the U.S. government. For that to happen, though, our friends on the left are going to have to confront their own racist practices in the guise of liberal guilt and exoticism.

Recommended

Deloria, Vine, Jr. *The Nations Within: The Past and Future of American Indian Sovereignty.* Pantheon, 1984.

Drinnon, Richard. *Facing West: The Metaphysics of Indian Hating and Empire Building.* Reprinted by Schocken Books, 1990.

Forbes, Jack D. *Native Americans and Nixon: Presidential Politics and Minority Self-Determination, 1969–1972.* American Indian Studies Program, UCLA.

Native American Rights Fund Legal Review. Quarterly. Contact NARF, 1506 Broadway, Boudler CO 80302.

Native Nations Magazine. A new monthly written and edited by American Indian people preparing for the Quincentenary. Writers include Leonard Peltier, John Mohawk, John Trudell, Suzan Shown Harjo, and Robert Warrior. Contact Solidarity Foundation, 310 W. 52 St., New York NY 10019.

The Day, the Pledge, the Myth

John Yewell

"Jubilee": A year of emancipation and restoration provided by ancient Hebrew law to be kept every 50 years by the emancipation of Hebrew slaves, restoration of alienated lands to their former owners, and omission of all cultivation of the land. —from Webster's Ninth New Collegiate.

Columbus Day, October 12, 1992, is three weeks and a day before the 1992 elections. The quincentennial of the arrival of Christopher Columbus in this hemisphere, and the hype being encouraged by the U.S. government-sponsored Christopher Columbus Quincentenary Jubilee Commission, promises to provide a boisterous if ultimately polarizing sideshow to the election, which, if history teaches us anything, will have little to do with a debate over governing and a lot to do with symbols such as Columbus has become. October 12, 1992, is also the putative centennial of the writing of President Bush's favorite political tract, the Pledge of Allegiance—which was written, in fact, for the Columbian Exposition and Columbus Quadricentennial of 1892-93.

Columbus has become a symbol for anyone's political inclinations. He is either a slave-trading, bloodthirsty colonial pirate, or the personification of the virtues of capitalism and an inspiration for generations of entrepreneurs. I will attempt here to examine the growth of the Columbus myth and how it resulted ultimately in the establishment of two cultural and political institutions: Columbus Day and the Pledge.

For the first hundred years or so after his first landfall in the Caribbean, the reputation of Christopher Columbus was generally that of an audacious if errant sailor who brought to Europe news of lands to the west. That those lands formed at least one distinct continent separate from Asia was *possibly* known by Columbus before his death (although most historians claim he did not), but in either case this knowledge would dawn slowly on the rest of Europe over the course of the next few generations. That it was a "new" world was a point of view that, once established, generally went unchallenged until recently. The existence of the Spanish and the lands to the east from which they came was certainly news — terrifying news — to the 15th century inhabitants of the Caribbean.

In 1507, a year after Columbus's death, he was still not well enough known to merit having the lands he "found" named after him. German mapmaker Martin Waldseemüller would inadvertently bestow that honor on Amerigo Vespucci, whose own fantastic writings and exaggerated claims of "discovery" were more widely disseminated at the time. Six years later Waldseemüller would realize his mistake, but the damage had been done.

From the beginning the Americas exercised a powerful influence on the European imagination. The writings of Vespucci and others set the stage for wide-ranging speculation on the nature of the western continents and their inhabitants. From this fascination came new images of the "noble savage" and the nature of utopia, including Thomas More's *Utopia,* published in 1516. Even when the story of how that utopia was being treated (which became known as the Black Legend) became better known, and as Spain was being roundly vilified by much of Europe (under the influence of the Reformation), little of the fallout would affect Columbus's own reputation. Since even those who condemned the horrible treatment of the Indians were generally Columbus supporters, such as Bartolomé de las Casas, "the Admiral" would grow steadily in stature throughout the 16th century as writings about him appeared all over Europe.

The first descriptions of his activities in the Caribbean appeared in 1504, and the first biography in 1516. In 1526 the Spanish historian Gonzalo de Oviedo wrote of him in a way intended to prepare the pedestal on which Columbus would be placed by later generations, declaring him to be "worthy of fame and glory." Some years later Columbus's son Fernando wrote a complete biography of his father, although it was not published until 1569 — and then in Italian.

Reality transmogrified itself effortlessly into legend, which by the 17th century acquired practical application. The ease with which the indigenous peoples of the Western Hemisphere had been shouldered aside and exterminated became the inspiration for the settlement policies of every European power with the means and interest to finance them, and it didn't take long for Columbus to become as important a symbol of political legitimacy to them as he had long been to Spain. But Columbus's fame was still incomplete and apocryphal, his example to a new generation of determined colonizers based on legend.

By the late 18th and early 19th centuries legend would begin to give way to idolatry, and — especially in the United States — myth. With independence for white males firmly secured, the new nation wasted no time in creating a pantheon of heroes, and with the proximity of the Columbian tricentennial to the country's birth, Columbus seemed the natural place to begin. The proposal was advanced to name the new country Columbia, or to replace "of America" with "of Columbia," and while the effort was unsuccessful, his supporters did at least succeed in having the new capital named in his honor. With the naming of the District of (then known as the "Territory of") Columbia in 1791, the finding of the mouth of the Columbia River in 1792, and the renaming of King's College in New York to Columbia College the same year, Columbus was well on his way to becoming the governing paradigm for a new society poised on the brink of a continent ripe for exploitation.

The first known celebration of the "discovery" of America was held by the Tammany Society on October 12, 1792. Monuments to Columbus were erected in New York (where a dinner was also held) and Baltimore. The Tammany Society, also known as the Columbian Order, had grown in part from the Sons of Liberty during the Revolution, and ironically claimed as its two guiding lights Columbus and Chief Tammany of the Delaware Indians, who had welcomed William Penn and his followers to their new colony in 1682. The affable Tammany, sometimes later referred to as "Saint" Tammany, was a supporter of the new settlers, and in his name an undercurrent of Indian societal emulation took root in the colonies that some contend led to the adoption of certain principles of Indian (in particular Iroquois) law into the American Constitution, such as a government of checks and balances. Dressing as Indians during the Boston Tea Party was not done merely on whim.

Then in 1828, Columbusmania broke out. Given access to newly uncovered primary source material and an enormous library with which to work, Washington Irving would proceed to misconstrue much of it and cut from whole cloth a man larger than myth for his hero-starved young nation. His biography, *The Life and Voyages of Columbus,* published in 1828, was the Big Bang of Columbiana.

It is thanks to Irving that we have our most brazen fictions about Columbus: the myth of Isabella's pawned jewels to finance his voyages, his valiant defense of the round earth "hypothesis" (which was of course no longer in question) before the disbelieving council of Salamanca University, his brave resistance to mutineers on his first voyage, and much more. The passive voice (*mistakes were made*) was as alive then as it is today, and Irving cloaked Columbus in a mantel of genius to cover his inevitable human faults.

Following the publication of this fawning and inaccurate book, interest in Columbus as a symbol for the entrepreneurial spirit of the new country soared. Columbus's name became shorthand, a metaphorical code for initiative, optimism and courage — qualities essential to a young country determined not to let indigenous peoples stand in the way of its exploration and expansion any more than Columbus had let their antecessors stand in the way of his.

The book was a huge success. But it can be argued that Irving, a down-

and-out author desperate for a literary success, only caught the crest of the Columbus wave.

Throughout the 19th century, and particularly after Irving, many new statutes, paintings, buildings, and monuments would be named for Columbus. While neither Latin America nor Canada (where they don't celebrate Columbus Day) would ever develop the same level of affection, other countries in North and South America (in particular Colombia), along with Spain and Genoa, Italy, rushed to get into the act. He would become the subject of hundreds of plays, novels, poems, and other writing. The number of cities and towns, place names, rivers, mountains, lakes, parks, schools, colleges, banks, space shuttles and broadcasting systems ultimately named after Columbus almost defy counting, but according to those who have done so he takes a close second in this country to George Washington.

In 1866, with the Civil War over and the troops shipped west to police the new neighborhoods, the Italian population of New York City held its first general if unofficial celebration of Columbus Day. By 1869 Italian communities in Philadelphia, St. Louis, Boston, Cincinnati, San Francisco (on October 17 that year for some reason), and New Orleans were doing likewise.

As the country approached the quadricentennial in 1892, interest in Columbus appeared to quicken further. In 1882 the Knights of Columbus were founded in New Haven. By the end of that decade, interest in a grand exposition to celebrate Columbus had developed into a campaign.

Westward-facing Chicago outbid New York for the rights, and on February 24, 1890, was selected by the House of Representatives to host the Columbian Exposition. By the time of the massacre at Wounded Knee in December, 1890, with the West "won" and Columbus more than ever a symbol of the nation's vitality, planning for the Exposition was well underway.

Potter Palmer, president of the World's Columbian Commission, planners of the fair, urged; "May we not hope that lessons here learned, transmitted to the future, will be potent forces long after the multitudes which will throng these aisles shall have measured their span and faded away?" In this spirit, Francis J. Bellamy, editor of the magazine, *The Youth's Companion,* had two seminal ideas: he urged that the opening day of the fair, October 12, be set aside as a national holiday, and as further promotion of the fair itself urged that children be taught to celebrate Columbus's achievements. To this end he wrote the Pledge of Allegiance, and with the cooperation of the Federal Bureau of Education circulated copies to teachers around the country — which has since provided an unlimited supply of political fodder for generations of jingoistic politicians.

While the fair was indeed dedicated on October 12, 1892, funding and other problems would delay the actual opening to May 1 the following year.

Still, President Benjamin Harrison did declare October 12, 1892, a national holiday, and a commemorative coin with a hypothetical likeness of Columbus (the first such coin in this country) was struck.

The fair itself sported a midway with "authentic" ethnic displays from around the world, whose ultimate purpose seemed to be to demonstrate the steady march of human progress to the pinnacle of social and technological progress in white European and American societies. As Robert Rydell wrote in *All the World's a Fair*: "the Midway provided visitors with ethnological, scientific sanction for the American view of the nonwhite world as barbaric and childlike and gave a scientific basis to the racial blueprint for building a utopia." It is a telling analysis that, after 400 years, utopia had been bleached white.

Some American Indians were persuaded to take part. Emma Sickles, who was on the exposition's planning staff, objected that the Indian display "has been used to work up sentiment against the Indian by showing that he is either savage or can be educated only by Government agencies. . . ." She was fired.

In 1892 New York held its own celebration, and the memorial to Columbus was placed at what is now Columbus Circle. Chauncey Depew, president of the New York Central Railroad, gave a speech at Carnegie Hall for the occasion, blasting then-recent criticism of Columbus:

> If there is anything which I detest more than another, it is that spirit of critical historical inquiry which doubts everything; that modern spirit which destroys all the illusions and all the heroes which have been the inspiration of patriotism through all the centuries.

A dozen years later, thanks to the lobbying of an Italian American printer and part-time politician named Angelo Noce, agitation for a formal Columbus Day holiday would bear its first fruit. In 1905, the governor of Colorado requested that his state observe the holiday, and in 1907 it became law.

In 1906 in Chicago, mayor Edward F. Dunne would do the same for his city. In 1908 in New York State a holiday bill was passed but vetoed. However, the following year a new bill was passed and signed by the new governor, Charles Evans Hughes. Other states also passed holiday bills in 1909: Connecticut, Maryland, Montana, New Jersey and Pennsylvania. Massachusetts and Rhode Island followed in 1910.

By the end of that year 15 states in all had passed Columbus holiday legislation. By 1938 the number had grown to 34. But in the meantime, in 1934, the U.S. Congress passed a joint resolution urging the declaration of

a Columbus Day holiday. After his relection in 1937, President Franklin
Roosevelt finally issued a proclamation to that effect.

Perhaps the ultimate irony to the mythologization of Columbus and the
institution of the Columbus Day holiday is that we celebrate it on the wrong
day. Since Columbus lived under the Julian calendar, which at the time was
11 days off, his actual landfall in this hemisphere occurred not on October 12,
but what would according to today's Gregorian calendar be October 23. Having taken no more historical care for Christmas Day itself, few have seemed
to care.

During the 1992 presidential campaign we can expect to relive the Hundred Hours' War against Iraq on television 30 seconds at a time. But with
Columbus being such convenient grist for the multicultural mill, don't be surprised to hear populist-sounding appeals for an assault in his name on the
ramparts of that latest right-wing red herring, political correctness. George
Bush may find the Columbus Day connection to the Pledge an irresistible tool
in trying to tar the Left with its own brush by showing how Columbus inspired the Pledge, and how the two are linked with what may be portrayed
as the subsequent development of the "greater good."

The president has already tipped his hand on this issue, as his 1989 proclamation on Columbus Day (see Appendix F) reveals. With his now legendary enthusiasm for the symbolism of the Pledge, can the president be expected on that holiday and anniversary, October 12, 1992, to do other than
pledge allegiance to the spirit of Columbus (which is the *real* meaning of the
Pledge)? Given the genocidal consequences of Columbus's arrival for the indigenous peoples of this hemisphere, do not the origins of the Pledge call into
question its appropriateness in our classrooms, not to mention its political
exploitation?

Sources

Cohen, Hennig, and Coffin, Tristram Potter, eds. *The Folklore of American Holidays*.
    Detroit: Gale Research Co., 1987.
Grinde, Donald A., Jr. "White Men as Indians, or The Appropriation of American
    Indian Ideas and Symbols during the Revolutionary War Period by the Constitu-
    tional Sons of St. Tammany, or Columbian Order," *Indigenous Thought*, June,
    1991.
Myers, Robert J. *Celebrations: The Complete Book of American Holidays*. Garden City,
    N.Y.: Doubleday, 1972.
Rydell, Robert W. *All the World's a Fair: Visions of Empire at the American International
    Expositions, 1876–1916*. Chicago: University of Chicago Press, 1984.
Sale, Kirkpatrick. *The Conquest of Paradise*. New York: Knopf, 1990.

Bibliography

Chris Dodge

Especially Notable

Crosby, Alfred W. *The Columbian Voyages, the Columbian Exchange, and Their Historians.* American Historical Association, 1987. 29 pages. Analysis of historical interpretations of Columbus, and of the intellectual, economic, nutritional and demographic effects of his voyages.

Curl, John. *Columbus in the Bay of Pigs.* Homeward Press (P.O. Box 2307, Berkeley, CA 94702), 1988. 72 pages. "A poetic account of Columbus's second voyage and his devastating contact with the friendly Taino Indians."

1492: Discovery? Encounter? Invasion? Michigan Interfaith Committee on Central American Human Rights (4835 Michigan Ave., Detroit, MI 28410), 1991. 16 pages. Tabloid which "tells the story of the conquest from the perspective of the indigenous people of Latin America and of North America." Includes discussion questions, graphics, crossword puzzle, and suggested activities. Single copies, $1.50 postpaid; 10–49 copies, 75 cents each plus $3 shipping; 50–99 copies, 50 cents each plus $6 shipping.

"1492–1992: Exploring the Past to Discover the Present." Central America Resource Center (317 17th Ave. SE, Minneapolis, MN 55414), 1991. Curriculum packets for grades K–6, 7–12, and for National History Day, compiled by CARC's Quincentennial Educational Project. The first two include teaching guidelines, bibliographies, and sample lessons, while the third includes articles and *Directory of Central America Classroom Resources.* K–6 and 7–12 packets, $6 postpaid; History Day packet, $15 postpaid.

huracán (P.O. Box 7591, Minneapolis, MN 55407; $15). "500 Years of Resistance." A publication of the Alliance for Cultural Democracy's "clearinghouse for information on the 500th anniversary of the European invasion of the Americas." The summer 1991 issue includes Quincentennial news briefs, "Periodicals of Note," a listing of art and media projects, and an article on the Christopher Columbus Quincentenary Jubilee Commission.

Indigenous Thought (6802 SW 13th St., Gainesville, FL 32608; $10). "A networking newsletter to link counter–Columbus Quincentenary activities," the 56-page second issue (March/June 1991) includes Ward Churchill's "Deconstructing the Columbus myth," a report on an AIM-Chicano counter–Quincentennial alliance in Corpus Christi, letters regarding libraries' response to the Quincentennial, and news about the "First Encounters" exhibit, as well as resource listings and an extensive bibliography.

Koning, Hans. *Columbus: His Enterprise.* Monthly Review Press, 1976. 128 pages. An unsparing, eminently readable classic describing Columbus's voyages and their ill effects.

———. *Columbus: His Enterprise: Exploding the Myth.* Monthly Review Press, 1991. 141 pages. Includes new introduction, as well as Bill Bigelow's essay, "Columbus in the Classroom."

Listing of Organizations Planning to Observe the Columbus Quincentennial. 13 pages. Racial Justice Working Group, National Council of Churches of Christ (475 Riverside Dr., New York, NY 10115), 1991.

Meltzer, Milton. *Columbus and the World Around Him.* Franklin Watts, 1990. 192 pages. Intended for middle grades, this book details Indian exploitation as does no other children's biography of Columbus. Describes the voyages, the terrible impact of the Spaniards on the Indians, and the ultimate cultural influence of the Native Americans on their white conquerors.

"1992: Rediscovering America." *Sojourners,* Oct. 1991. Includes Winona LaDuke's "We are still here," Yvonne V. Delk's "A Moment of Turning: An African-American Vision for the Kairos of 1992," Native Hawaiian Kaleo Patterson's "All Is Not Well in Paradise" and S. Michael Yasutake's "Asians and the Legacy of Columbus" (Box 29272, Washington, DC 20017).

Pelta, Kathy. *Discovering Christopher Columbus: How History Is Invented.* Lerner Publications, 1991. 112 pages. Intended for middle grades, this book includes material on Columbus's voyages to the Americas subsequent to 1492, Columbian historiography from las Casas to Washington Irving, the 1893 Columbian Exposition, and the meaning of the Quincentennial, as well as "You, the Historian."

"Rediscover the History of the Americas: 1492-1992." *CALC Report,* Aug. 1991. Includes "Action Suggestions," bibliography, a list of organizations and Quincentennial publications, "Resources for 1992" (buttons, bumperstickers, etc.), and an update on Columbus in Context activities. 1-5 copies, $1 each, postpaid; 5-20 copies, $.50 each, postpaid; 21+ copies, $.25 each, plus 20 percent for postage (Clergy and Laity Concerned, 340 Mead Rd., Decatur, GA 30030).

Rethinking Columbus: Essays and Resources for Teaching about the 500th Anniversary of Columbus's Arrival in the Americas. Rethinking Schools (1001 E. Keefe Ave., Milwaukee, WI 53212), 1991. 96 pages. Single copies, $6 postpaid; 10-49 copies, $2 each plus shipping. For other bulk order prices, phone 414-964-9646. Special edition of *Rethinking Schools* published in collaboration with the Network of Educators on Central America.

Re-View (P.O. Box 801, New York, NY 10009). Newsletter providing "information and contacts for people and projects engaged in a critical re-interpretaton of the 1492-1992 anniversary." The second issue (August 1990) includes Jan Elliott's "Five Hundred Years of Resistance Continued," information about the Alliance for Cultural Democracy's 1990 annual conference, and the Quincentennial resolution passed by members of the American Library Association.

Sale, Kirkpatrick. *The Conquest of Paradise: Christopher Columbus and the Columbian Legacy.* A.A. Knopf, 1990. 453 pages. A "revisionist" history, featuring material about the writings of such previous Columbus idolater-biographers as Washington Irving and Samuel Eliot Morison.

Small, Deborah, with Maggie Jaffe. *1492: What Is It Like to Be Discovered?* Monthly Review Press (122 W. 27th St., New York, NY 10001; $15), 1991. 160 pages. "Weaves together a narrative history of Columbus's invasion . . . with poetry, quotations and illustrations."

Thornton, Russell. *American Indian Holocaust and Survival: A Population History Since*

1492. University of Oklahoma Press, 1987. 292 pages. Illustrated with drawings, tables, graphs, maps and photographs.

"View from the Shore." *Northeast Indian Quarterly.* Fall 1990. Includes José Barreiro's "A Note on Tainos," "500 Years: Preliminary Results of a Quincentennial Survey," John Mohawk's "Discovering Columbus: The Way Here," Jorge Quintana's "Thoughts on the Next 500 Years," Robert Venables's "The Cost of Columbus," Dave Warren's "American Indians and the Columbus Quincentenary," a "Select Bibliography of Caribbean Encounters," and an extensive 1992 resource directory (American Indian Program, 300 Caldwell Hall, Cornell University, Ithaca, NY 14853).

Zinn, Howard. "Columbus, the Indians, and Human Progress." *A People's History of the United States.* Harper and Row, 1980. pp. 1–22. Looks at the Spanish invasion through the eyes of Bartolomé de las Casas, describes the subsequent patterns of Indian annihilation, and analyzes the ideological distortions of past historians. Elsewhere in the book is material on Indian wars and removals of the 19th century.

Other Sources

Achenbach, Joel. "Columbus, Rediscovered." *Washington Post,* July 14, 1991. pp. F1, F4–5.

Allen, Martha Sawyer. "Celebrate Columbus? Some Churches Debate It." *Star Tribune,* Oct. 9, 1990, p. 1B.

"American Indian Movement Wants Columbus Day Out." *The Circle,* Oct. 1990, p. 8.

Anner, John. "500 Years of Sorrow." *Minority Trendsletter,* winter 1990/91, pp. 16–17.

Axtell, James. "Europeans, Indians and the Age of Discovery in American History Textbooks." *American Historical Review,* June 1987, pp. 621–632.

Bauerlein, Monika. "The Specter of Chris Columbus." *The Circle,* July 1991, p. 21.

Berg, P. "Starting Over Without Columbus." *Raise the Stakes,* fall 1989, p. 1.

Buffalohead, Roger. "Celebrating Columbus's Voyage: A Case of Historical Amnesia." *Star Tribune,* March 24, 1990, p. 15A.

Burton, Bruce. "Literature, Paradigm, and Plunder in the New World." *Northeast Indian Quarterly,* fall 1990, pp. 56–65.

"Call to a Campaign for a Post-Columbian World: 1992 and the Next 500 Years." *Cultural Democracy,* fall 1989, pp. 6–7.

"CARC Quincentennial Education Project." *The Connection* [Central America Resource Center, Minnesota], May 1991, p. 7.

Carew, Jan. "Columbus and the Origins of Racism in America." *Fulcrums of Change.* Africa World Press, 1988. pp. 3–48.

Carothers, Andre. "The First People." *E Magazine,* Sept./Oct. 1991, p. 72.

"Churches and the Quincentennial." *Christianity and Crisis,* Feb. 4, 1991, pp. 10–11.

Colon, Willie. "Quinientos Anos" (Five Hundred Years). *Honra y Cultura* (Phonograph album). Sony Discos, 1991.

"Columbus, Stay Home! A Bitter Debate Over His 500th Anniversary." *Newsweek,* June 24, 1991, pp. 54–55.

"Countering the Columbus Myth: Action Ideas for 1992." *CALC Report* [Clergy and Laity Concerned], March 1990, p. 18.

Crawford, John. "Short [Alliance for Cultural Democracy 'After Columbus'] Conference Reading List." *People's Culture,* Sept. 1990, pp. 3–7.

176   Confronting Columbus

Crosby, Alfred W. "The Biological Consequences of 1492." *Report on the Americas,* Sept. 1991, pp. 6–13.

Culture. "Pirate Days." *Two Sevens Clash* (Phonograph record/audio cassette/compact disc). Shanachie Records, 1987.

Curl, John. "The Dance of the Condor and the Eagle." *The Circle,* July 1991, pp. 17–18. A report on the First Continental Meeting of Indigenous Peoples on the First 500 Years of Indian Resistance.

―――. "Resistance 500 and Estanislao's Revolt." *Ecology Center Newsletter,* Oct. 1991, pp. 1–5. A chronicle of repression and resistance in 19th century California.

Cytron, Barry D. "In 1492, Jews Set Sail from Spain — In Exile." *Star Tribune,* June 2, 1991, p. 21A.

Dixon, Susan R. "Points of View: The Art of Encounter." *Northeast Indian Quarterly,* fall 1990, pp. 88–92.

Dodge, Chris. "Chris Dodge's Public Ear." *Artpaper,* Jan. 1991, p. 7.

Douglas, Marjory Stoneman. "The Discoverers." *The Everglades: River of Grass.* Revised edition. Pineapple Press, 1988. pp. 80–106.

Dunbar-Ortiz, Roxanne. "Columbus and 'The Stink Hiding the Sun': An Interview with Joy Harjo." *CrossRoads,* Oct. 1990, pp. 16–23.

Durham, Jimmie. *Columbus Day.* West End Press, 1983. 104 pages. "Poems, drawings and stories about American Indian life and death in the Nineteen-Seventies."

Ehlert, Bob. "Critics of Columbus Ask: 'What's to Celebrate?'" *Star Tribune,* May 2, 1991, pp. 1E, 4E.

"End the Columbus Myth!" *Educators Against Racism and Apartheid,* Oct. 1990, pp. 1–3.

Ferguson, James. "A Lighthouse That Won't Pierce the Gloom." *The Progressive,* Oct. 1991, pp. 24–26. Article about the construction of a giant lighthouse in Santo Domingo, intended as a monument to Columbus.

Fimrite, Peter. "Columbus Day Celebration Called 'Insult.'" *San Francisco Chronicle,* Bay Area Edition, March 26, 1991, p. A4.

"500 Years of Indian Resistance." *SAIIC* [South and Meso-American Indian Information Center] *Newsletter,* fall 1989/winter 1990, pp. 16–24.

Fogel, Daniel. *Junipero Serra, the Vatican, and Enslavement Theology.* Ism Press, 1988. "A detailed history of the Spanish mission system in California," focusing on "the friars' cultural and psychological impact on the Indians they recruited to the mission."

Galeano, Eduardo. "The Blue Tiger and the Promised Land." *NACLA Report on the Americas,* Feb. 1991, pp. 13–17.

―――. *Memory of Fire: Genesis.* Pantheon Books, 1985. 293 pages. "The turbulent saga of the conquest of the Americas."

―――. *Open Veins of Latin America: Five Centuries of the Pillage of a Continent.* Monthly Review Press, 1973, 313 pages.

Gamarekian, Barbara. "Grants Rejected; Scholars Grumble." *New York Times,* April 10, 1991, p. B1. "Dispute over . . . rejection of a series of grants for projects marking the 500th anniversary of Christopher Columbus's discovery of the New World."

Gerth, Jeff. "Columbus Celebration Under Cost Inquiry." *New York Times,* Dec. 10, 1990, p. A1, A15.

Gilman, Rhoda R. "Some Thoughts on Columbus." *Collective Voice,* March/April 1991, p. 10.

Goss, Carol. "Thoughts on the Quincentenary: Five Hundred Years After Columbus." *Bulletin* [Institute of American Indian Studies], winter 1990, pp. 15–16.

Greendigger, Emmett. "500 Years of Resistance!" *Katuah Journal,* fall 1991, p. 25.

Reviews the environmental impact of Columbus's landfall, notes the counter–Quincentennial activities, and lists several alternative resource packets available.

Grossmann, Mary Ann. "Some Will Not Salute Christopher Columbus." *Saint Paul Pioneer Press,* April 14, 1991, p. 6D. A look at Uruguayan author Eduardo Galeano.

Harjo, Suzan Shown. "We Were Here Before Columbus." *New World Times,* spring 1991, p. 11.

"International Call to 'Year 499' Conference." *News from Indian Country,* Aug. 1991, p. 16.

Iwanski, Len. "Ditch Columbus Day in Favor of 'Native Americans Day.'" *The Circle,* Feb. 1991, p. 8.

Jamies, M. "Discovering the Truth About Columbus." *Akwesasne Notes,* winter 1990, p. 27.

Jojola, Ted. "American Indian Stereotypes." *Northeast Indian Quarterly,* fall 1990, pp. 26–28.

Kilian, Michael. "New World of Hype." *Chicago Tribune,* Aug. 12, 1990, pp. 1+ .

Kluznik, Michael. "The Women Who Upstaged Columbus." *Star Tribune,* April 25, 1991, p. 23A. (Published in slightly different form as "Columbus Quincentenary Celebration or the First Four Women?" *The Circle,* June 1991, p. 23.)

Knauer, Lisa Maya. "Columbus Exhibits Miss the Boats." *The Guardian,* July 31, 1991, pp. 10–11.

_____. "Roll Out the Hoopla, It's Columbus's Big '500'." *The Guardian,* Sept. 12, 1990, p. 9.

Kohn, Moshe. "Rediscovering Columbus." *Jerusalem Post,* International Edition, week ending Oct. 27, 1990, p. 16.

Koning, Hans. "Don't Cheer What Columbus Set in Motion." *Star Tribune,* Aug. 17, 1990, p. 19A.

_____. "Should We Celebrate Columbus Day?" *Briarpatch,* March 1991, p. 3.

Kovel, J. "Talk About Understatement." *Lies of Our Times,* March 1990, p. 15.

Krenkel, Noele. "Preparing for 1992: The Makings of an International Coalition Among Environmentalists, Indigenous Peoples, and Peace and Justice Communities." *Ecology Center Newsletter,* Oct. 1991, pp. 6–8. Includes listing of books, periodicals, organizations, and events.

las Casas, Bartolomé de. *Devastation of the Indies.* Seabury Press, 1974.

Leo, John. "The North American Conquest." *U.S. News and World Report,* May 13, 1991, p. 25.

Levins Morales, Ricardo. "Art for Our Sake." *Artpaper,* Dec. 1990, p. 7.

Lippard, Lucy. "Discover Ups." *Z Magazine,* Feb. 1991, pp. 84–86.

Lumbreras, Luis Guillermo. "Misguided Development." *NACLA Report on the Americas,* Feb. 1991, pp. 18–22.

McDonald, Peter. "Columbus in Context: Rediscovering the Americas." *CALC Report* [Clergy and Laity Concerned], summer 1990, pp. 20–21.

MacEoin, Gary. "1492–1992; To Bury Columbus or Praise Him." *National Catholic Reporter,* Sept. 21, 1990, pp. 11–12.

_____. "Rediscovering America: New World, Old Wounds: Indigenous Groups Tell Their Side of the Story." *National Catholic Reporter,* Nov. 2, 1990, p. 15.

Martinez, Felipe. "1992: What's to Celebrate?" *Christianity and Crisis,* Feb. 4, 1991, pp. 10–11.

Meyer, Matt. "Resisting the New World (Order)." *Nonviolent Activist,* July/Aug. 1991, pp. 11–13.

Mohawk, John. "Discovering Columbus: The Way Here." *Northeast Indian Quarterly,* fall 1990, pp. 37–46.

_____. "Looking for Columbus." *Native Nations,* Jan. 1991, pp. 16–17.

Mollenhoff, Lori. "Another View of Columbus Day." *The Connection,* Oct. 1990, p. 7.

_____. "Challenging the Lies." *CALC Report* [Clergy and Laity Concerned], March 1990, p. 5.

Montgomery, Peter. "Holy Columbus! His 500th Anniversary Won't Be Till 1992, But for a Small Circle of Insiders, the Fun Has Already Begun." *Common Cause,* Nov./Dec. 1989, pp. 24–6.

Moseley, Ray. "Expo '92 in Seville Celebrating Age of Discovery." *Chicago Tribune,* Nov. 3, 1991, p. 14 (Travel section). Describes buildings and exhibits at Expo '92, including a U.S. pavilion "destined to become . . . an embarrassment."

Murphy, Sheridan. "Celebrating 500 Years of Resistance and Struggle." *Blue Ryder,* Aug./Sept. 1991, p. 22.

Nash, Philip Tajitsu. "Columbus and the Classroom: Strategies for Teachers and Parents." *Rethinking Schools,* Oct./Nov. 1990, p. 15.

_____. "Re-'discovering' Columbus: An Agenda for Progressives." *CALC Report* [Clergy and Laity Concerned], summer 1990, pp. 12–14.

National Council of the Churches of Christ in the U.S.A. *A Faithful Response to the 500th Anniversary of the Arrival of Christopher Columbus: Resolution Adopted by the Governing Board, May 17, 1990.* 5 pages.

Nicolai, Dan. "Contesting the Columbus Day Quincentennial." *Artpaper,* Nov. 1989, pp. 12–13.

Novak, Viveca. "Quincentenary quandary." *Common Cause,* Jan./Feb. 1991. p. 5.

"Organizations and Resource Persons Involved in Alternative 1992 Activities." *CALC Report* [Clergy and Laity Concerned], summer 1990, p. 15.

Pardo, Mercedes. "Against Celebrating the Fifth Centennial of the 'Discovery of America.'" *Green Letter,* summer 1990, p. 18. A critical view from Spain.

Peterson, Bob. "Unlearning the Columbus Myth: A Bibliography of Resources." *Rethinking Schools,* Oct./Nov. 1990, p. 14.

Quammen, David. "Columbus and Submuloc." *Outside,* June 1990, pp. 31 + . "A gentle plot to reverse five centuries of dubious history."

Quijana, Anibal, "Recovering Utopia." *NACLA Report on the Americas,* Feb. 1991, pp. 34–40.

"The Quincentennial: Time for Reconciliation, Not Celebration." *Indian Report,* summer 1990, p. 4.

"Quincentennial Resources." *The Connection* [Central America Resource Center, St. Paul, Minnesota], April 1991, p. 3.

Raphael, David. "Something Is Wrong with Plans for Sepharad '92 Celebrations." *American Jewish World,* May 24, 1991, p. 5.

Rodriguez, Roberto. "1492 Brought Genocide; Why Celebrate?" *Los Angeles Times,* July 23, 1990, p. B5.

Rojas Mix, Miguel. "Reinventing Identity." *NACLA Report on the Americas,* Feb. 1991, pp. 29–33.

Sale, Kirkpatrick. "Columbian Legacy: We'd Better Start Preparing." *Earth First!,* Feb. 2, 1990, p. 25.

_____. "What Columbus Discovered." *The Nation,* Oct. 22, 1990, pp. 444–446.

Shadow. "Columbus Lied." *Columbus Lied* (Audio cassette/compact disc). Shanachie Records, 1991.

Stedman, Raymond William. "The Enemy." *Shadows of the Indian: Stereotypes in American Culture.* University of Oklahoma Press, 1982, pp. 134–138. Includes "Outline by Columbus."

Stiddem, David R. "It's Time We Rethink Our History." *CALC Report* [Clergy and Laity Concerned], March 1990, pp. 6–8.

Sugnet, Charlie, and Joanna O'Connell. "Discovering the Truth About Columbus." *Utne Reader,* March/April 1990, pp. 24, 26.

Sullivan, John. "An Ongoing Voyage, 1492–1992: The Library of Congress Quincentenary Program." *Library of Congress Information of Bulletin,* Jan. 29, 1990, pp. 51–55.

"A Teachable Moment." *MSRRT Newsletter,* Dec. 1990, pp. 4–5.

"A Time for Cheers or Tears? Mexico and Peru See the Colonial Era Differently." *Newsweek,* Jan. 23, 1989, p. 10.

Todorov, Tzvetan. "Discovery." *The Conquest of America: The Question of the Other.* Harper and Row, 1984. pp. 3–50.

Turner, Frederick. "Penetration." *Beyond Geography: The Western Spirit Against the Wilderness.* Viking Press, 1980. pp. 144–170.

Villagran, Nora. "The Great Columbus Chase." *San Jose Mercury News,* July 7, 1991, pp. 1T +. Presents accounts of Columbian cruelties, thoroughly covers counter–Quincentennial activities (with a focus on those organized by indigenous peoples), and includes a sidebar listing over two dozen "groups planning alternative Columbus celebrations."

Vogel, Virgil J. "The Indians Discover Columbus: 1492–1493." *The Country Was Ours: A Documentary History of the American Indian.* Harper and Row, 1972. pp. 33–34.

Wallis, J. "1992: A Call for Reconstruction." *Sojourners,* July 1990, p. 50.

Warrior, Robert Allen. "Indian Confab Reclaims 1992 Agenda." *Guardian,* Oct. 24, 1990, p. 13.

_____. "A Quincentenary Agenda." *Lies of Our Times,* Jan. 1991, p. 8.

White, Dale. "An Encounter with Controversy: New Exhibit Reveals Explorers' Dark Side." *Sarasota Herald-Tribune,* Feb. 4, 1990, p. 1D.

Wichman, Julie. "Columbus Rediscovered." *Shepherd Express,* Oct. 10, 1991, pp. 1 +. Investigates the lesser known history of Columbus's voyages, describes Quincentennial organizing efforts in Wisconsin, interviews Native Americans and other people concerned about the celebratory nature of the commemoration, and talks about the *Rethinking Schools* Columbus project.

Wilford, John Noble. "Discovering Columbus." *New York Times Magazine,* Aug. 11, 1991, pp. 24 +.

Williams, Eric. *From Columbus to Castro: The History of the Caribbean, 1492–1992.* Harper and Row, 1970. 576 pages.

Winkler, Karen J. "Humanities Agency Caught in Controversy Over Columbus Grants." *Chronicle of Higher Education,* March 13, 1991, p. A5 +.

Wrone, David R., and Russell S. Nelson, editors. *Who's the Savage?* R.E. Krieger Publishing, 1982. "Collection of documents that describes the mistreatment of the Native North American from the days of the Vikings to the present."

"The Year of Indigenous People: The 1992 Alliance." *Native Nations,* Jan. 1991, pp. 10–11.

Yewell, John. "To Growing Numbers, Columbus No Hero." *Saint Paul Pioneer Press,* Oct. 13, 1990, p. 5B.

Selected Addresses

Artpaper, 2402 University Ave. W., #206, St. Paul, MN 55114.
Blue Ryder, P.O. Box 587, Olean, NY 14760.

Briarpatch, 2138 McIntyre St., Regina, Saskatchewan, Canada, S4P 2R7.
CALC Report, P.O. Box 1987, Decatur, GA 30031.
Christianity and Crisis, 537 W. 121st St., New York, NY 10027.
The Circle, 1503 Franklin Ave., Minneapolis, MN 55404.
Collective Voice, 1929 S. 5th St., Minneapolis, MN 55454.
Common Cause, P.O. Box 220, Washington, DC 20077.
The Connection, Central America Resource Center, 317 17th St. SE, Minneapolis, MN 55414.
CrossRoads, P.O. Box 2809, Oakland, CA 94609.
E Magazine, 28 Knight St., Norwalk, CT 06851.
Earth First! P.O. Box 7, Canton, NY 13617.
Ecology Center Newsletter, 2530 San Pablo Ave., Berkeley, CA 94702.
Educators Against Racism and Apartheid, 164-04 Goethals Ave., Jamaica, NY 11432.
Green Letter, P.O. Box 14141, San Francisco, CA 94114.
Guardian, 33 W. 17th St., New York, NY 10011.
Indian Report, Friends Committee on National Legislation, 245 Second St. NE, Washington, DC 20002-5795.
Ism Press, P.O. Box 12447, San Francisco, CA 94112.
Katuah Journal, P.O. Box 638, Leicester, NC 28748.
Lies of Our Times, 145 W. Fourth St., New York, NY 10012.
Minority Trendsletter, 3861 Martin Luther King, Jr. Way, Oakland, CA 94609.
MSRRT Newsletter, Minnesota Library Association/Social Responsibilities Round Table, 4645 Columbus Ave. S., Minneapolis, MN 55407.
NACLA Report on the Americas, see *Report on the Americas.*
National Council of the Churches of Christ in the U.S.A., 176 Riverside Dr., Room 850, New York, NY 10115.
Native Nations, 175 Fifth Ave., New York, NY 10010.
New World Times, 625 Ashbury St., #14, San Francisco, CA 94117.
News from Indian Country, Rt. 2, Box 2900-A, Hayward, WI 54843.
Nonviolent Activist, 339 Lafayette St., New York, NY 10012.
Northeast Indian Quarterly, American Indian Program, 300 Caldwell Hall, Cornell University, Ithaca, NY 14853.
The Progressive, 409 E. Main St., Madison, WI 53703.
Raise the Stakes, P.O. Box 31251, San Francisco, CA 94131
Report on the Americas, 475 Riverside Dr., Suite 454, New York, NY 10115.
Rethinking Schools, 1001 Keefe Ave., Milwaukee, WI 53212.
SAIIC Newsletter, P.O. Box 28703, Oakland, CA 94604.
Shepherd Express, 1123 N. Water St., Milwaukee, WI 53202.
Sojourners, P.O. Box 29272, Washington, DC 20077-5290.
Utne Reader, 1624 Harmon Pl., Minneapolis, MN 55403.
Z Magazine, 150 W. Canton St., Boston, MA 02118.

Resource Directory

Jan DeSirey

The following list is not inclusive of all organizations with counter–Quincentennial events or activities planned. The focus is on more permanent national and regional organizations, whose existence does not depend on a single event. A broad spectrum of activities is included, from conferences to concerts, from pow-wows to plays, in order to provide a look at the many ways of "confronting Columbus" and his legacy. A caveat — as with any list of organizations: addresses, phone numbers and names are subject to change. The list is current as of November 1991.

Alliance for Cultural Democracy. P.O. Box 7591, Minneapolis, MN 55407. A national network aimed at empowering artists and cultural workers at the grassroots level, ACD also serves as a clearinghouse for information on the Quincentennial, publishes *huracán* ("500 Years of Resistance"), and is creating a 32-page handbook for designing Quincentennial-related grassroots resistance and education projects (*How to '92*, available fall 1991, for $2.00, from Lucy Lippard, 138 Prince St., New York, NY 10012).

American Indian Law Alliance. 488 Seventh Ave., Room 5K, New York, NY 10018. 212-268-1347. The Law Alliance, with the Solidarity Foundation, is involved in planning events with the Native American Council of New York City for 1992.

American Indian Law and Policy Center. University of Oklahoma, College of Law, 300 Timberland Rd., Norman, OK 73019-0701. Planning "New Voices for Native Visions: Beyond 1992," a conference scheduled for June 1992, which will explore issues of concern to Native Americans over the next 500 years.

American Indian Movement. 2300 Cedar Ave. South, Minneapolis, MN 55404. 612-724-3129. AIM, with its offshoot, League of Indigenous Sovereign Indian Nations (LISIN), plans to become a "presence" at the United Nations for one year, beginning October 12, 1991, while working to achieve a representative seat in the U.N. by 1992.

Arctic to Amazonia Alliance. P.O. Box 73, Strafford, VT 05072. 802-765-4337. Operates a regional clearinghouse for organizing efforts focused upon the Quincentennial (including a database on resource sharing), and publishes a newsletter (*The Arctic to Amazonia Alliance Report*).

Atlanta Quincentennial Alliance. Contact: AQUA, c/o Sandy Corley, 765 Myrtle St. NE, Atlanta, GA 30308. The Alliance is a group of educators, artists, performers and others planning a series of alternative programs for the Quincentennial. Besides a video and film festival and storytelling events, a symposium is planned for spring 1992, at Georgia State University, which will address issues of curriculum and education about Columbus, European colonization, and indigenous cultures.

ATLATL. 402 W. Roosevelt, Phoenix, AZ 85003. 602-253-2731. A national Indian arts service organization, which, together with Submuloc Society, produced a traveling exhibit ("Submuloc, or the Columbus Wohs"), featuring conceptual and performance art, slides and videos by Native American artists, all portraying an alternative view of the Quincentennial celebration. The exhibit was curated by artist Jaune Quick-to-See Smith.

Boston Indian Council. 105 South Huntington, Boston, MA 02130. 617-232-0343. The Council, along with nearby museums, universities and Indian organizations, is planning a conference for October 3-9, 1992, which will feature an international pow-wow, and will cover topics of traditional and modern concern.

Center for the Study of Political Graphics. 8124 W. 3rd St., Suite 211, Los Angeles, CA 90813. The Center has prepared an exhibit — available for touring — on the arrival of Columbus from the perspective of conquered peoples.

Central America Resource Center Quincentennial Committee. 317 17th Ave. SE, Minneapolis, MN 55414-2077. 612-627-9445. CARC serves as a clearinghouse for alternative Quincentennial curricula and other educational materials.

Clergy and Laity Concerned. P.O. Box 1987, Decatur, GA 30031. 404-377-1983. A national, "multi-racial network for people of faith and conscience," CALC has available an information packet ("Rediscovering the History of the Americas") which includes a bibliography and a list of resource people and groups involved in counter-Quincentennial activities.

Columbus in Context Coalition/Rethinking the History of the Americas Project. c/o Clergy and Laity Concerned, 198 Broadway, New York, NY 10038. 212-964-6730. A New York-based group of educators, artists, community activists, and others networking to challenge the "celebration" and to re-examine education, law, media and the arts in terms of the "discovery" and conquest. Sponsored the July 1990 program, "Columbus in Context: Rediscovering the Americas."

Committee for American Indian History (CAIH). 6802 SW 13th St., Gainesville, FL 32608. 904-378-3246. "Works to introduce contemporary Indian problems into school curricula . . . and to introduce Native perspectives on historical events," and publishes a bimonthly magazine linking counter-Quincentenary activities (*Indigenous Thought*). Along with the University of Florida and the Florida Endowment for the Humanities, CAIH co-sponsored a December 1991 conference titled, "The Ethics of Celebration and De-celebration, a Native American Perspective."

Confederation of Indian Nations of Ecuador (CONAIE). Casilla Postal 92-C, Sucursal 15, Quito, Ecuador. CONAIE, along with the South and Meso-American Indian Information Center and the Organization of Indian Nations of Colombia, organized the "500 Years of Indian Resistance" conference held in 1990. For 1992, the three organizations are planning a 500-person redress delegation to Spain.

Continental Meeting of Indigenous and Popular Organizatons. c/o Secretaria Operativa, Apartado Postal 7-B, Sucursal El Trebol, 01903 Guatemala Ciudad, Guatemala. 502-2-29040, 80375. The Continental Campaign is coordinating actions of indigenous people in the Americas to combat the official Quincentennial celebration and to develop a network of "communication, encounter and coordination" among indigenous people and "popular sectors." The First Continental Meeting was held in Quito, Ecuador, in 1990. The Second Continental Meeting took place October 7-12, 1991, in Guatemala.

Educators Against Racism and Apartheid. 164-04 Goethals Ave., Jamaica, NY 11432.

A New York–based educators' group which is developing student projects in a variety of subject disciplines that counter the Columbus myth.

Europilgrim. c/o Hans W. Horeman, Vrienden Van Epp '92, A. Sniederslaan 14, NL 5615 GE Eindhoven, The Netherlands. A coalition of Belgian, Dutch and German people planning a 7-month walk across the U.S. in 1992 to draw attention to the oppression of Native Americans (as well as to the ongoing mining of uranium for nuclear purposes).

500 Years of Resistance Coalition (500YRC). P.O. Box 8901, Denver, CO 80201. A broad-based multiracial coalition dedicated to correcting the cultural, sociopolitical, economic, and spiritual wrongs done to indigenous people of the Americas, 500YRC is also recognizing 1992 as the 50th anniversary of the internment of Japanese-Americans.

Global Awareness Project of Northwestern Ontario, Counter-Columbus Committee. 283 Bay St., Thunder Bay, Ontario, Canada P7B 1R7. The Committee has a two-year program intended to deal with the teaching of history to young people, to encourage action against celebrations of Columbus's landing, and to make connections between the history of colonialism and present-day repression of indigenous and other peoples.

In the Heart of the Beast Puppet and Mask Theatre. 1500 East Lake St., Minneapolis, MN 55407. 612-721-2535. The Theatre has done several productions as part of a three-year project exploring Columbus and the Quincentennial, one of which is a touring show, "Discover America."

Indigenous America Media Project. P.O. Box 864, Wendell, MA 01379. 508-544-8313. A collaboration of Turning Tide Productions, Eclipse Communications, and Arctic to Amazonia Alliance for the Earth, to produce a series of documentary television programs examining the Columbus legacy from the perspectives of contemporary indigenous peoples.

Indigenous Communicatons Resource Center. American Indian Program, 400 Caldwell Hall, Cornell University, Ithaca, NY 14850. The ICRC is planning a hemispheric Indian conference for 1992, as well as a multiethnic encounter at Cornell. The Center is also publishing a resource book on 1992 (*View from the Shore*) and publishes a scholarly journal (*Northeast Indian Quarterly*).

Indigenous Women's Network. P.O. Box 174, Lake Elmo, MN 55042. 612-770-3861. The Network is planning a Third Conference of Indigenous Women, 1992, in Cuernavaca, Mexico, to focus on 500 years of resistance by the indigenous peoples of the Americas, and also publishes a journal (*Indigenous Woman*).

Indio-Innu 1492–1992. 2135 Rue Beaudry, Montreal, Quebec, H2L 364 Canada; or P.O. Box 800, 1089 Dequen, Sept-Iles, Quebec, G4R 4L9 Canada. Indio-Innu is organizing an International Meeting of Native Peoples on Peace and the Environment, which will include a conference, concerts, a cultural festival and a meeting of Native spiritual leaders from the Americas, to reflect on the coexistence of Native and non–Native peoples, and to look ahead to the next 500 years. The group is also urging all Native peoples to drum or play other traditional instruments for one hour at noon on October 12, 1992.

International Council for Adult Education. 720 Bathurst St., Suite 500, Toronto, Ontario, Canada M5S 2R4. The Council is working with the World Council of Indigenous Peoples, and using the Quincentennial as a starting point, in efforts to reach indigenous communities through training, research, seminars, and other educational means, to promote the development of humankind.

International Indian Treaty Council (IITC). 710 Clayton St. #1, San Francisco, CA 94117. 415-566-0251. The legal and political section of AIM is planning an international

pow-wow October 9–10, 1992, followed by a tribunal, October 10–11, at which Columbus, Pizarro, Cortés, and DeSoto will be put "on trial." IITC is also planning to form
a flotilla ("Peace Navy") of 500 vessels, which will form a blockade to meet the replicas
of Columbus's ships as they sail into San Francisco Bay on October 12, 1992.

Minnesota Library Association, Social Responsibilities Round Table (MSRRT). c/o
Chris Dodge, 4645 Columbus Ave. South, Minneapolis, MN 55407. 612-541-8572.
Serves as a regional clearinghouse for counter–Quincentennial activities and
materials, and has available a continually-revised bibliography of Columbus-related
materials. MSRRT also organized panel discussions for the 1990 Minnesota Library
Association Conference and for the 1991 Midwest Federation of Library Associations
Conference in Minneapolis, titled "The Columbus Quincentennial: Is There
Anything to Celebrate?"

National Council for the Social Studies. 3501 Newark St. NW, Washington, DC
20016. 202-966-7840. The Council is preparing curriculum materials for the study of
the historical and contemporary effects of Columbus's landing.

National Council of the Churches of Christ. 475 Riverside Dr., New York, NY 10115.
212-870-2298. The NCC Racial Justice Working Group produced and disseminated
a packet of materials ("Responding Faithfully to the Quincentenary") to be used "to
reflect upon what 1492 continues to mean in 1992 to indigenous, poor, oppressed and
ethnic people . . . throughout the Americas."

1992 Alliance. c/o Richard Hill, American Indian Art Institute Museum, P.O.
Box 20007, Santa Fe, NM 87504. 505-988-6281. Represents the efforts of Indian
organizations, foundations and the media to respond to the mainstream version of the
Quincentennial. Other goals include education of the public about the beliefs of
Native Americans, their history, culture and natural law, protection of indigenous
rights, and strengthening "Indian values, traditions and philosophies." Plans include
establishing a 1992 clearinghouse and a newsletter.

Northland Poster Collective. c/o Ricardo Levins Morales, 1613 E. Lake St., Minneapolis, MN 55407. 612-721-2273. The Collective has available buttons, stickers,
T-shirts, posters, and a calendar reflecting alternative views of Columbus's landing.

Origen Project. Hans Braumuller, Los Almendros 3898, Nuñoa, Santiago, Chile.
A mail art project on the theme, "500 Years of Genocide and Colonialism."

Resistance 500. c/o South and Meso-American Indian Information Center, P.O.
Box 28703, Oakland, CA 94604. 415-834-4263. A coalition of environmental, education, human rights and other progressive groups, including the South and Meso-
American Indian Information Center, Alliance for Cultural Democracy and the International Indian Treaty Council. The coalition was formed at the All Peoples Network
Conference in Davis, California, with the goal of implementing activities that present
an alternative to the Eurocentric Quincentennial programs, for 1992 and beyond.

Seminole Tribe of Florida. 6073 Stirling Road, Hollywood, FL 33024. The
Seminole Tribe is planning a grand pow-wow during the summer of 1992, to focus
on Native contributions to the U.S. and their intent to continue this contribution.

Sephardic Educational Center. 6505 Wilshire Boulevard, Suite 403, Los Angeles,
CA 90048. 213-653-7365. The Center is planning an international conference
dedicated to exploring the consequences of the repression and exile of Sephardic Jewry
under the Spanish Inquisition of 1492.

South and Meso-American Indian Information Center (SAIIC). P.O. Box 28703, Oakland, CA 94604. 415-834-4263. Serves as a clearinghouse for many Spanish-speaking
Native organizations and provides information about Quincentennial-related activities
via their publication, *SAIIC Newsletter.* SAIIC was also one of the convenors of the First
Continental Meeting of Indigenous Peoples in Quito, Ecuador, in 1990.

Submuloc Society. c/o Kathryn Steward, P.O. Box 6157, Bozeman, MT 59715; or Salish Kootenai College, P.O. Box 117, Pablo, MT 59855. Submuloc (Columbus spelled backwards) is the response of a group of five Native American artists to the traditional view of Columbus. The intention is "to generate a better understanding of American Indians and their many contributions to all of mankind," and to reverse the impact Columbus has had on Native peoples.

Syracuse Cultural Workers. P.O. Box 6367, Syracuse, NY 13217. 315-474-1132. SCW is producing several resources featuring Native American perspectives on the Quincentennial. Planned are posters, notecards and a calendar combining Native American images with dates which reveal the Americas' pre–1492 cultures.

Underground Railway Theatre. 41 Foster St., Arlington, MA 02174. 617-643-6916. The Theatre has produced a play for school and family audiences ("The Discovery of Columbus"), using actors, audience participation, puppets and live music, available for touring in Fall 1991. For 1992 they are preparing "The Christopher Columbus Follies: An Eco-Cabaret," in which Columbus returns to the Americas in 2092.

WBAI-FM. c/o Marie Murillo, WBAI-FM, 505 Eighth Ave., New York, NY 10018. 212-279-0707. The New York affiliate of Pacifica Radio is coproducing (with Columbus in Context) a monthly radio program, "Rediscovering Columbus: Countdown to 1992," focusing on progressive analyses of issues related to the Quincentennial, as well as providing resources for activists and information about alternative events. Tapes are available for rebroadcast or educational uses.

World Council of Indigenous Peoples. 555 King Edward Ave., Ottawa, Ontario, Canada K1N 6N5. The Council functions at the global level to create an awareness of the work being done by indigenous groups and has also issued a call for papers on the theme, "Beyond 1992." "Themes of interest include perceptions on social development, philosophy, social and cultural organization, national indigenous disappearance and co-existence."

World's Columbian Jubilee. c/o Jim Koehnline, P.O. Box 85777, Seattle, WA 98145-1777. Artist Koehnline is soliciting entries for a new calendar of saints, from among those "who planted their gardens of dreams in the cracks and at the margins (along with those who ate of their fruits and saved the seeds)." The intent is to celebrate the true spirit of jubilee with a focus on emancipation and restoration.

Declaration of Quito

Appendix A

Indigenous Alliance of the Americas on 500 Years of Resistance, July 1990

The Continental Gathering "500 Years of Indian Resistance," with representatives from 120 Indian Nations, along with International and Fraternal organizations, met in Quito, Ecuador on July 17–20, 1990. The gathering was organized by the Confederation of Indian Nations of Ecuador (CONAIE), the Organization of Indian Nations of Colombia (ONIC) and South and Meso-American Information Center (SAIIC). The following is the Declaration from this gathering. The North, South and Meso-American conference participants declare before the world the following:

We Indians of America have never abandoned our constant struggle against the conditions of oppression, discrimination and exploitation which were imposed upon us as a result of the European invasion of our ancestral territories.

Our struggle is not a mere conjunctural reflection of the memory of 500 years of oppression which the invaders, in complicity with the "democractic" governments of our countries, want to turn into events of jubilation and celebration. Our struggle as Indian People, Nations and Nationalities is based on our identity, which shall lead us to true liberation. We are responding aggressively, and commit ourselves to reject this "celebration."

The struggle of our People has acquired a new quality in recent times. This struggle is less isolated and more organized. We are now completely conscious that our total liberation can only be expressed through the complete exercise of our self-determination. Our unity is based on this fundamental right. Our self-determination is not just a simple declaration.

We must guarantee the necessary conditions that permit complete exercise of our self-determination; and this, in turn must be expressed as complete autonomy for our Peoples. Without Indian self-government and without control of our territories, there can be no autonomy.

The achievement of this objective is a principal task for Indian Peoples. However, through our struggles we have learned that our problems are not different, in many respects, from those of other popular sectors. We are convinced that we must march alongside the peasants, the workers, the marginalized sectors, together with intellectuals committed to our cause, in order to destroy the dominant system of oppression and construct a new society, pluralistic, democratic and humane, in which peace is guaranteed.

The existing nation states of the Americas, their constitutions and fundamental laws, are judicial/political expressions that negate our socio-economic, cultural and political rights.

At this point in our struggle, one of our priorities is to demand a complete structural change which allows for the recognition of Indian People's rights to self-determination, and the control of our territories through our own governments.

Our problems will not be resolved through the self-serving politics of governmental entities which seek integration and ethno-development. It is necessary to have an integral transformation at the level of the state and national society; that is to say, the creation of a new nation.

In this Gathering it has been clear that territorial rights are a fundamental demand of the Indigenous Peoples of the Americas. Based on these aforementioned reflections, the organizations united in the First Continental Gathering of Indigenous Peoples reaffirm:

1. Our emphatic rejection of the Quincentennial celebration, and the firm promise that we will turn that date into an occasion to strengthen our process of continental unity and struggle towards our liberation.

2. Ratify our resolute political project of self-determination and our autonomy, in the framework of nation states, under a new popular order, with respect for whatever forms of organization each Nation determines appropriate for their situation.

3. Affirm our decision to defend our culture, education, and religion as fundamental to our identity as Peoples, reclaiming and maintaining our own forms of spiritual life and communal coexistence, in an intimate relationship with our Mother Earth.

4. We reject the manipulation of organizations which are linked to the dominant sectors of society and have no Indigenous representation, who usurp our name for (their own) imperialist interests. At the same time, we affirm our choice to strengthen our own organizations, without excluding or isolating ourselves from other popular struggles.

5. We recognize the important role that Indigenous women play in the struggles of our Peoples. We understand the necessity to expand women's participation in our organizations and we reaffirm that it is one struggle, men and women together, in our liberation process, and a key question in our political practices.

6. We Indian Peoples consider it vital to defend and conserve our natural resources, which right now are being attacked by transnational corporations. We are convinced that this defense will be realized if it is Indian People who administer and control the territories where we live, according to our own principles of organization and communal life.

7. We oppose national judicial structures which are the result of the process of colonization and neo-colonization. We seek a New Social Order that embraces our traditional exercise of Common Law, an expression of our culture and forms of organization. We demand that we be recognized as Peoples under International Law, and that this recognition be incorporated into the respective Nation States.

8. We denounce the victimization of Indian People through violence and persecution, which constitutes a flagrant violation of human rights. We demand respect for our right to life, to land, to free organization and expression of our culture. At the same time we demand the release of our leaders who are held as political prisoners, an end to repression, and restitution for the harms caused us.

A Faithful Response to the 500th Anniversary of the Arrival of Christopher Columbus

Appendix B

Resolution of the National Council of the Churches of Christ in the USA, May 17, 1990

As U.S. Christians approach public observances marking the 500th anniversary of Christopher Columbus's first landing in the Western hemisphere, we are called to review our full history, reflect upon it, and act as people of faith mindful of the significance of 1492. The people in our churches and communities now look at the significance of the event in different ways. What represented newness of freedom, hope and opportunity for some was the occasion for oppression, degradation and genocide for others. For the Church this is not a time for celebration but a time for a committed plan of action insuring that this "kairos" moment in history not continue to cosmetically coat the painful aspects of the American history of racism.

1. In 1992, celebrations of the 500th anniversary of the arrival of Christopher Columbus in the "New World" will be held.[1] For the descendants of the survivors of the subsequent invasion, genocide, slavery, "ecocide" and exploitation of the wealth of the land, a celebration is not an appropriate observation of this anniversary.

- For the indigenous people of the Caribbean islands, Christopher Columbus's invasion marked the beginning of slavery and their eventual genocide.
- For the indigenous people of Central America, the result was slavery, genocide and exploitation leading to the present struggle for liberation.
- For the indigenous people of South America, the result was slavery, genocide and the exploitation of their mineral and natural resources, fostering the early accumulation of capital by the European countries.
- For the indigenous people of Mexico, the result was slavery, genocide, rape of mineral as well as natural resources and a decline of their civilization.
- For the peoples of modern Puerto Rico, Hawaii and the Philippines the result was the eventual grabbing of the land, genocide and the present economic captivity.

- For the indigenous peoples of North America, it brought slavery, genocide and theft and exploitation of the land which has led to their descendants' impoverished lives.[2]
- For the peoples of the African Diaspora, the result was slavery, an evil and immoral system steeped in racism, economic exploitation, rape of mineral as well as human resources and national divisiveness along the lines of the colonizing nations.
- For the peoples from Asia brought to work the land, torn from their families and culture by false promises of economic prosperity, the result was labor camps, discrimination and today's victimization of the descendants facing anti–Asian racism.
- For the descendants of the European conquerors the subsequent legacy has been the perpetuation of paternalism and racism into our cultures and times.[3]

2. The Church, with few exceptions, accompanied and legitimized this conquest and exploitation. Theological justifications for destroying native religious beliefs while forcing conversion to European forms of Christianity demanded a submission from the newly converted that facilitated their total conquest and exploitation.[4]

3. Therefore, it is appropriate for the Church to reflect on its role in that historical tragedy and, in pursuing a healing process, to move forward in our witness for justice and peace.[5]

Towards that end, we are called to:

a. reflect seriously on the complexities and complicities of the missionary efforts during this period of colonization and subjugation that resulted in the destruction of cultures and religions, the desecration of religious sites and other crimes against the spirituality of indigenous peoples;[6]
b. review and reflect on the degree to which current missiologies tend to promote lifestyles that perpetuate the exploitation of the descendants of the indigenous people, and that stand in the way of enabling their self-determination;
c. identify and celebrate the significant voices within the Church that have consistently advocated the rights and dignities of indigenous peoples;
d. recognize that what some historians have termed a "discovery" in reality was an invasion and colonization with legalized occupation, genocide, economic exploitation and a deep level of institutional racism and moral decadence;
e. reflect seriously on how the Church should and might accomplish its task of witness and service to and with those of other faiths, recognizing their integrity as children of God, and not contributing to new bondages.

4. Therefore, the Governing Board of the National Council of the Churches of Christ in the USA:

a. Declares 1992 to be a year of reflection and repentance, and calls upon its member communions to enter into theological and missional reflection, study and prayer as a faithful observance of that year;
b. Commits itself to be involved in activities that bring forward the silenced interpretation of the 1492 event including:

- taking action to influence how governments or other institutions plan to celebrate the "discovery" of America;
- using its television, radio and print media resources to educate the Church and its constituency about the factual histories of indigenous people, the colonization of their lands and the effects today of colonization, including the loss of land, lives and cultures; and
- advocating the inclusion of the accurate factual history of indigenous people, including African Americans, in textbooks to be used in public and parochial education systems in the United States;[7] and

- cooperating with other hemispheric interfaith bodies in a gathering in the Caribbean islands to analyze the effects of the European invasion and colonization of the Americas from the perspective of their descendants;

c. Calls upon its member communions to join in affirming and implementing this resolution in dialogue with indigenous people of the Americas;

d. Requests that the Division of Church and Society (or its legal successor) in cooperation with the Division of Overseas Ministries (or its legal successor) develop programmatic materials for the speedy implementation of this resolution;

e. Requests appropriate units to explore convening a gathering of representatives of traditional tribes, urban Indian and tribal governments to discuss ways to strengthen Indian ministries;

f. Supports the endeavors of theological schools and seminaries to help open alternative understandings of 1492/1992;

g. Declares this resolution to be our humble and faithful first step contribution towards a deep understanding among peoples of our country. It is our hope that in a new spirit of reconciliation, we move forward together into a shared future as God's creatures honoring the plurality of our cultural heritage.

Policy Base

Human Rights (Policy Statement adopted by the General Board, 1961)
Racial Justice (Policy Statement adopted by the Governing Board, 1981)

Notes

1. A 30-member federal agency, the Christopher Columbus Quincentenary Jubilee Commission, was created by the U.S. Congress. Members appointed by President Reagan include James Baker, Robert Mosbacher and John Goudie. Spain, Italy and Portugal have designated observors to the U.S. Commission. A national program of commemorative activities is planned for 1991–1992. Twenty-two states have Quincentenary commissions. Among the projects: the Grand Columbus Regatta of tall ships to New York and Boston; commemorative coins; deployment of three space caravels. In Spain events will lead up to the 1992 World's Fair Expo with the theme of "The Age of Discovery."

2. "Chief Seattle Speaks," December 1854.

3. Howard Zinn, *A People's History of the United States* (New York: Harper & Row, 1980). See also the Final Document of the European Ecumenical Assembly *Peace with Justice for the Whole Creation,* May 1989, Basel, Switzerland, issued by the Conference of European Churches and the Council of European Bishop's Conference (Doct.id. 0116MPC/fm), June 2, 1989, which states that, "1992 will moreover mark the 500th anniversary of the beginning of a period of European expansion to the detriment of other peoples."

4. Chief Seattle, *ibid.*

5. See Basel Document, *ibid.*, where European churchpersons acknowledge having "failed to challenge with sufficient consistency political and economic systems which misuse power and wealth, exploit resources for their self-interest and perpetuate poverty and marginalisation. We consider it to be a scandal and a crime how human rights are violated. We commit ourselves to struggle against all violations of human rights and the social structures which favor them."

6. "A Public Declaration to the Tribal Councils and Traditional Spiritual Leaders of the Indian and Eskimo Peoples of the Pacific Northwest," Bishop Thomas L. Blevins, Pacific Northwest Synod, Lutheran Church in America, and eight Bishops and leaders of other denominations, November, 1987. This statement speaks of "unconscious and insensitive" attitudes and actions by the church which reflect "the rampant racism and prejudice of the dominant culture with which we too willingly identified." In September 1987 Pope John Paul II spoke to Indian leaders of the Northwest Territories and assured them that the Roman Catholic Church "extols the equal human dignity of all peoples and defends their right to uphold their own cultural character, with its distinct traditions and customs." See Marsha King, "Prejudice Recalled: Churches Pledge to Support Indian Spiritual Practices," *The Seattle Times,* November 22, 1987. See also 1969 Report from the Anglican Church of Canada which acknowledges the problems of Canadian Indians and the complicity of missionaries.

7. Bartolomé de las Casas, *Historia de los Indios* (ca. 1550), *Tears of the Indians* (ca. 1550), *In Defense of the Indians* (ca. 1550); Vine Deloria, Jr., *Custer Died for Your Sins* (1970), *God Is Red* (1983); Eduardo Galeano, *Memory of Fire: Genesis* (New York: Pantheon, 1985); Helen Hunt Jackson, *A Century of Dishonor* (1881); Francis Jennings, *The Invasion of America: Indians, Colonialism and the Cant of Conquest* (Chapel Hill: University of North Carolina Press, 1975); Winthrop Jordan, *White Over Black: American Attitudes Toward the Negro 1550–1812* (Baltimore: Penguin, 1968); Patricia Nelson Limerick, *The Legacy of Conquest: The Unbroken Past of the American West* (New York: W.W. Norton, 1987).

The Columbian Quincentenary: An Educational Opportunity

Appendix C

Statement by the National Council for the Social Studies, October, 1991.

Nineteen ninety-two is the 500th anniversary of Columbus's first voyage to the Americas. The voyage of Columbus is a much too significant event in human history for the nation's schools and colleges to ignore or to treat romantically or trivially. The most fitting and enduring way in which educators can participate in commemorating the Quincentenary is to examine seriously the available scholarship to enhance our knowledge about 1492 and, in turn, to enhance the knowledge of our students. Specifically, educators should: (a) help students comprehend the contemporary relevance of 1492, and (b) provide students with basic, accurate knowledge about Columbus's voyages, their historical setting, and unfolding effects.

Sixty years after Columbus's first landfall in the Americas, Francisco López de Gómara wrote: "The greatest event since the creation of the world (excluding the incarnation and death of Him who created it) is the discovery of the Indies." In the year the 13 English colonies declared their independence from Britain, Adam Smith observed: "The discovery of America, and that of a passage to the East Indies by the Cape of Good Hope, are the two greatest and most important events recorded in the history of mankind."

Although these two famous assessments of the significance of 1492 in human history may be overstatements, it is certainly true that the world as we know it would not have come to be were it not for the chain of events set in motion by European contact with the Americas.

The Contemporary Relevance of 1492

One of the most significant and visible features of the contemporary United States is its multiethnic and culturally pluralistic character. Scholars describe the United States as one of history's first universal or world nations—its people are a microcosm of humanity with biological, cultural and social ties to all other parts of the earth. The origin of these critical features of our demographic and our civil life lies in the initial encounters and migrations of peoples and cultures of the Americas, Europe and Africa.

Another significant feature of the United States is the fact that the nation and its citizens are an integral part of a global society created by forces that began to unfold in 1492. Geographically, the Eastern and Western hemispheres were joined after millennia of virtual isolation from one another. Economically, the growth of the modern global economy was substantially stimulated by the bullion trade linking Latin America, Europe and Asia; the slave trade connecting Africa, Europe and the Americas; and the fur trade joining North America, Western Europe and Russia. Politically, the contemporary worldwide international system was born in the extension of intra–European conflict into the Western Hemisphere, the establishment of European colonies in the Americas, and the accompanying intrusion of Europeans into the political affairs of Native Americans, and the Native Americans' influence on the political and military affairs of European states. Ecologically, the massive transcontinental exchange of plants, animals, microorganisms and natural resources initiated by the Spanish and Portuguese voyages modified the global ecological system forever.

Basic Knowledge About the Historical Setting and Effects of Columbus's Voyages

Educators should ensure that good contemporary scholarship and reliable traditional sources be used in teaching students abut Columbus's voyages, their historical settings and unfolding effects. Scholarship highlights some important facets of history that are in danger of being disregarded, obscured, or ignored in the public hyperbole that is likely to surround the Quincentenary. Particular attention should be given to the following:

1. Columbus did not discover a new world and, thus, initiate American history.
Neither did the Vikings nor did the seafaring Africans, Chinese, Pacific Islanders or other people who may have preceded the Vikings. The land that Columbus encountered was not a new world. Rather, it was a world of peoples with rich and complex histories dating back at least 15,000 years or possibly earlier. On that fateful morning of October 12, 1492, Columbus did not discover a new world. He put, rather, as many historians have accurately observed, two old worlds into permanent contact.

2. The real America Columbus encountered in 1492 was a different place from the precontact America often portrayed in folklore, textbooks and the mass media.
The America of 1492 was not a wilderness inhabited by primitive peoples whose history was fundamentally different from that of the peoples of the Eastern Hemisphere. Many of the same phenomena characterized, rather, the history of the peoples of both the Western and the Eastern hemispheres, including: highly developed agricultural systems, centers of dense populations, complex civilizations, large-scale empires, extensive networks of long-distance trade and cultural diffusion, complex patterns of interstate conflict and cooperation, sophisticated systems of religious and scientific belief, extensive linguistic diversity and regional variations in levels of societal complexity.

3. Africa was very much a part of the social, economic and political system of the Eastern hemisphere in 1492.
The Atlantic slave trade, which initially linked western Africa to Mediterranean Europe and the Atlantic islands, soon extended to the Americas. Until the end of the 18th century, the number of Africans who crossed the Atlantic to the Americas exceeded the number of Europeans. The labor, experiences and cultures of the African American

people, throughout enslavement as well as after emancipation, have been significant in shaping the economic, political and social history of the United States.

4. *The encounters of Native Americans, Africans and Europeans following 1492 are not stories of vigorous white actors confronting passive red and black spectators and victims.*

Moreover, these were not internally homogeneous groups but represented a diversity of peoples with varied cultural traditions, economic structures and political systems. All parties pursued their interests as they perceived them—sometimes independently of the interests of others, sometimes in collaboration with others, and sometimes in conflict with others. All borrowed from and influenced the others and, in turn, were influenced by them. The internal diversity of the Native Americans, the Africans and the Europeans contributed to the development of modern American pluralistic culture and contemporary world civilization.

5. *As a result of forces from 1492, Native Americans suffered catastrophic mortality rates.*

By far the greatest contributors to this devastation were diseases brought by the explorers and those who came after. The microorganisms associated with diseases such as smallpox, measles, whooping cough, chicken pox and influenza had not evolved in the Americas; hence, the indigenous peoples had no immunity to these diseases when the Europeans and Africans arrived. These diseases were crucial allies in the European conquest of the Native American. The ensuing wars between rival European nations that were played out in this hemisphere, the four centuries of Indian and European conflicts, as well as the now well-documented instances of genocidal and displacement policies of the colonial and postcolonial governments further contributed to the most extensive depopulation of a group of peoples in the history of humankind. Despite this traumatic history of destruction and deprivation, Native American peoples have endured and are experiencing a cultural resurgence as we observe the 500th anniversary of the encounter.

6. *Columbus's voyages were not just a European phenomenon but, rather, were a facet of Europe's millennia-long history of interaction with Asia and Africa.*

The "discovery" of America was an unintended outcome of Iberian Europe's search for an all-sea route to the "Indies"—a search stimulated in large part by the disruption of European-Asian trade routes occasioned by the collapse of the Mongol Empire. Technology critical to Columbus's voyages such as the compass, the sternpost rudder, gunpowder and paper originated in China. The lateen sail, along with much of the geographical knowledge on which Columbus relied, originated with or was transmitted by the Arabs.

7. *Although most examinations of the U.S. historical connections to the Eastern hemisphere tend to focus on northwestern Europe, Spain and Portugal also had extensive effects on the Americas.*

From the Columbian voyages through exploration, conquest, religious conversion, settlement and the development of Latin American mestizo cultures, Spain and Portugal had a continuing influence on life in the American continents.

The Enduring Legacy of 1492

Certain events in human history change forever our conception of who we are and how we see the world. Such events not only change our maps of the world, they alter our mental landscapes as well. The event of 500 years ago, when a small group of Europeans and, soon after, Africans, encountered Native Americans is of this magnitude. Educators contribute to the commemoration of the quincentenary in intellectually significant and educationally appropriate ways when they assist students in becoming knowledgeable about this event and about its critical role in shaping contemporary America as a universal nation within an interdependent world.

Columbus Quincentennial Resolution

Appendix D

American Library Association

WHEREAS: A Presidential Commission is planning a massive celebration to take place in 1992 on the 500th anniversary of Columbus's voyage, with festivities including a trip to Mars by three solar-powered "space caravels," the sale of commemorative coins, and a scholarship program designed to "both honor the achievements of Columbus and encourage young people who embody his spirit and accomplishments to carry forward his legacy into the next century,"

AND WHEREAS: Columbus's voyage to America began a legacy of European piracy, brutality, slave trading, murder, disease, conquest and ethnocide, and further, engendered the Native American Holocaust which saw a population of over 5,000,000 American Indians in the land area of the United States decline to about 250,000 by the last decade of the 19th century.

THEREFORE, BE IT RESOLVED: The American Library Association urges libraries to provide Columbus Quincentennial programs and materials which examine the event from an authentic Native American perspective, dealing directly with topics like cultural imperialism, colonialism and the Native American Holocaust.

Introduced by the Minnesota Library Association Social Responsibilities Round Table (MSRRT) and passed by ALA membership, June 1990.

The Santo Domingo Statement*

Appendix E

As the time approaches for the celebration of the 500th anniversary, the controversy grows regarding the "discovery" and the evangelization of this continent. The following statement issued by the Commission for Studies on the History of the Church in Latin America (CEHILA), is offered for serious reflection.

The Commission for Studies on the History of the Church in Latin America (CEHILA), attentive to the clamor of the indigenous and Afro-American peoples and in solidarity with the Christian Communities in Santo Domingo, met to reflect on the historic significance of the 500th anniversary of Western colonial expansion in our lands.

I. Identities

For us the historic significance of the V Centenary springs from concrete identities and clearly distinguishable faces. There are the millions of faces of the many indigenous peoples, the autochthonous inhabitants of these lands. They are the ones invaded by Europe, which turned them into strangers in their own land. There are also the faces of millions of Africans transplanted here to our lands in a monstrous exile. They were enslaved by Europe and uprooted from their own land.

Since 1492 the West has set itself up as the world's center. In its pride the West has tried to found a world in its own image through invasions and the weight of its imperial will. It has denied the identity of Indians and Africans and their own descendants of mixed bloods; all those cursed bloods and their rebellious, creative and resistant issues.

But those are the identities which form the foundation of our history and our historical significance. The illusions of the Western lords, with their economic, political and ideological pretensions, all of them violent and homicidal, have all been in vain. In spite of everything, for 500 years these grassroots identities, conflictive, rejected and marginated, have continued to grow, mature; they intertwine, provoke us and make us what we are.

Translated from a document written by Guillermo Melendez, October 12, 1989.

The invaders, as a background for their pride and supposed superiority in the world, used the Christian God, transforming him into a symbol of power and oppression. Indians, Blacks, mixed bloods, Afro-Americans and Caribbeans were judged to be pagans, infidels, superstitious creatures, lost in the darkness of sin and error. God had to arrive here with the Europeans. This was, we believe, the idolatry of the West.

Looked at from our historical perspective, God, the creator of life, had already been here in our lands for thousands of years as the vital, spiritual force of aboriginal and African cultures. It was the Spirit who gave life, well-being and sustenance to all peoples, as the mother of this land.

The Western Churches will insist on the 500 years of evangelization. But they will cover up the Spirit of life and liberation active since time immemorial, and which Europe often smothered or interrupted by its sense of superiority and contempt for the oppressed peoples and their descendants. "What can he save us from?" the Indians said, with every right, referring to the invaders' god. (cf. AGI, Charcas, Leg. 12, fs. 1–5). All Christians, Catholics and Protestants, from the North and the South, are in some way responsible for this sin and we ask for forgiveness.

II. The Invasions

1492: Year of glory for the conquerors!
Of criminal activity and misfortune for the conquered!
The West still talks about the "discovery of America," or the more up to date "encounter of cultures." For the peoples colonized in 1492, it was the beginning of the invasion and uprooting. The invasion and plundering of lands which already had owners. The uprooting of millions of Africans, deported and enslaved by the colonial powers. The conquest was, as José Martí said, "an historical calamity and a crime against nature." The conquest and colonization of America is a 500-year long process of invasion and oppression. The plundering of land and destruction of nature hasn't ceased since the end of the 15th century. The genocide, the ethnocide, and the destruction of the culture and religion of the autochthonous peoples hasn't ceased. The destruction and oppression of colonialism fell especially heavily on the indigenous women and children.

The greatest genocide in human history took place in the 16th century. And still, today, 300 million of our brothers and sisters survive in a situation of extreme poverty under the impact of U.S. imperialism. The Western economic, financial, military, cultural and religious powers, in an alliance with internal dominating powers, continue to destroy our life, our culture and our religion.

Victims of the so-called "spiritual conquest," we have suffered a violent, deceitful evangelization, in league with colonial and neo-colonial powers, for 500 years. Indian and African peoples have been forced to become Christians. A theology which brought death and a spirituality which repressed bodies hovered over us.

Up to the present time the dominating system multiplies the idols of death in order to continue its boundless repression "in good conscience." Money, power, the market, consumerism, racism, and sexism are today's idols which destroy life and culture.

Fortunately, this violent and deceitful evangelization, which rather than introduce Christ among us, brought Satan (as Pineda y Bascunan denounced in Chile during the 17th century) has been unmasked by the liberating evangelization of our people. The oppressed, but never defeated, peoples were capable of discovering the presence of the Gospel in spite of the violence of the States and the Churches. They recognized God as the one who listens to the clamor of the oppressed (cf. Exodus, ch. 3).

The autochthonous and mixed-blood peoples, the Afro-American and Caribbean groups, have gone on rebuilding their own religious world. Thus the discovery of Jesus Christ tended less to come from Christendom to the people than from them to the overall society. The poor people of God felt the Spirit of God hovering, urging them to proclaim the Good News to their brothers and sisters (cf. Luke, ch. 4).

The European culture, originally Spanish and Portuguese, in spite of the structures of domination, managed to give us its positive cultural and religious values and its own version of the Christianity of the poor. These values were integrated into the religious and cultural tradition of the oppressed. In that way a grassroots religion and culture of resistance and struggle against domination was born. A new way of being Church, a sign of hope for all people, was being born.

III. The Struggles

In the final analysis, the historical significance of the Five Hundredth Anniversary has to do with the peoples' struggles. The remembrance of all the freedom-loving races which have managed to recover subjugated lives, cultures, and religions awakens our peoples' memory.

Today we joyfully call to mind all the rebels:

The aborigines of the land, the struggles of the Guaraníes and Mapuches, the Caribbeans and the Cakchiqueles; Túpac Amaru in Peru, Canindé from Ceará in Brazil, Lautaro in Chile, Canek from the Yucatan in Mexico, so many other men and women; the struggles of the Afro-Americans and Afro-Caribbeans, Zumbí from Palmares in Brazil, Lemba in Santo Domingo; all the women who have struggled for our liberation, among them Gaitana from Colombia, Mamá Tingó from Santo Domingo.

These men and women are the protagonists, those who, through their challenging lives, point out the path of history, the historical significance of these 500 years and the future of the Churches.

Last of all we recall those who understood the peoples' struggles and were capable of listening to their cries of pain and protest, from Bartolomé de las Casas to Oscar Arnulfo Romero. The people of God are reborn today in the grassroots movements and Christian communities and reaffirm hope in the Church's ecumenical and prophetic path.

Santo Domingo, October 12, 1989

Columbus Day, 1989

Appendix F

By the President of the United States of America

A Proclamation

On Columbus Day, we pause as a Nation to honor the skilled and courageous navigator who discovered the Americas and in so doing, brought to our ancestors the promise of the New World. In honoring Christopher Columbus, we also pay tribute to the generations of brave and bold Americans who, like him, have overcome great odds in order to chart the unknown.

For nearly half a millennium, Americans have followed the example of this great explorer, challenging the frontiers of knowledge. Throughout our Nation's history, the spirit of discovery has been demonstrated by scholar and student, expert and novice, alike. While the efforts of men such as Lewis and Clark, Thomas Edison, Eli Whitney and Alexander Graham Bell are well known, we should also remember the thousands of pioneers who quietly tamed the American wilderness. With courage, ingenuity, hard work and sacrifice, these men and women helped to build a Nation.

Generations of American entrepreneurs and business people have likewise accepted great risks in order to pursue their dreams. Their vision and initiative, allowed to flourish in this land of liberty, have helped the United States grow strong and prosperous.

From test pilots and astronauts to scientists and researchers in virtually every field of endeavor, Americans have continued to explore not only the wonders of our planet, but also the great mysteries of space. Like Christopher Columbus, all of these Americans have faced the unknown, not with a reckless sense of adventure, but with a great sense of purpose and opportunity.

Just a few years from now, in 1992, the United States will commemorate the 500th anniversary of the arrival of Columbus on these shores and proudly participate in events honoring this great explorer. A number of educational and commemorative events and programs are also being planned by the members of the Christopher Columbus Quincentenary Jubilee Commission, which was established by the Congress in 1984.

Americans of Italian and Spanish descent will have special reason to join in this quincentenary celebration. As we reflect on the achievements of this famous son of Genoa, and the generous support he received from Spanish monarchs Ferdinand V and Isabella I, we are also reminded of the many contributions that men and women of Italian and Spanish descent have made and continue to make to our Nation.

200

In tribute to Christopher Columbus, the Congress of the United States, by joint resolution of April 30, 1934 (40 Stat. 857), as modified by the Act of June 28, 1988 (82 Stat. 250), has requested the President to proclaim the second Monday in October of each year as "Columbus Day."

NOW, THEREFORE, I GEORGE BUSH, President of the United States of America, do hereby proclaim October 9, 1989, as Columbus Day. I call upon the people of the United States to observe this day with appropriate ceremonies and activities. I also direct that the flag of the United States be displayed on all public buildings on the appointed day in honor of Christopher Columbus.

IN WITNESS WHEREOF, I have hereunto set my hand this sixth day of October, in the year of our Lord nineteen hundred and eighty-nine, and of the Independence of the United States of America the two hundred and fourteenth.

George Bush

1492: Fact and Fancy

Appendix G

Letter to Lies of Our Times (LOOT), *by Hans Koning, April 1991*

As I write this, the debate whether to commemorate, celebrate, or mourn 1492 has moved to the wings and has left center stage to the Gulf. But no apology is needed for writing about the coming Quincentenary. There are *links,* as there usually are in matters historical, and the way we were taught about Columbus and our past surely helps explain the American character. It may even throw light on the dark thought processes of our politicians and president.

Fifteen years ago Monthly Review Press in New York first published my short biography, *Columbus: His Enterprise.* It is a revisionist history, but not because it tries to squeeze history into a radical or any other ideological mold; it is revisionist because it lists the perfectly well-known facts and tries to look at them from the viewpoint of the victims, the *hastily* exterminated Indians of the Caribbean. Its message was summed up by me in an Op-Ed piece in the *New York Times* last August, and at that time it might have been assumed (as Robert Allen Warrior, a journalist from the Osage nation, put it in *LOOT* of January 1991) that the *Times* was set to "mediate" the debate, though without interrupting any celebrations. It was not much to expect, but six months after they printed that Op-Ed, I am even less optimistic on that score than Warrior. *Times* editorial mechanics work in such a way that any letters which object to an Op-Ed generally have the last word. This may be acceptable in an opinion battle, but it works havoc upon truth when misinformation cannot be refuted. When my answers to the letters of my opponents remained unpublished, I felt that the entire exchange might even have left a negative balance.

One letter claimed that "Spain was the first European power to outlaw slavery while at the same time introducing Christianity to the native Indians," making the writer "proud and thankful" for the Conquest. *Actually,* in 1873 (last listing in the *Encyclopaedia Britannica,* 11th edition) Cuba, a Spanish colony, had half a million slaves; there is not one record of a conversion to Christianity in Columbus's time (Indians were strung up, though, under his governorship, in rows of 13 "in honor of the Redeemer and His twelve Apostles").

A second *Times* reader quoted a letter written by Columbus on January 2, 1493, about the need "to keep the love and friendship" of the Indians. In that same document he wrote at length (to his king and queen) of the Indians' gentleness and generosity. The *Times* letter writer used the quote to show me wrong in calling Columbus "cruel in small as in vast matters." *Actually,* it proves to all serious historians that his later diatribes about the Indians were false, alibis for the ruthless system he had put in place for squeezing wealth out of them — wealth to replace the "mountains of gold" he had promised his backers but had not found.

A third letter claimed that my facts were but a fantasy to make the man "a symbol of American failure" and that the proper reaction was to see him as our "first immigrant," establishing the happy theme of "American diversity." *Actually,* Columbus and his followers used their slaves to feed and indeed to carry them; they disdained work, they hated the land. All they wanted to do was to go back to Spain with their plunder.

These unfounded objections then remained the final record. Moreover, nothing in the *Times*'s own editorials on the subject since, or in its routine reporting on our official 1992 plans for celebration, indicated that there was anything controversial here.

I am not questioning the importance of the letters the paper printed, for they demonstrate the huge emotional charge our Eurocentric, tilted, and just plain falsified schoolbooks have given to the subject. They have left many Americans refusing to be confused by facts. Solid historical data become "insults to the Italian community," or to the Hispanics, or to the whole country. I received a phone call from a Native American woman in Ridgefield, Connecticut, which has a large Italian-American constituency. She had become afraid of their hostility when she taught what she knew to be the truth. Could I give her the name of a genuine Italian hero she could mention to placate them?

It is painful to let go of dear national lore, but this pain means that the debate must not be constricted but made as wide and open as possible. We must let the air in. Our false heroes have for too long burdened our national spirit. The facts of our history must move from the Op-Ed page to the editorial pages.

Hans Koning

Prize Essay

Appendix H

In the early 1940s, the editors of the Wyoming Farmer-Stockman *printed a picture of a deserted farm house in a desolate sand-swept field and offered a prize for the best 100-word essay on the disastrous effects of land erosion. An Indian boy from Oklahoma won the contest with this graphic description:*

"Picture show white man crazy. Cut down trees. Make too big teepee. Plow land, water wash, wind blow soil. Grass gone, door gone, squaw gone. Whole place gone to hell. No pig, no corn, no pony.

Indian no plow land. Keep grass. Buffalo eat grass. Indian eat buffalo. Hide make plenty big teepee. Make moccasin. All time Indian eat. No work—no hitch-hike. Ask no relief. No build dam. No give damn. White man heap crazy."

Index

205